ECSTATIC RELIGION
THIRD EDITION

D0140012

States of spirit possession, in which believers feel themselves to be 'possessed' by the deity and raised to a new plane of existence, are found in almost all known religions. From Dionysiac cults to Haitian voodoo, Christian and Sufi mysticism to shamanic ritual, the rapture and frenzy of ecstatic experience forms an iconic expression of faith in all its devastating power and unpredictability. *Ecstatic Religion* has, since its first appearance in 1971, become the classic investigative study of these puzzling phenomena. Exploring the social and political significance of spiritual ecstasy and possession, it considers the distinct types and functions of mystical experience – in particular, the differences between powerful male-dominated possession cults which reinforce established morality and power, and marginal, renegade ecstatics expressing forms of protest on behalf of the oppressed, especially women.

I. M. Lewis's wide-ranging comparative study looks at the psychological, medical, aesthetic, religious and cultural aspects of possession, and covers themes including soul-loss, ecstatic trance, divination, erotic passion and exorcism. Probing the mysteries of spirit possession through the critical lens of anthropological and sociological theory, this fully revised and expanded Third Edition is of crucial importance for students of psychology, sociology, religious mysticism and shamanism.

I. M. Lewis, a former Professor of Anthropology and head of department at the London School of Economics, is the author of several works on anthropology and religion including *Religion in Context* (1996) and *Blood and Bone* (1994).

ECSTATIC RELIGION

A Study of Shamanism and Spirit Possession

Third Edition

I. M. LEWIS

 Routledge
Taylor & Francis Group

LONDON AND NEW YORK

First published 1971
by Penguin Books

Second edition published 1989
by Routledge

Third edition published 2003
by Routledge
11 New Fetter Lane, London EC4P 4EE

Simultaneously published in the USA and Canada
by Routledge
29 West 35th Street, New York NY 10001

Routledge is an imprint of the Taylor & Francis Group

© 1971, 1989 and 2003 I. M. Lewis

Typeset in Times by
Keystroke, Jacaranda Lodge, Wolverhampton
Printed and bound in Great Britain by
TJ International Ltd, Padstow, Cornwall

British Library Cataloguing in Publication Data
A catalogue record for this book is available from the British Library

Library of Congress Cataloging in Publication Data
Lewis, I. M.
    Ecstatic religion: a study of shamanism and spirit possession/
I. M. Lewis. – 3rd ed.
        p. cm.
    Includes bibliographical references and index.
    ISBN 0–415–30508–X (hb) – ISBN 0–415–30124–6 (pbk.)
    1. Ecstasy. 2. Shamanism. 3. Spirit possession.
    4. Religion and sociology. I. Title.

BL626 .L48 2003
306.6′9142–dc21   2002027542

ISBN 0–415–30124–6 (PB)
ISBN 0–415–30508–X (HB)

For Ann

'Pour soulever les hommes il faut avoir le diable au corps'
BAKUNIN

CONTENTS

PREFACE TO THE THIRD EDITION

I

Since the last edition of this book in 1989, the 'possession' of human beings by alien spirits, an exotic condition that seemed to have virtually disappeared from Western culture, returned with a bang in the shape of what psychiatrists call 'Multiple Personality Disorder'. This striking phenomenon of contemporary, especially American, life, involving possession by an assorted collection of spirit entities (including frequently aliens), with its specialist diagnosticians and therapists, has become big business. It is legitimated and promoted by a mushrooming popular literature and by highly successful films such as 'The three faces of Eve', 'Rosemary's Baby', 'Alien', 'Others' etc.

The current appeal of New Age beliefs and practices has encouraged a similar, if more exclusive, market for 'Neo-Shamanism', as individuals and groups in contemporary Western society adapt what they take to be exotic shamanistic lore for ritual healing and other spiritual purposes (cf. Perrin, 1995; Jakobsen, 1999; Ogudina, 1999). This is a kind of 'psychic aerobics' as Clifton (1989) dubs 'armchair shamanism', and if you have the money to spare, you can enrol in practical courses and not only at such famous sites as Big Sur in California. Successful Western entrepreneurs even finance international conferences for academic researchers on 'traditional' shamanism (the real mackay), as well as for practitioners like themselves. This is truly the era of guru globalisation!

For its part, Multiple Personality Disorder connects with another popular contemporary preoccupation: satanism. The standard explanation of MPD by its diagnosticians and therapists is in terms of childhood sexual assault, often in a satanic ritual context. Typically, therapy which is designed to recover repressed memories, often with the aid of hypnotism, reveals that the patient, typically a female, was sexually abused in childhood by a senior male relative, usually the father. By the early 1990s, therapists claimed that a quarter of the estimated MPD 200,000 victims in the US were survivors of ritual Satanic abuse (Schnabel, 1994). This interpretation revives Freud's early theory that hysteria, in later life, is a consequence of childhood sexual abuse. Freud himself, of course, later revised this formulation, treating the theme of child sexual abuse by a parent as, in the Oedipus context, an extremely powerful wish-fulfilling fantasy, not an actual fact. Without this crucial reclassification of childhood incest as a fantasy rather than reality, as the feminist analyst Juliet Mitchell (2000) points out, there would have been no scope for the elaboration of the key constructs of Freudian psychoanalysis.

This new (or revisionist) version of Freud's theory casts the parent (usually the father) in the unenviable role of incestuous child molester — a very powerful denunciation by the 'innocent' MPD 'victim' (Ross, 1995). This terrifying scenario, with its normally disastrous outcome for the accused parents or other relatives, whose lives are usually literally destroyed in the wake of the accusations, has striking parallels with the social dynamics of possession and witchcraft in many Third World cultures which we explore later in this book (cf. also Lewis, 1996; Littlewood, 1996). As we shall see, witchcraft accusations (by definition implying incest) may be made by spirit-possessed victims, when the latter impute their possession illness to the malevolent acts of a 'witch' (in the case of MPD a parent). In these circumstances, the effect of the accusation is to deny or destroy the relationship which, of course, is exactly what happens when therapists encourage their MPD patients to 'recover' memories of sexual abuse by a father or other male relative. The presenting symptoms of this fashionable malady, in a climate strongly interested in 'satanism' and UFO's, also often include possession by aliens as well as less exotic human agents (see Schnabel, 1994). 'Alien' is of course a relative term and spirit entities of various degrees and kinds of alienness are commonplace in possession cosmologies in the Third World.

Over the thirteen years since the last edition of this book, there has been an impressive growth of anthropological (and other) literature on both spirit possession and shamanism, as the bibliographical surveys referred to at the end of this preface indicate. The Sudanese/Ethiopian *zar/bori* cult to whose inspiration this book owes so much, has been further studied and analysed by a number of anthropologists and historians (see Lewis, al-Safi and Hurreiz, eds. 1991). In terms of new fieldwork, the rich study by Boddy (1989) in a Sudanese village in 1977 and 1984 deserves particular mention as the fullest ethnographic account so far published. Boddy treats the spirit cult as 'counter hegemonic' for women in the male dominated local Islamic context. Sudanese women, she claims, are culturally 'over-determined' to be fertility objects where their socialisation deprives them of any sense of individuality and fails to provide them with a way of dealing 'conceptually and actively with infertility, or other significant contraventions of femininity'. By preventing pregnancy and causing premature and still births, as is believed locally, *zar* spirits assume responsibility for disrupting human fertility. Possession, thus, lifts from the women's shoulders a measure of responsibility for reproduction. At the same time, by paying for the woman's treatment, her husband and kin are forced to acknowledge some liability.

Thus far Boddy repeats previous analyses (cf. below, pp.90–114). But she seeks to go further, invoking literary analogies to treat possession and trance episodes as 'texts' (as advocated by her colleague, M. Lambeck, 1981). More daringly, she claims that Sudanese spirit possession is designed to promote free-thinking, encouraging reflection on the taken-for-granted world by the possessed, and thus promotes enhanced self-consciousness. In consequence, oppressed women are led to enjoy 'more felicitous outcomes in their encounters with others'. However, no evidence is offered in this ambitious account to suggest that in consequence of the intellectual refocusing or re-framing postulated, possessed women do actually think and feel differently. Boddy does not provide information on how women comport themselves, and on what they say about themselves and others before and after their possession experiences.

This rather precious 'literary' analysis thus conceals the familiar 'If I were a horse' series of suppositions (cf. Lewis, 1990). Indeed, as a number of other critics have noted, Boddy slips back into the kind of analysis she sets out to replace. Possession for her is an 'allegory', the 'words and dances of mediums refer "allegorically" to social factors such as gender, class and personal history' (Nourse, 1996). She thus remains imprisoned by her own intellectual perceptions, and the spirit realities she sets out to explore remain 'interpretatively opaque' as Karp (1990, p.79) delicately puts it. It is a pity that she did not concentrate more on the conceptions of the Sudanese women themselves with more substantial ethnographic reporting. Adopting the historical approach to how possession and the spirit galaxy respond to social change which I have long advocated (below, pp.121ff), Makris (2000) documents the associated *tumbura* possession cult. This involves marginalised men and women of slave descent in the urban Sudan, and extends our understanding of *zar-bori* and its derivatives.

So many historical figures — General Gordon, Earl Cromer, the Pashas and other characters expressive of the Anglo-Egyptian period people the *zar/bori* cosmology that it is impossible not to view it, in part, as a kind of historiography of 'repressed memories'. (On the wider geographical and historical reach of this multifaceted subterranean cult linked to various kinds of social exclusion in Islam in Africa and the Middle East, see Lewis, al-Safi and Hurreiz, eds. 1991.)

Possession in other areas of the world continues to be identified, documented and analysed, generating a rapidly expanding, if uneven literature. As has recently been observed in a Latin American context, this ramifying written documentation (as well as a host of films and recordings of possession music), shows *inter alia* how anthropologists are prone to reproduce 'their own logic, converting the possessed into a medium through which they speak to their own (anthropological) agenda'. (Placido, 2001, p.208). Possession studies do thus indeed tend to mirror the current fashions of anthropological theory and, if we are not careful, the voices of those we seek to report are in danger of being silenced as we pursue our own ethnocentric preoccupations.

II

This undesirable tendency seems to me to be especially promoted by the vogue for Post-Modernist 'interpretative writing' which certainly reveals much about the anthropological writer, but often disappointingly little about his or her informants (cf. Lewis, 1999). A number of the more recent possession studies follow the literary style criticised above, privileging the possessed persons utterances as 'texts' in a wider 'discourse', while tending to ignore, or undervalue, the dramatic character of the séance in which they take place, and the roles played by key performers in possession ritual (contrast, for instance, the collection of self-consciously interpretative essays assembled by Behrend and Luig, 1999, with the more staid, but more scholarly collection of Mastromattei, 1999). What the possessing spirits actually say, as they in effect speak for their human vehicles, is obviously an important initial clue to understanding what is going on as we emphasise in this book. But, this is only part of the picture in any satisfactory sociology of possession which must ask 'what do the women and men involved in possession themselves think it is about? In what circumstances do people become possessed? What are the social (and political) implications of possession? How does it demonstrably affect peoples' lives?' The textual, 'cultural account' approach does not adequately elucidate these questions. A case in point is Kapferer's (1983) unconvincing attempt to explain the prevalence of possessed female victims in Buddhist Sri Lanka in terms of what he calls 'cultural typification' which, he claims, 'places women in a special and significant relation with the demonic'. This observation should be the starting point, not the end of analysis. As Isabelle Nabokov (1997, p.298) shrewdly remarks, Kapferer fails to explain why 'it is not women as a whole, but predominantly new brides who are most at risk'. The difficulties of their novel marital situation, and their 'emotional entrapment' makes them especially vulnerable to seduction by hedonistic spirits who, not only sexually enjoy their victims, but also incite them to resist the sexual attentions of their legitimate mortal spouses. Hence culturological accounts — which may reproduce local social representations and stereotypes (e.g. women are especially vulnerable to possession) — do not in themselves explain the incidence of possession which is the prime sociological concern. The key question in that context is: Why new brides rather than other women? The answer, as suggested, lies in the difficulties some brides experience in adapting to their new marital situation, especially if the husband proves to be unsatisfactory.

This book seeks to answer such questions in relation to possession and shamanism, viewing both as social rather than specifically cultural phenomena, exploring which social categories of people are most vulnerable to spirits, and what social consequences follow from this. We also examine how the character of possessing spirits relates to the social circumstances of the possessed.

Here, since as we shall see, shamans are regularly possessed, I reject Luc de Heusch's outright 'dialectical' distinction between possession and shamanism (which follows Mircea Eliade's classical dichotomy, based on the latter's misreading of the relevant primary sources). But, I adopt (with reservations) de Heusch's valuable insights into the implications of responding to possession by exorcism, as distinct from the contrary process of domesticating spirits, which he calls 'adorcism'. Interest in how these cults based on adopting rather than expelling spirits, develop from an initial traumatic experience into what are often effectively mystery religions, does not commit the researcher to a medical interpretation of possession.

Nor, pace Boddy (1994, p.410) do I see how my sociological distinction between main and marginal cults contributes to a 'medicalization' of possession (cf. Csordas, 1987). The differentiation (which is relative) between 'central' and 'peripheral' cults (discussed more fully in chapters 5 and 6) does not rest on their therapeutic (or medical) scope, but on whether they are inspired by spirits which directly uphold public morality (central) or those 'peripheral' agencies that threaten public order. For an alternative formulation of this distinction see Kramer (1993). Defined by their social significance, the former constitute shamanistic religions, the latter subversive marginal cults (albeit internally perceived as 'secret religions').

It would be perverse, moreover, to ignore the explicit views of those involved who choose to present possession as therapeutic and in modern terms 'medical' (cf. de Heusch, 1997). This comes out clearly in Brown's (1986) study of Brazilian Umbanda where spirit mediums wear nurses' uniforms and, in the name of their spirits, hold clinics for spiritual healing. In a recent short field-study in Malaysia, I found exactly the same 'medicalization' well established in the healing practise of spirit-inspired *bomohs* with 'clinics' modelled on those of local doctors.

This criticism seems all the more surprising since the ensuing pages emphasise, how gender influences the interpretation of possession, and the manner in which an initially negative possession indisposition is regularly transformed retrospectively into a beatific revelation. In male chauvinist societies, women's secret religions are apt to be represented to outsiders (especially males) as harmless therapies, whose practise is in everyone's interest. I readily confess, also, an interest in the psychiatric significance of possession. But, following Shirokogoroff and others, I argue that Western psychiatry (and especially psychoanalysis) constitutes an alternative framework for understanding perceptions and behaviour which elsewhere are couched in the language and logic of spirit possession (cf. Littlewood and Lipsedge, 1982). As Shirokogoroff long ago put it, 'spirits are hypotheses'.

Typically, possession makes its initial appearance as a traumatic experience, even a crippling 'illness', or other personal disaster. However, the ensuing definition and redefinition of this involuntary spirit intrusion depends upon how the onset symptoms respond to subsequent treatment and the changing condition of the possessed victim. Where the forces at play are initially interpreted as dangerous and terrifying, exorcism is the preferred response (particularly by men). If this proves ineffective, treatment switches to attempting to reach an accommodation with the spirit, placating and domesticating it, by paying it cult (adorcism). As the cliché has it, what begins in agony ends in ecstasy.

According to her own testimony, this was the case with the famous Christian mystic St. Teresa of Avila (1515–1582) whose initial experiences were fraught with pain and difficulty. Her most sublime transports, however, she describes as unfolding in three phases: 'union', 'rapture', and the climatic 'wound of love'. De Heusch refers to her as a mystic spouse, devoured by amorous passion. But she also had an extremely ambitious and powerful personality and steely determination as well as practical skills. These qualities, which led to her being regularly referred to as 'Eagle and Dove', were amply displayed in her campaign to establish the reformed (barefoot) Carmelite movement.

Her family background would not, however, have indicated such a career. As has recently been highlighted by the American philosopher Evan Fales (1996), St. Teresa was a member of a family forced to convert from Judaism to Christianity during the religious persecutions of the Inquisition in fifteenth century Spain. As a woman, a spinster and convert, despite her family's wealth, she was in several significant respects a marginal figure, and like her counterparts in traditional societies, a strong candidate for spiritual attention. Against the patriarchal odds of her times, she appears to have successfully mobilised her spiritual intimacy with Christ to legitimise her sharp political criticism of the aristocratic power structure of the Spanish monarchy, based as it was on the concept of 'honour'. Fales adopts the general arguments of this book to claim that the empowerment, conferred by possession on those disadvantaged by gender and other social disabilities, provides an adequate explanation of mystical experience. This, he contends, is more logically compelling and inherently plausible than taking religious experience at face value as conclusive evidence for the existence of God. Although his argument goes somewhat beyond the more limited objectives of this book, it is gratifying that our study should be cited in this philosophical debate on the existential status of theistic beliefs!

III

As a rebellious figure, the ecstatic experiences of St. Teresa (canonised after her death) always risked being refuted, and re-classified by the ecclesiastical authorities as demonic episodes. Had St Teresa been less successful in treading this tightrope, she would almost certainly have been subject to exorcism. Exorcism, which we see as the logical opposite to adorcism, is indeed frequently employed to control and contain unruly and excessively enthusiastic ecstatics (especially women).

This is particularly marked in strongly patriarchal traditional cultures where exorcism is gender-biased and is the preferred treatment applied by husbands to treat their possessed wives. Men clearly sense the rebellious undertones (which we discuss in detail in later pages) and seek to respond by re-imposing patriarchal order and obedience. Nabokov, cited above, provides a convincing account of this situation amongst the Tamils of southern India. An equally telling literary demonstration comes from the famous eleventh century classic *The Tale of the Gengi* where the brilliant female author, Murasaki Shikibu ('Japan's Shakespeare'), shows how in the Heian period (794–1186), spirit possession (*mono noke*) was rampant amongst the grand ladies of the imperial court. In this patriarchal, polygynous society, this 'woman's weapon', as Doris Bargen (1997) puts it in her magisterial study, was invoked to counter incestuous transgression by male nobility and courtiers and the unwelcome attentions of peeping-toms. However distant in time, and space and culture this was evidently thus not all that remote in its aetiology from Multiple Personality Disorder. This women's condition in ancient Japanese society was not, it seems, allowed to flourish into a full-blown female cult. It was held in check by the vigorous practise of exorcism, mainly by male priests.

Nevertheless, the picture here is complicated. For women, initiated as spirit mediums, usually served as vehicles for the spirits possessing the victim. The possessing spirits then spoke and acted on their behalf during the drama of exorcism so that: 'the possessed, the possessing spirits, and the medium formed a powerful female triad engaged in resolving gender-related conflict' (Bargen, 1997, p.15).

Despite their logical opposition and the sociological value of de Heusch's division between exorcism and adorcism, when we examine a wider range of evidence carefully, it becomes evident that the contrast is less clear cut than at first appeared. This is not simply, as de Heusch (1997) himself appears to suppose in a recent revision of his schema, that, as we have seen from a gender perspective, both exorcism and adorcism regularly operate as alternative procedures in the same society. This fuller complexity becomes evident when we turn to modern Japan, where possession is one of the commonest problems leading women to join the exorcistic 'New Religions', often themselves founded by women. Members of these religions are not exorcised once and for all but, rather, repeatedly attend their exorcistic rituals. This, obviously, makes the status of exorcism problematic. We find the same phenomena in the Catholic exorcisms performed in Rome (until in 2001 the Vatican refused to allow him to practise) by the well-known African Archbishop Milingo (Lanternari, 1988; ter Haar and Ellis, 1988). Similar cases of the same individuals repeatedly attending the same 'exorcistic' rites and experiencing ecstatic 'possession' on each occasion are reported in the north

African cult of Islamic saints (Virolles-Souibes, 1986; Ferchiou, 1991; Hell, 1997).

In such cases, although carried out in the name of the local established male-dominated religion, repeated exorcism seems paradoxically to stimulate and clandestinely incorporate (and effectively co-opt) what amounts to an implicit ecstatic cult. If as I argue, exorcism is regularly employed to control wayward female mystical tendencies (and those of men of similar subordinate status), and adorcism does not succeed in achieving a formal existence, it may nevertheless surface as an undercurrent within the process of exorcism itself (cf. Bastide, 1972, p.102). When we look more closely at the mechanics of exorcism this paradox is not as surprising as it first appears. For, as we note later in this book, possession is usually expected to reach a dramatic climax at the critical moment when the struggle between the exorcist and the possessing spirit is about to culminate in the expulsion of the latter. Exorcism, thus, paradoxically serves to stimulate possession trance. Since expulsion (exorcism) and induction (adorcism) may in their trance manifestations coincide, the essential ambiguity of these two formally opposite processes becomes apparent. This helps to explain why professional exorcists seem usually to be regarded as ambiguous, potentially dangerous figures of uncertain moral virtue.

This also recalls the essential ambivalence of the typical initial possession experience, at first in the form of a terrifying trauma or illness, but which once brought under control, and mastered, signifies the attention of the Gods and the onset of the inspired healer's career. This is how the leaders of women's spirit cults are recruited and accredited. It is equally the standard route to the assumption of the male shaman's career. In the Christian tradition, we see a typical example in the case of the divine calling of the Apostle Paul, whose shamanistic conversion on the road to Damascus, as John Ashton (2000) argues in his exciting new study, is clearly recorded in the famous revelatory passage in Romans 7: 13–25. The term *shaman*, as we see later (pp.45–50), comes originally from the Tungus reindeer herders of Siberia, who for centuries have provided the *locus classicus* of shamanism. As explained by specialists on Tungus culture and language, this originally ethnographically specific term, meaning a spirit inspired priest and healer, comes from the root *sam* signifying the violent bodily movement and agitated dancing of the shaman as he vigorously beats his drum to summon the spirits to his séance. According to the French Tungus specialist, Roberte Hamayon (1990), in the séance which is highly charged with sexual symbolism, the shaman wears the animal skin of one of his spirits to whom he is 'married', and his dramatic movements in his dance mime the act of rutting with this spirit partner. This more recent and admirably detailed documentation confirms the classic account of the Russian medical doctor and pioneering ethnologist, S.M. Shirokogoroff, to whom we owe our fundamental understanding of the spirit-inspired shaman. We may note in passing that Hamayon seeks to question the significance of the shaman's 'trance' experience. Despite its obvious sexual appropriateness as signalling the climax of the shaman's dance with his spirit partner, she claims that trance is a psychological phenomenon beyond the scrutiny of anthropology. This idiosyncratic view, criticised by de Heusch and Rouget, seems irrelevant to the séance drama where what is at issue is not whether or not the shaman is 'really' in trance but the effectiveness of his performance (see Lewis, 2002).

IV

Some years ago, faced with the difficulty of defining Social Anthropology, a witty commentator opted for a 'functionalist' definition as 'what social anthropologists do'. Rather similarly from the sociological perspective advocated in this book, we can define shamanism as the work of shamans who, as we see, are spirit-inspired priests (masters of spirits). This view emphasises the coincident importance of spirit possession and rejects the shaman's 'celestial voyage', as the determining feature insisted on by Eliade and his successors. As we see below, Shirokogoroff and other first-hand sources (which Eliade was not) describe the shaman's mystical voyages, with the aid of his spirits, as travelling both above and below, as well as on our terrestrial world. Unlike the tradition generally pursued by historians of religion, in privileging the shaman's role we detach it from any particular cosmology. The former culturological approach, which is natural to American anthropology, has other disadvantages to which I return in a moment.

In firmly following Shirokogoroff I also follow a more recent Siberian specialist who, writing after the publication of the first edition of this book, says: 'To be a shaman does not signify professing particular beliefs, but rather refers to a certain mode of communication with the supernatural' (Lot-Falck, 1973). The supposed mutually exclusive distinction between spirit possession religions and shamanic ones was first mooted by Eliade, and then developed by de Heusch in his imaginative model contrasting ecstatic religiosity with spirit possession which we examine later. Both writers share the view that shamanism necessarily involves celestial voyages, whereas as an incarnation, possession is an earth-bound phenomenon. Celestial flight, they argue, excludes spirit possession: but, in fact, as we emphasise, possessing spirits may take their human hosts (in one form or another) on exciting spirit trips to the heavens as well as elsewhere. De Heusch applies this false dichotomy to develop his structuralist theory of religion, in which shamanism and possession feature as opposed 'metaphysics', and the former is seen primarily as a culturally specific Tungus product. As indicated, I prefer to see shamanism as a general, cross-cultural phenomenon based on the shaman's mastery of spirits and the practise of his art with the aid of spirits. In common with other charismatic figures, 'mastery' here is never a secure property, since it is regularly contested, making the shaman's role inherently insecure and problematic.

The old-fashioned view of shamanism, emphasising mystical flight, still continues to haunt the writings of historians of European religion as well as some historians of early society. These include the influential Italian historian, Carlo Ginzburg (1989), whose neo-Frazerian fantasy, *Storia Notturna* (English title: *Ecstasies*), conjures up a misty 'shamanic' complex, rooted in early Europe and with wide-flung tentacles in time and space, to explain the ecstatic features of the 'witch's Sabbath' in sixteenth century Italian popular culture. Inevitably, as Ginzburg acknowledges, this remarkable enterprise recalls the theories on European witchcraft of the English folklorist Margaret Murray (1962). Her discredited notion of a pan-European fertility cult, associated with the Goddess Diana, with significant traces surviving into modern times, is too well-known to require further comment here. As we see below witchcraft is in fact very often linked with spirit possession, but this topic is rather undeveloped in Ginzburg's notion of shamanism. A number of Italian anthropologists have remarked on this omission. They point out that this neglect is all the more surprising given the well-known prominence in southern Italian popular culture of the cult of tarantism, involving possession by the hybrid tarantula spider — Saint Paul (Pizza, 1995, 1997; see also below, pp.81–83).

Nevertheless, the artificiality, as I hold, of separating possession and shamanism in water-tight compartments, seems to be becoming increasingly evident to specialists in these fields, especially those who study religion as a social phenomenon (cf. Johansen, 1999). Here feminist analyses have contributed by pointing out that 'shamanism' has tended to be invoked where male priests are involved, in contrast to possession dominated by women. Since men also experience possession (and trance), it cannot, however, be the case that possession is inherently gendered and rooted in the female's physical experience of heterosexual intercourse and pregnancy (see Sered, 1994, p.190). By the same token, as 'masters of spirits', shamans might be expected always to be cast as 'husbands' in their unions with spirits. But this is by no means inevitably the case, the superior status of spirits *vis à vis* mortals is often expressed by classifying their shaman partners (irrespective of sex) as 'wives'. The gender of their human hosts may also change in the course of a séance as they are possessed in succession by male or female deities.

Beyond gender, consideration of the wider political co-ordinates of shamanism (advocated in this book) is increasingly explored in a number of recent publications often, but not always, in the neo-Marxist political-economy style (see e.g. Atkinson, 1989; Balzer, 1990; Santos-Granero, 1991; Thomas and Humphrey, 1994; Taussig, 1987). This work does not usually exclude spirit possession but treats it as a related and, frequently linked socio-political phenomenon.

In America, however, where the term 'shamanism' has been much more widely used than in Britain, the ambient culturological bias tends to encourage the separate treatment of the two phenomena (for a useful survey of the field see Atkinson, 1992). Illustrating yet again the dominance of the cultural over the social paradigm in American anthropology, Atkinson also seeks to represent the culturally distinct varieties of shamanism she recognises as so many 'shamanisms', thus side-stepping the core definition, based on the shaman's role, which our sociological approach advocates.

Yet, despite this American tendency to celebrate cultural specificity, it is probably significant that an increasing number of international conferences and collected papers by academic specialists breach the gap, here following the sensible lead of the open-minded International Society for Shamanic Research and the policy of its journal, *Shaman*.

Finally, it is gratifying to note that Janice Boddy's (1994) review of the field should judge that in the analysis of possession, 'the model and assumptions' set out in this book 'have guided a generation of scholarship'. As our subject — possession-shamanism ('ecstatic religion', for short) continues to develop with new material and new analyses, I hope that these ideas may continue to have some utility. Above all, I hope that they may serve as a guide to what is known and, therefore, does not need to be re-invented by young researchers seeking a novel topic. The existing literature on possession and shamanism is truly vast. But like the shaman's guiding spirits, this store of knowledge requires to be convincingly mastered by those who aspire to add significantly to it, thus contributing further to our understanding of possession and shamanism.

Ioan Lewis
London, December 2001

References

Aigle, D., Brac de la Perriere, B., and. Chaumeil, J-P., *La Politique des Esprits*, Paris, Societe d'Ethnologie, 2000

Arens, W. and Karp, I. (eds) *The Creativity of Power*, Washington, Smithsonian Institute, 1989

Atkinson, J.M., *The Art and Politics of Wana shamanship*, Berkeley, University of California Press, 1989

―― 'Shamanisms Today', *Annual Review of Anthropology*, vol. 21, 1992, pp.307–330.

Balzer, M. (ed.) *Shamanism: Soviet Studies of Traditional Religion in Siberia and Central Asia*, London, M.E. Sharp Inc., 1990

Bargen, D.G. *A Woman's weapon: Spirit Possession in the Tale of the Gengi*, Honolulu, University of Hawai Press, 1997

Bastide, R. *Le Reve, La Transe, et la Folie*, Paris, Flamarion, 1972

Behrend, H. and Luig, U. (eds), *Spirit Possession, Modernity, and Power in Africa*, Oxford, James Curry, 1999

Boddy, J. 'Spirit Possession Revisited: Beyond instrumentality', *Annual Review of Anthropology*, vol. 23, 1994, pp. 407–34

Brown, D.G. *Umbanda: Religion And Politics in Urban Brazil*, Ann Arbor, University of Michigan Press, 1986

Csordas, T. 'Health and the body in African and Afro-American spirit possession', *Social Science and Medicine*, 24, (1), 1987, pp.1–11

Fales, E. 'Scientific explanations of mystical experiences, Part I: the case of St. Teresa', *Religious Studies*, 32, 1996, pp.143–163

―― 'Part II: the Challenge of Theism', *Religious Studies*, 32, 1996, pp.299–313

Ferchiou, S. 'The possession cults of Tunis', in Lewis, I.M., al-Safi, A. and Hurreiz, S. (eds), *Women's Medicine*, Edinburgh University Press, 1991, pp.209–219

Ginzburg, C. *Storia Notturna*, Turin, Einaudi, 1989 (English translation by R. Rosenthal, *Ecstasies: deciphering the witches' sabbath*, London, Penguin, 1992

Hacking, I., 'Multiple Personality Disorder and its Hosts', *History of Human Society*, 5, pp.3–31, 1992

Hamayon, R. *La Chasse a l'ame*, Paris, 1990

—— 'Pour en finir avec la 'transe' at 'l'extase' dans l'etude du Chamanisme', in Beffa, M.I. and Even, M.D. *Variations Chamaniques*, 2, Paris, University of Paris X, 1996

ter Haar, G. and Ellis, S. 'Spirit possession and healing in modern Zambia', *African Affairs*, 87, 347, pp.185–206, 1988

Hell, B. *Possession et Chamanisme: les Maitres de Desordre*, Paris, Flammarion, 1999

—— 'travailler avec ses genies: de la possession sauvage a la possession maitraise chez les Gnawa du Maroc', in Aigle D. etc. (eds) *La Politique des Esprits*, Paris, 2000, pp.411–434

Heusch, de L. 'Pour en revenir a la Transe', Paper given at the IVth ISSR Conference on Shamanism, Chantilly, 1997

Jakobsen, M.D. *Shamanism: traditional and contemporary approaches to the mastery of Spirits and Healing*, New York, Berghan Books, 1999

Johansen, U., 'Further thoughts on the History of Shamanism', *Shaman*, vol. 7, No. 1, 1999, pp.40–58

Kapferer, B. *A Celebration of Demons*, Bloomington, Indiana University Press, 1983

Karp, I. in Jackson, M. and Karp, I. (eds) *Women's Medicine*, Edinburgh University Press, 1991

Kenny, M.G. *The Passion of Ansel Bourne: Multiple Personality in American Culture*, Washington, Smithsonian Institution, 1986

Kramer, F. *The Red Fez: Art and Spirit Possession in Africa*, London, Verso, 1993

Lambek, M. *Human Spirits: a Cultural Account of Trance in Mayotte*, Cambridge University Press, 1981

Lanternari, V. 'L'Africa cattolica A Roma: il cuito terapeutico di Emmanuel Milungo', *Metaxo*, 6, pp.65–81, 1988

Lewis, I.M., 'In the house of Spirits', *Times Literary Supplement*, 1990

—— *Arguments with Ethnography*, London, Athlone Press, 1999

—— 'Is there a shamanic Cosmology?', in Mastromattei, R. and Rigopoulos, R. (eds), *Shamanic Cosmos*, New Delhi, D.K. Printworld, Ltd., 1999, pp.117–128

—— 'Music, Trance, Shamanism and Sex', in press, 2002

—— *Religion in Context*, Cambridge, Cambridge University Press, 1996

Lewis, I.M., al-Safi, A. and Hurreiz, S. (eds) *Woman's Medicine*, Edinburgh University Press, 1991

Littlewood, R. *Reason's necessity in the specification of the Multiple Self*, RAI Occasional Paper No. 43, London, 1996

Littlewood, R. and Lipsedge, M. *Aliens and Alienists: ethnic minorities and psychiatry*, Penguin, Harmondsworth, 1982

Loftus, E. and Ketcham, K. (eds), *The Myth of Repressed Memory: False Memories and Allegations of Sexual Abuse*, New York, St. Martin's Press, 1994

Mageo, J.M. and Howard, A. (eds) *Spirits in Culture History and Mind*, London, Routledge, 1996

Lot-Falck, E. 'Le chamanisme en Siberie: essai de mise au point', *Asie du Sud-Est et Monde Insulindien*, 4, No.3, pp.1–10

Mageo, J.M. 'Spirit girls and Marines': possession as historical discourse in Samoa', *American Ethnologist*, 23(12), pp.61–82, 1996

Makris, G.P. *Changing Masters. Spirit Possession and Identity Construction among Slave Descendants and other Subordinates in the Sudan*, Evanston, Northwestern University Press, 2000

Masquelier, A. 'Consumption, prostitution and reproduction: the poets of sweetness in Bori(Niger)', *American Ethnologist*, 22, pp.883–906, 1995

Mitchell, J., *Mad Men and Medusas*, London, Allen Lane, 2000

Murray, M., *The Witch Cult in Western Europe*, London, 1921

—— *The Witch Cult in Western Europe*, Oxford University Press, 1962

Nabokov, I., 'Expel the Lover, recover the wife: symbolic analysis of a South Indian exorcism', *Journal Royal Anthropological Institute*, vol. 3, No. 2, 1997

Nourse, R. 'The voice of the winds versus the masters' of cure: contested notions of spirit possession among the Lauje of Sulawesi', *Journal Royal Anthropological Institute*, vol. 2, No. 3, 1996

Ogudina, G., 'A look at the New Shamans', in Mastromattei and Rigopoulos (eds), *Shamanic Cosmos*, 1999, pp.181–206

Perrin, M. *Le Chamanisme (Que sais-je?)*, Paris, Presses Universitaires de France, 1995

Pizza, G. 'The Virgin and the Spider: Revisiting Spirit possession in southern Europe', unpublished ms., IVth Conference, International Society for Shamanic Research, Chantilly, 1997

Placido, B. 'It's all to do with words: an analysis of spirit possession in the Venezuelan cult of Maria Lionza', *Journal Royal Anthropological Institute*, 7, 2, pp.207–224, 2001

Ross, C.A. *Satanic Ritual Abuse: principles of treatment*, Toronto: University of Toronto Press, 1995

Santos-Granero, F., *The Power of Love: the moral use of knowledge amongst the Amuesha of Central Peru*, London, Athlone Press, 1991

Schnabel, J., *Dark White: aliens, abductions, and the UFO obsession*, London, Hamish Hamilton, 1994

Sered, S.S., *Priestess, Mother, Sacred Sister: Religions dominated by women*, New York, Oxford University Press, 1994

Shapiro, D.J., 'Blood, oil, honey and water: symbolism in spirit-possession sects in North East Brazil', *American Ethnologist*, 22, No. 4, pp.828–847, 1995

Stoller, P. *Embodying colonial memories: spirit possession, power and the Hauka in West Africa*, New York, Routledge, 1995

Virolle-Souibes, M. 'Femmes, possession et chamanisme: exemples algeriens' in *Transe, Chamanisme, et possession*, Nice, Editions Serre, 1986

Taussig, M. *Shamanism, Colonialism, and the Wildman*, Chicago University Press, 1987

Thomas, N. and Humphrey, C. (eds.), *Shamanism, History, and the State*, Ann Arbor, University of Michigan Press, 1994

Wafer, J. *The Taste of Blood: Spirit Possession in Brazilian Candomble*, Philadelphia, University of Pennsylvania Press, 1991

Chapter One

TOWARDS A SOCIOLOGY
OF ECSTASY

I

This book explores that most decisive and profound of all religious dramas, the seizure of man by divinity. Such ecstatic encounters are by no means uniformly encouraged in all religions. Yet it is difficult to find a religion which has not, at some stage in its history, inspired in the breasts of at least certain of its followers those transports of mystical exaltation in which man's whole being seems to fuse in a glorious communion with the divinity. Transcendental experiences of this kind, typically conceived of as states of 'possession', have given the mystic a unique claim to direct experiential knowledge of the divine and, where this is acknowledged by others, the authority to act as a privileged channel of communication between man and the supernatural. The accessory phenomena associated with such experiences, particularly the 'speaking with tongues', prophesying, clairvoyance, and transmission of messages from the dead, and other mystical gifts, have naturally attracted the attention not only of the devout but also of sceptics. For many people, in fact, such phenomena seem to provide persuasive evidence for the existence of a world transcending that of ordinary everyday experience.

Despite the problems inevitably posed for established ecclesiastical authority, it is easy to understand the strong attraction which religious ecstacy has always exerted within and on the fringe of Christianity. We can also readily appreciate how modern Spiritualism has won the interest not only of Christians of all shades of opinion, but also of agnostics and atheists. The comforting message that it 'proves survival' has much to do with its appeal for the recently bereaved; and this obviously contributes to Spiritualism's popularity in times of war and national calamity. Yet the phenomena in which it deals continue to command the serious attention of experimental scientists. And if scientists are prepared to give their cautious assent to some psychic phenomena, we can scarcely be surprised that certain churchmen should still search in the séance for conclusive proof of the divine powers of Jesus Christ. Indeed, whether in the séances of suburbia, or in more rarefied surroundings, those mystical experiences which resist plausible rational interpretation are seen, even sometimes by cynics, as pointing to the possibility that occult forces exist.

There is also a vast literature on the occult which has no doubts at all on the matter. The metaphysical meaning of trance states has been expounded by hundreds of writers in many languages and from many different points of view. Something of the character of much of this literature, or at least of that produced by enthusiastic partisans of the occult, can be gauged from the breath-taking predictions made by the editor of a popular book on trance (Wavell, 1967). 'Once the use of trance becomes as easily available as electricity,' this writer assures us,

immense new opportunities potent for good or evil will be open to all people. Conquests which spring to mind are those on which we currently expend many of our resources — space travel, physical and psychological warfare, espionage, pop music, and mass organized leisure. Its greatest practical application may be in space exploration . . . the light barrier . . . need prove no obstacle to spirits of astronauts bent on visiting the other regions of the universe.

Perhaps not. However, the golden age of trance which this inspired writer foresees is not without its darker side. 'Its greatest danger', he solemnly warns us, 'lies in providing our planet, already divided into hostile nations, with a new dimension for conflict-spirit hosts in mass formations manipulated by demoniac shamans annihilating the human race and all its hopes of reincarnation.'

This remarkable passage must seem on a different astral plane, to put it mildly, from the secluded world of Origen, or any other of the great Christian mystics. As recently as a decade ago it would also have struck most people as ridiculous in the extreme. Today, however, such seemingly far-fetched views are not so discordant with much of the climate of opinion in which we live. Far from being relegated to obscure publications on dusty shelves in seedy bookshops, as used to be the case, the occult is now very much part of the contemporary scene.

By the young, at any rate, the message of the Maharishi is widely listened to — at least until it has been displaced in popularity by some other brand of mysticism. In the same vein, the Sunday colour supplements in 'serious' newspapers sententiously bid us contemplate the therapeutic potentialities of healing magic and 'white' witchcraft; some psychiatrists even rally to the cry: 'Spiritualism proves survival', and a trendy bishop or two throws in his weight for extra measure.

Other indications point in the same direction. Scientology may be more successfully organized as a business venture than most of the Spiritualist churches which it succeeds and to some extent supplants. But it has much in common with them in seeking to blend pseudoscience and occult experience in that special package-deal which sells so well today. These and a host of other new competing cults strive to fill the gap left by the decline of established religion and to reassert the primacy of mystical experience in the face of the dreary progress of secularism. In thus appealing to the ever-present need for mystical excitement and drama, these new sects naturally often find themselves in conflict, not only with each other, but also with that longer established rival, psychiatry, which has already taken over so many functions formerly fulfilled by religion in our culture. Here the fanatical rantings of Scientologists against psychiatry are a revealing, if unreassuring, testimony to their rival common interests.

All this suggests that we live in an age of marginal mystical recrudescence, a world where Humanists seem positively archaic. Our vocabulary has been enriched, or at any rate added to, by a host of popular mystical expressions which, if enshrined in the special argot of the Underground, also spill over into general usage. We know what 'freak-outs' are, what 'trips' are, and any one who wants to can readily participate in psychedelic happenings in dance halls with evocative names like 'Middle Earth'. Although much of this language relates to drug-taking, in its original and more extended usage it also carries strong mystical overtones. Certainly the Eskimo and Tungus shamans, whom we consider later, would find a ready welcome in that most successfully publicized sector of our contemporary society, the pop scene. With its pronounced magical aura, and shamanic superstars like Jimi Hendrix and the Beatles (cf. Taylor, 1985), in this clamorously assertive sub-culture, far from being dismissed as excessive crudities of questionable religious value, the trance and possession experiences of exotic peoples are seriously considered, and often deliberately appropriated as exciting novel routes to ecstasy. It is thus perhaps not surprising that readings from an earlier edition of this book were included in the American public service religious radio series, 'Rock and Religion', broadcast from Sacramento, California, in 1979.

II

In this eclectic climate little special pleading is needed to introduce an anthropological study of trance and possession which, as the reader would expect, draws many of its examples from exotic tribal religions. Contrary to what might be anticipated, the fact that so much has already been written on these topics, largely by historians of religion, provides an added incentive for the development of a fresh approach. Most of these writers have had other ends in view, and have consequently not been concerned to pose the sort of question which the social anthropologist automatically asks. Few of the more substantial works in this area of comparative religion pause to consider how the production of religious ecstasy might relate to the social circumstances of those who produce it; how enthusiasm might wax and wane in different social conditions; or what functions might flow from it in contrasting types of society. In a word, most of these writers have been less interested in ecstasy as a social fact than in ecstasy as an expression, if a sometimes questionable one, of personal piety. And where they have ventured outside their own native tradition to consider evidence from other cultures their approach has generally been vitiated from the start by ethnocentric assumptions about the superiority of their own religion. This is not to say that no interesting sociological conclusions emerge from any of this work; but rather where they do, it is more by accident than by design.

Let me illustrate and at the same time move towards the position from which the arguments of this book stem. Here Ronald Knox's splendidly erudite study of Christian enthusiasm provides an excellent starting point (Knox, 1950) Beginning with the Montanists, Knox traces the erratic history of Christian enthusiasm, which he defines as a definite type of spirituality. He makes no attempt to explain by reference to other social factors the ebb and flow of ecstatic phenomena — possession, speaking with tongues, and the rest — whose wavering course he charts through so many centuries. These he views as the inevitable product of an inherent human tendency, almost of a failing — the disposition to religious emotionalism which John Wesley summed up in the word 'heart-work'. 'The emotions must be stirred to their depths, at frequent intervals, by unaccountable feelings of compunction, joy, peace, and so on, or how could you be certain that the Divine touch was working within you?' Knox is concerned to point the moral that ecstasy is less a 'wrong tendency' than a 'false emphasis'. But if he stresses the dangers of an excessive and unbridled enthusiasm, he also recognizes that organized religion must allow ecstasy some scope if it is to retain its vitality and vigour. These are the lessons which Knox seeks to impress upon the reader and which he finds little difficulty in illustrating in the mass of evidence which he so skilfully marshals.

Knox writes, as he says, primarily from a theological point of view. Yet certain interesting sociological insights almost force themselves upon him. Thus, with greater sociological perspicacity than Christian charity, he sees enthusiasm as the means by which men continually reassure themselves, and others, that God is with them. This view of ecstasy, as a prestigious commodity which could readily be manipulated for mundane ends, opens the door to the sort of sociological treatment which this book advocates, and which I shall enlarge upon shortly.

By confining his attention to the Christian tradition, and arguing in effect that spirituality is to be judged by its fruits, Knox was not faced with the problem of relating mystical experiences in other religions to those in his own. This tendentious issue has been left to plague other Christian authorities. Thus R.C. Zaehner (1957), the orientalist, has boldly sought to establish criteria with which to assess objectively the relative validity of a host of mystical encounters. The examples range from the recorded experiences of celebrated Christian and oriental mystics at one extreme, to the author's own and Huxley's experiments with drugs at the other. The critical sophistication of his argument is impressive, but the result is too predictable to be entirely convincing. Indeed, only those who share his assurance will accept Zaehner's conclusion, that Christian mysticism represents a more lofty form of transcendental experience than any other.

Not all Christian writers in this field are so adamant of course. Where Zaehner re-erects and fortifies the barriers of Christian complacency, Professor Elmer O'Brien's concise and useful survey, mainly of Christian mysticism, knocks them down again (O'Brien, 1965). Perhaps because he is a professional theologian he can afford to be more tolerant and practical. He is again concerned with the problem of establishing the authenticity of different mystical experiences. But the homely recipes, which he recommends should be applied in the assessment of the mystic, do not contain such glaring, inbuilt assumptions about the superiority of Christian or any other experience. O'Brien suggests that the following tests are crucial. First, the reputed mystical experience should be contrary to the subject's basic philosophical or theological position. Thus 'when the experience (as that of St Augustine) does not fit in at all with the person's speculative supposition, the chances are that it was a genuine experience'. Secondly, the experience, which the would-be mystic claims, is all the more convincing if it can be shown to be contrary to his own wishes, and cannot then be dismissed simply as a direct wish-fulfilment. Finally, the experience alone gives meaning and consistency to the mystic's doctrines.

Here, clearly, O'Brien is less concerned than Zaehner to pronounce upon the quality of ecstatic experience in any final or ultimate sense. His object is not to extol some brands of mysticism as superior, because more fully endowed with divine authenticity than others, but simply to provide criteria for distinguishing between the genuine and simulated mystical vocation. Here involuntariness and spontaneity become the touch-stones in assessment. It can, I think, be argued that O'Brien's first criterion depends too directly upon the special circumstances of the Christian tradition to make it universally applicable in all cultural contexts. But there is no doubt at all that in emphasizing the mystic's reluctance to assume the burdens of his vocation Professor O'Brien is pointing to a characteristic which, as we shall see later, applies widely in many different religions. Indeed it is a condition that most cultures which encourage mysticism and trance take as axiomatic.

But if O'Brien's tolerant catholicity can help to speed us on our path towards the comparative study of divine possession in a wide range of different cultures, his view of the incidence of mysticism seems to spell disappointment to all our hopes. Where Knox assumed a constant if partly regrettable human proclivity to indulge in enthusiasm, to some extent varying in its expression in different social conditions, O'Brien holds that apparent variations in the mystical 'outputs' of different ages are an illusion. The explanation for the seeming lack or abundance of mystics at any given period is 'not that a time and place favourable to mysticism brings mystics into existence'. On the contrary, it is merely a question of whether more or less attention is paid to mystics in different ages. Where mysticism is fashionable and accepted it is fully reported; where it is not nobody bothers to keep any record of it.

This steady state theory of mystical productivity would, if it were correct, divorce transcendental experience from the social environment in which it occurs and make totally irrelevant the sorts of sociological questions which I have urged should be applied to the data. Indeed it would almost close the door to sociological analysis; for all that would be left to discuss would be the significance of changing fashions concerning the desirability or otherwise of mystical experiences.

Powerful arguments against this stultifying conclusion come from a direction from which social anthropologists do not always like to accept help — psychology. T.K. Oesterreich, whose magisterial study of possession within as well as outside the Christian tradition is the most substantial work by a psychologist in this field, takes a very different view (Oesterreich, 1930). Acknowledging the universal character of possession phenomena, which he explains in terms of suggestion and the development of multiple personalities in the self, Oesterreich emphasizes how belief in the existence of spirits encourages psychic experiences which are interpreted as possession by these spirits. These transcendental encounters tend in turn to confirm the validity of the pre-existing beliefs in the existence of spirits. As he says (p. 377):

> By the artificial provocation of possession, primitive man has to a certain degree had it in his power to procure voluntarily the conscious presence of the metaphysical, and the desire to enjoy that consciousness of the divine presence offers a strong incentive to cultivate states of possession. In many cases it is probable that, exactly as in modern Spiritualism, the impervious desires for direct communication with departed ancestors and other relatives also play a part. Possession begins to disappear among civilized races as soon as belief in spirits loses its power. From the moment that they cease to entertain seriously the possibility of being possessed, the necessary auto-suggestion is lacking.

True enough. Yet as we now see in our own contemporary world, when, through drugs and other stimuli, people find a ready means to achieve trance states, these experiences quickly become invested with metaphysical meaning (see e.g. Young, 1972). There are also striking similarities in the patterns of imagery in which such experiences are expressed (see Grof, 1977).

Writing over fifty years ago, Oesterreich thus pushes further along the road towards a genuinely objective cross-cultural study of possession and trance than any of the more recent authorities I have mentioned. He also confirms that we are right to pursue our aim of relating these phenomena to the wider social circumstances in which they are produced. But if Oesterreich makes the connection for us between ecstasy in the great religions of the world and in the tribal religions studied by anthropologists, it is naturally to the latter that we should look for guidance in their own field. So far, however, the results of their labours have been singularly disappointing. Only one major comparative work has been produced — Mircea Eliade's study, *Shamanism and Archaic Techniques of Ecstasy* (Eliade, 1951). Here Eliade, who regards himself as a historian of religions, traces easily and convincingly the many common symbolic themes which occur in ecstatic cults in different cultures. However, his concern with the internal structures of these symbolic motifs and their historical relation leaves him little space for sociological analysis. In fact, he candidly acknowledges that the sociology of ecstasy has still to be written. The thirty years which have elapsed since this harsh judgement was delivered have, I am afraid, produced little that would require it to be revised.

III

At least until quite recently, anthropologists have scarcely displayed any more interest in the sociology of possession and trance than their colleagues who have studied these phenomena under the guise of ecstasy or enthusiasm in other cultural traditions. With a few notable exceptions they have thus simply not asked the important questions which, I glibly asserted above, automatically roll off the tongues of anthropologists. On the contrary, the majority of anthropological writers on possession have been equally fascinated by its richly dramatic elements, enthralled — one might almost say — by the more bizarre and exotic shamanistic exercises, and absorbed in often quite pointless debates as to the genuineness or otherwise of particular trance states. Their main interest has been in the expressive or theatrical aspect of possession; and they have frequently not even troubled to ask themselves very closely what precisely was being 'expressed' — except of course a sense of identity with a supernatural power.

This fixation with all that is dramatic in possession contrasts sharply with the social anthropologist's approach to the study of witchcraft and sorcery. In that dark corner of comparative religion where, at least in my opinion, sociological research has made its most successful impact, the anthropologist focuses squarely on the social nexus in which sorcery and witchcraft accusations are made. He passes beyond the beliefs to examine the incidence of accusations in different social contexts. He is thus able to show convincingly how witchcraft charges provide a means of mystical attack in tension-fraught relationships, where other means of pursuing conflict are inappropriate or unavailable. It is possible that this objective and thoroughly sociological approach, which sees the accused witch as the real victim rather than the 'be-witched' subject, is encouraged by the simple fact that by and large anthropologists do not themselves believe in the reality of witchcraft or sorcery. Where religious ecstasy and all its many theatrical accessory manifestations are concerned, however, many anthropologists appear to display a much more open, and certainly a far less dispassionate attitude. This is even true of those anthropologists who flaunt their atheism. For atheists, after all, frequently believe in extra-sensory perception, if not in all the more sensational manifestations of the occult.

For whatever reasons, the fact is that social anthropologists have in general shown a quite remarkable reluctance to ask the really significant questions when dealing with possession. This, of course, is not to say that no sociological interpretation whatsoever has been attempted. A number of anthropologists have considered the social role of the possessed priest or 'shaman', and the manner in which religious ecstasy may serve as the basis for a charismatic leader's authority. Others have emphasized the significance of the evasion of mortal responsibility implied where decisions are made not by men, but by gods speaking through them. And if some have stressed the employment of ecstatic revelations to conserve and strengthen the existing social order, others have shown how these can equally well be applied to authorize innovation and change.

This short catalogue, however, practically exhausts the range of most current preoccupations in the sociological study of possession. The crucial bread-and-butter questions still remain to be asked. How does the incidence of ecstasy relate to the social order? Is possession an entirely arbitrary and idiosyncratic affair; or are particular social categories of person more or less likely to be possessed? If so, and possession can be shown to run in particular social grooves, what follows from this? Why do people in certain social positions succumb to possession more readily than others? What does ecstasy offer them? It is these basic issues concerning the social context of possession that this book examines.

I referred earlier to the possible relevance of the anthropologist's personal equation in influencing his approach to his data. I hasten therfore to say that the adoption of this sociological line of inquiry does not necessarily imply that spirits are assumed to have no existential reality. Above all, it is not suggested that such beliefs should be dismissed as figments of the disordered imaginations of credulous peoples. For those who believe in them, mystical powers are realities both of thought and experience. My starting point, consequently, is precisely that large numbers of people in many different parts of the world do believe in gods and spirits. And I certainly do not presume to contest the validity of their beliefs, or to imply, as some anthropologists do, that such beliefs are so patently absurd that those who hold them do not 'really' believe in them. My objective is not to explain away religion. On the contrary, my purpose is simply to try to isolate the particular social and other conditions which encourage the development of an ecstatic emphasis in religion.

Nor, of course, have I any ambition to follow Zaehner or other ethnocentric writers in seeking to distinguish between 'higher' and 'lower', or 'more' or 'less' authentic forms of ecstatic experience. The anthropologist's task is to discover what people believe in, and to relate their beliefs operationally to other aspects of their culture and society. He has neither the skills nor the authority to pronounce upon the absolute 'truth' of ecstatic manifestations in different cultures. Nor is it his business to assess whether other people's perceptions of divine truth are more or less compatible with those embodied in his own religious heritage, whatever he may feel about the latter. Indeed I would go further. Such judgements might be more fittingly left to the jurisdiction of the powers which are held to inspire religious feeling. Certainly, at least, it is not for the anthropologist to attempt to usurp the role of the gods whose worship he studies.

Hence the reader who expects any cross-cultural calculus of the relative authenticity of the ecstatic experiences discussed in this book will be disappointed. Judgements concerning the truth or falsity of inspiration will only be relevant to our sociological analysis where they are made by the people in whose midst these experiences occur. Only where the actors themselves hold that some ecstatic states are false, whereas others are true, does this assessment form part of the evidence which we have to consider.

Perhaps I should also add that in treating tribal and Christian beliefs, and sometimes those of other world religions within the same

24

frame of reference no disrespect is intended to the adherents of any of these faiths. I can only ask that the validity of my comparisons should be judged by their inherent plausibility, and by the extent to which they contribute to the understanding of religious experience.

IV

I make these declarations because the study of religious enthusiasm is peculiarly sensitive to subjective judgement. My slogan, if one is still necessary, is: let those who believe in spirits and possesion speak for themselves!

Now let me summarize my argument which, I repeat, is based on the assumption that, notwithstanding all its richly dramatic aspects and, from one point of view, its highly personal character, religious enthusiasm can be treated as a social phenomenon.

I begin in the next chapter by trying to unravel a number of largely semantic confusions which bedevil the objective comparison of ecstatic experiences, showing how the non-mystical conception of trance held by medical science is shared by some tribal peoples, but not by others. Those for whom trance connotes a mystical state tend to adopt one of two partly conflicting theories. They consider that trance is due either to the temporary absence of the subject's soul ('soul-loss'), or that it represents possession by a supernatural power. The first interpretation stresses a loss of personal vital force, a 'de-possession', the second emphasizes an intrusion of external power. In some cultures both these views are entertained simultaneously, so that the 'de-possessed' person is 'possessed' by the spirit or power. For the most part, however, our concern in this book is with those who regard trance primarily as a form of supernatural possession. If I use the term 'trance' to denote some degree of mental dissociation, it is extremely important that we should grasp that in other cultures people are frequently considered to be possessed who are very far from being in a trance state. Often the onset of an illness if regarded as possession by an alien mystical power, long before the subject is in anything approaching a condition of trance. Possession thus has a much wider range of meanings than our denatured term trance.

Following this, I move on to examine briefly some of the most striking common elements in imagery and symbolism which so many different ecstatic religions share. If I pursue here only those themes which relate directly to my sociological preoccupations and ignore others which are more tangential, I do this deliberately and not because

I consider the latter unimportant. Those who seek a fuller treatment of the symbolic content of possession will readily find it in Eliade's book.

After these necessary preliminaries, I begin in the third chapter to look closely at the social contexts in which ecstasy and possession flourish. Far from being arbitrary and haphazard in its incidence, there we shall see how a widespread form of possession, which is regarded initially as an illness, is in many cases virtually restricted to women. Such women's possession 'afflictions' are regularly treated not by permanently expelling the possessing agency, but by reaching a viable accommodation with it. The spirit is tamed and domesticated, rather than exorcized. This treatment is usually accomplished by the induction of the affected women into a female cult group which regularly promotes possession experiences among its members. Within the secluded cult group, possession has thus lost its malign significance.

Hence what men consider a demoniacal sickness, women convert into a clandestine ecstasy. And this of course is my justification for treating as a religious experience something which, on the surface, appears to be its precise opposite. If the reader still feels that this dramatic apotheosis is unconvincing, he should remember how frequently the great mystics of the Christian and other world religions have received their first illumination either in circumstances of extreme adversity, or in a form which appeared initially as a searing affliction. He should recall also how aptly the conception of this first call as a dreaded sickness meets the requirements for mystical authenticity so clearly formulated by Professor O'Brien.

For all their concern with disease and its treatment, such women's possession cults are also, I argue, thinly disguised protest movements directed against the dominant sex. They thus play a significant part in the sex-war in traditional societies and cultures where women lack more obvious and direct means for forwarding their aims. To a considerable extent they protect women from the exactions of men, and offer an effective vehicle for manipulating husbands and male relatives. This interpretation coincides closely with Ronald Knox's brilliant, if caustic, aside that in Christianity, 'from the Montanist movement onwards, the history of enthusiasm is largely a history of female emancipation, and it is not a reassuring one'. I do not subscribe to the latter judgement. But this conclusion — which Knox does not pursue systematically — offers striking corroboration, from a somewhat unexpected quarter, of the validity of our findings in very different cultural circumstances.

So far we have said nothing of the character of the spirits involved in this type of possession. It is I believe of the greatest interest and importance that these spirits are typically considered to be amoral: they have no direct moral significance. Full of spite and malice though they are, they are believed to strike entirely capriciously and without any grounds which can be referred to the moral character or conduct of their victims. Thus the women who succumb to these afflictions cannot help themselves and at the same time bear no responsibility for all the annoyance and cost which their subsequent treatment involves. They are thus totally blameless; responsibility lies not with them, but with the spirits.

Because they play no direct part in upholding the moral code of the societies in which they receive so much attention, I call these spirits 'peripheral'. They are in fact very often also peripheral in a further sense. For typically these spirits are believed to originate *outside* the societies whose women they plague. Frequently they are the spirits of hostile neighbouring peoples, so that animosities between rival local communities become reflected in this mystical idiom. And if their favourite victims are usually women who, as jural minors in traditional societies, also in a sense occupy a dependent — and in a sense also peripheral position, we have here a very direct concordance between the attributes of the spirits, the manner in which the afflictions they cause are evaluated, and the status of their human prey. Peripherality, as I use the term, has this three-fold character.

Such peripheral cults, as I try to show in Chapter Four, also frequently embrace downtrodden categories of men who are subject to strong discrimination in rigidly stratified societies. Peripheral possession is consequently far from being a secure female monopoly, and cannot thus be explained plausibly in terms of any innate tendency to hysteria on the part of women. And where men of low social position are involved, although ostensibly existing only to cure spirit-caused illnesses, such cults again express protest by the politically impotent. Our own contemporary experience of fringe protest groups and cults should help us to appreciate what is involved here.

In addition to explaining illness, peripheral possession can thus be seen to serve as an oblique aggressive strategy. The possessed person is ill through no fault of his own. The illness requires treatment which his (or her) master has to provide. In his state of possession the patient is a highly privileged person: he is allowed many liberties with those whom in other circumstances he is required to treat with respect.

Moreover, however costly and inconvenient for those to whom his normal status renders him subservient, his cure is often incomplete. Lapses are likely to occur whenever difficulties develop with his superiors. Clearly, in this context, possession works to help the interests of the weak and downtrodden who have otherwise few effective means to press their claims for attention and respect. This process, Gomm (1975) aptly calls, 'bargaining from weakness'.

This interpretation of peripheral possession as a form of mystical attack immediately suggests parallels with the employment of witchcraft accusations to express aggression between rivals and enemies. To accuse someone of bewitching you is, however, to attack them openly and directly, and represents a much more drastic strategy than is implied in the devious manoeuvre of peripheral possession. The possessed person exerts pressure on his superior without radically questioning his superiority. He ventilates his pent-up animosity without questioning the ultimate legitimacy of the status differences enshrined within the established hierarchical order. If peripheral possession is thus a gesture of defiance, it is also, usually, one of hopelessness. It follows from these distinctions that we should expect these two separate strategies to operate, in different social context, and this is largely what we find in practice. However, a highly significant synthesis is also achieved between them. We shall find that those who, as masters of spirits, diagnose and treat illness in others, are themselves in danger of being accused as witches. For if their power over the spirits is such that they can heal the sick, why should they not also sometimes cause what they cure? Reasoning in this fashion, the manipulated establishment which reluctantly tolerates bouts of uncontrolled possession illness among its dependants, rounds on the leaders of these rebellious cults and firmly denounces them as witches. Thus, I argue, the most ambitious and pushing members of these insurgent cults are kept in check, hoist, as it were, with their own petard.

It will be clear that whatever mystical or psychological benefits peripheral possession confers, it also regularly achieves other more tangible rewards. Following this up, we move on in Chapters Five and Six to explore the functions of possession where this has ceased to be solely the resort of the weak and humiliated and has become the mystical idiom in terms of which men of substance compete for positions of power and authority in society at large. Here enthusiasm emerges from its seclusion on the fringes of society into the full light of day. Now we are on more familiar ground since we are concerned with the ecstatic aspects of mainline religions. The path we shall follow has already been indicated for us by Knox's observation that religious leaders turn to ecstasy when they seek to strengthen and legitimize their authority. Whereas those cults we called peripheral involved spirits which were sublimely indifferent to the moral conduct of mankind, now we are concerned with mystical powers which are regarded frankly as sternly moralistic. While they inspire men to high positions, they also act as the censors of society. Their intervention in human affairs is a direct product of human misdemeanours and the commission of moral wrongs. Their task is to uphold and sustain public morality.

In distinction to the peripheral cults with their more limited and specialized functions, I shall refer to these thoroughly moralizing systems of ecstatic beliefs as 'main morality possession religions', or, more simply and less barbarously, as 'central possession religions'. I shall distinguish two types: those involving ancestor spirits (Chapter Five); and those involving more autonomous deities which are not simply sacralized versions of the living (Chapter Six). In both cases we shall examine how the inspired priest, or shaman, who has privileged access to these supernatural powers, diagnoses sins and prescribes the appropriate atonement. The political and legal authority wielded by the holders of these religious commissions is, as we shall see, largely a function of the availability of other more specialized agencies of political and social control. In highly atomized societies without secure and clearly defined political positions, the shaman comes into his own as an omni-competent leader, regulating the intercourse both between man and man and between men and the spirits.

If certain exotic religions thus allow ecstasy to rule most aspects of their adherents' lives, all the evidence indicates that the more strongly-based and entrenched religious authority becomes, the more hostile it is towards haphazard inspiration. New faiths may announce their advent with a flourish of ecstatic revelations, but once they become securely established they have little time or tolerance for enthusiasm. For the religious enthusiast, with his direct claim to divine knowledge, is always a threat to the established order. What then are the factors which inhibit the growth of this attitude towards ecstasy and keep possession on the boil? The empirical evidence, which we review, suggests that part at least of the answer lies in acute and constantly recurring social and environmental pressures which militate against the formation of large, secure social groups. For, as we shall see, those societies in which central possession cults persist seem to be usually composed of small, fluid, social units exposed to particularly exacting physical conditions, or conquered communities lying under the yoke of alien oppression. Thus, as in peripheral cults, the circumstances which encourage the ecstatic response are precisely those where men feel themselves constantly threatened by exacting pressures which they do not know how to combat or control, except through those heroic flights of ecstasy by which they seek to demonstrate that they are the equals of the gods. Thus if enthusiasm is a retort to oppression and repression, what it seeks to proclaim is man's triumphant mastery of an intolerable environment.

This brings us directly to the crucial question of the psychological significance of possession. If I have relegated discussion of psychological interpretations of ectasy to my final chapter, this is not because I consider these unimportant. My objective is to bring us back finally to our world, relating these largely exotic experiences from alien cultures to our own contemporary circumstances through psychology and psychiatry, since it is primarily within the subject matter studied by these disciplines that we find directly comparable material today. As I have already revealed so much of the hand that I try to play in this book, I leave the reader to explore for himself the arguments of the final chapter. I would only add, that such is the incidence of mental stress and illness in our contemporary culture, that we do well to ponder how so many beliefs and experiences, which we relegate to abnormal psychology, seem to find in other cultures a secure and satisfying outlet in ecstatic religion.

Finally, my aplogy, if an apology is needed, for this extended summary of the arguments of this study is that where one seeks to open up a largely novel line of approach and to look at old data from a fresh angle, the writer owes it to the reader to indicate the general direction he intends to follow. I am not particularly wedded to the analytical terms 'peripheral' and 'central' which I find so useful. But since I hold very definite views about the realities to which I consider they refer, it has seemed essential to make it perfectly clear from the start how these concepts are applied. Much of my treatment of the evidence on possession and shamanism will be found to correspond closely to that modish approach which is now often dignified with the title of 'transactional analysis'. For what it is worth, my own more limited slogan in the present context is, that to a significant extent, possession is as possession does.

In thus pointing to certain social functions fulfilled by possession I do not maintain that these exhaust the phenomenon's functional capacities, nor do I consider that in any complete sense they explain its existence. Once they have shown what for secular ends is done in the name of religion, some anthropologists naïvely suppose that nothing more remains to be said. Thus they leave largely unexplained the characteristic mystical aspects which distinguish the religious from the secular, and they totally fail to account for the rich diversity of religious concepts and beliefs. Although my ambitions do not extend to explaining these particularistic aspects of different ecstatic religions, I do seek to uncover some of the foundations, psychological as well as social, upon which the ecstatic response is based. In pursuing these aims, I realize of course that I must sometimes seem to have allowed myself to be carried to conclusions which impose some strain on the existing evidence. Where this is the case I would only plead that enthusiasm is catching. Although I don't myself fall in this category, I might add that some of those anthropologists who have studied shamanism in other cultures have followed Carlos Castaneda to become themselves practising shamans in their own culture.

Chapter Two

TRANCE AND POSSESSION

I

The great Danish Arctic explorer and ethnographer, Rasmussen, records how one of the Eskimo shamans, or inspired priests, whom he encountered had in vain sought instruction in his mystical vocation from other shamans. Finally, like St Antony, the founder of the Anchorites, this Eskimo neophyte sought inspiration in solitude and wandered off to pursue a lonely vigil in the wilderness. 'There,' he told Rasmussen,

> I soon became melancholy. I would sometimes fall to weeping and feel unhappy without knowing why. Then for no reason all would suddenly be changed, and I felt a great, inexplicable joy, a joy so powerful that I could not restrain it, but had to break into song, a mighty song, with room for only one word: joy, joy! And I had to use the full strength of my voice. And then in the midst of such a fit of mysterious and overwhelming delight I became a shaman, not knowing myself how it came about. But I was a shaman. I could see and hear in a totally different way. I had gained my enlightenment, the shaman's light of brain and body, and this in such a manner that it was not only I who could see through the darkness of life, but the same bright light also shone out from me, imperceptible to human beings but visible to all spirits of earth and sky and sea, and these now came to me to become my helping spirits (Rasmussen, 1929, p. 119).

This vivid recollection of an Eskimo shaman's calling echoes countless descriptions of similar ecstatic experiences in the world's universalistic religions as well as in the more exotic tribal religions with which this book mainly deals. It is directly analogous too to the growing volume of reports of mystical experiences engendered by the so-called 'sacramental drugs' of the LSD type. One typical American subject, for example, has described this common response to a session with this drug in similar, if more pretentious language:

> But then in a flash of illumination, I understood that this perfect genius of which I conceived was nothing more than a minute and miserable microcosm, containing but the barest hint of the infinitely more complex and enormously vast macrocosmic Mind of God. I knew that for all its wondrous precision this man-mind even in ultimate fulfilment of all its potentials could never be more than the feeblest reflection of the God-Mind in the image of which the man-mind had been so miraculously created. I was filled with awe of God as my Creator, and then with love for God as the One Who sustained me even, as in my images, I seemed to sustain the contents of my own mind . . . I marvelled all the more at the feeling I now had that somehow the attention of God was focused upon me and that I was receiving enlightenment from Him. Tears came into my eyes and I opened them upon a room in which it seemed to me that each object had somehow been touched by God's sublime Presence (Masters & Houston, 1967, p. 264).

Attempts to diminish the status of such drug-induced mysticism by dubbing it 'instant religion' need not detain us here. Nor need we be unduly disturbed by the fact that psychiatric case-records abound in descriptions of similar subjectively evaluated mystical experience. The problem of distinguishing between madmen and mystics, which we shall take up later, is one most religious communities have had to face.

For our purposes all we need to note for the moment is the universality of mystical experience and the remarkable uniformity of mystical language and symbolism. We also require, however, a neutral term to denote the mental state of the subject of such experiences. Here I shall employ the word 'trance', using it in its general medical sense which the *Penguin Dictionary of Psychology* conveniently defines as: 'a condition of dissociation, characterized by the lack of voluntary movement, and frequently by automatisms in act and thought, illustrated by hypnotic and mediumistic conditions.' So conceived, trance may involve complete or only partial mental dissociation, and is often accompanied by exciting visions, or 'hallucinations', the full content of which is not always subsequently so clearly recalled as in the two experiences quoted earlier.

As is well known, trance states can be readily induced in most normal people by a wide range of stimuli, applied either separately or in combination. Time-honoured techniques include the use of alcoholic spirits, hypnotic suggestion, rapid over-breathing, the inhalation of smoke and vapours, music, and dancing; and the ingestion of such drugs as mescaline or lysergic acid and other psychotropic alkaloids. The specific and non-specific effects of these drugs and the extent to which drug experiences vary with the socio-cultural setting in which they occur has received much attention (see eg. Furst, 1972; Harner, 1973; Grof, 1977; Schultes and Hofmann, 1980). Even without these aids, much the same effect can be produced, although usually in the nature of things more slowly, by such self-inflicted or externally imposed mortifications and privations as fasting and ascetic contemplation (e.g. 'transcendental meditation'). The inspirational effect of sensory deprivation, implied in the stereotyped mystical 'flight' into the wilderness, has also been well documented in laboratory experiments. The most exciting scientific discoveries here, surely, are those of the endorphins — natural opiates in the human brain — whose production and release is promoted by such traditional methods of trance induction (Ahlberg, 1982; Prince, 1982). The presence of these natural euphoriants in the human body — which seem to be released by such mundane activities as jogging (cf. Banyai, 1984) makes Marx's famous epithet about 'religion as the opium of the people' literally and materially true in a most unexpected way! The existence of this natural endorphin (and possibly other similar) endogenous systems also explains how states of altered consciousness and analgesia associated specifically with the ingestion of hallucinogenic or psychotropic drugs can be produced without these external aids to trance.

However they are produced, our immediate concern is with the interpretation given by different cultures to trance states. Here we take up the question of the culturally standardized, and therefore 'normal', meaning of trance in different communities. In conformity with our own Christian tradition, we tend to equate trance and possession, thus following what — as we shall see in a moment — is one of the most widespread cultural explanations of mental dissociation. As with other established religions, however, orthodox Christianity has generally sought to belittle mystical interpretations of trance where these were claimed by those who experienced them to represent Divine revelation. Thus though it is difficult to ignore the countless visions of Christian mystics, where the church has approved or honoured these ascetic figures it has often done so on other grounds. The sanction of heresy has proved a powerful deterrent in curtailing and discrediting wayward personal mystical experiences. Indeed, it is mainly in the context of trance states ascribed to the work of the Devil that we meet official ecclesiastical recognition of possession. But today, within the Catholic church, the wide range of cases, which in the middle ages were unhestitatingly diagnosed as demoniacal possession, has shrunk to those few instances which Catholic psychiatrists feel unable to explain in more prosaic terms. This small residuum is all that remains of the vast spectrum of trance and hysterical behaviour formerly attributed to the work of the Devil and his agents. All other cases are treated as 'pseudo-possessions' explicable in terms of modern science.

Outside the Catholic church, for most psychiatrists and psychoanalysts there is no such thing as true possession in our modern world. All cases involving the ideology of possession are considered to be satisfactorily explained without invoking belief in the existence of the Devil — or of God. Indeed, psychiatry today itself uses a wide range of therapies which are specifically designed to provoke trance and trance-like states in which the patient, liberated by drugs or hypnosis from his customary restraints, is freed to disgorge repressed traumatic experiences through abreaction. Here, for most psychiatrists, if not for all psychoanalysts, there is no implication that these techniques are inherently mystical. Rather they are held to work on the central nervous system by scientific processes which, if not yet fully understood in detail, are certainly not considered to be unfathomable.

This non-mystical secular interpretation of trance and dissociation which, of course, is not fully shared by Western Spiritualists, Pentecostalists, some Quakers, or many of the new 'pop' cult-groups, is by no means a monopoly of modern science. Amongst the conservative Samburu pastoral nomads of northern Kenya, Paul Spencer (Spencer, 1965) has vividly described trance states which in their own local cultural setting involve no mystical aetiology. Here Samburu men in the unmarried warrior age-group of fifteen to thirty years called *morans*, readily fall into trance in particular circumstances. These 'odd men out', suspended between boyhood and adulthood in an uncomfortably prolonged adolescence, regularly go into trance, shaking with extreme bodily agitation, in frustrating situations. Typical precipitating circumstances are those where one group of *morans* is out-danced by a rival group in front of girls; or when one of their own girls is led off in marriage; during initiation; or when they are about to be replaced by a new age-group of younger men. Similarly outside these traditional settings, Samburu soldiers may get the shakes on parade, or when ambushed. All the evidence here shows conclusively that this is a culturally conditioned response to tension and danger which is not interpreted mystically, and is indeed viewed by the Samburu as a sign of manliness and self-assertion. Once men have passed through the *moran* grade, have married, and become elders, they stop shaking. It would no longer be culturally appropriate for adult men to make this response. In all these trance experiences there is no implication at all that those who shake are possessed by spirits. Possession is not part of Samburu ideology.

Rather similarly, amongst the Abelam tribe of New Guinea (Forge), young deprived bachelors sometimes exhibit all the symptoms which in many other societies would be interpreted as signs of possession. Known in this state by a word which means literally 'deaf' and clearly well describes their dissociation, these men behave with hysterically agitated gestures and (apparently) uncontrolled violence. Such outbursts are tolerated for those in this position, and indeed temporarily earn them a measure of special respect. Again, there is no idea that this state is due to spirit possession. Although the evidence is not entirely clear, it seems that this is also the case with that wider New Guinea phenomenon, known as 'mushroom madness', where trance behaviour is associated with the eating of certain fungi.

This non-mystical interpretation of trance also applies, although not completely, to that medieval dancing mania called tarantism, which in the fifteenth century swept through Italy in the wake of the Black Death. This was the Italian version of the extraordinary epidemic which had earlier spread like a contagion through Germany, Holland, and Belgium. In those countries, the malady had become associated with the names of St Vitus and St John the Baptist, since it was at shrines dedicated to these saints that the dancers sought relief from their affliction. Whether it was known as St Vitus's Dance or tarantism, its symptoms, and the circumstances in which it occurred, were generally the same. In times of privation and misery, the most abused members of society felt themselves seized by an irresistible urge to dance wildly until they reached a state of trance and collapsed exhausted — and usually cured, if only temporarily. Contemporary reports record how peasants left their ploughs, mechanics their workshops, house-wives their domestic duties, children their parents, servants, their masters — all swept headlong into the Bacchanalian revelry. The frenetic dancing would last for hours at a stretch, the dancers shouting and screaming furiously, and often foaming at the mouth. Many enjoyed strange apocalyptic visions, as the heavens seemed to open before their eyes to reveal the Saviour on His throne with the Blessed Virgin at his side. Sometimes individuals were seized first by epileptic-like attacks. Panting and labouring for breath, they fell swooning to the ground, only to leap up again to dance with powerful convulsive movements.

Although this 'dancing mania', as Hecker calls it, was remarkably uniform in its incidence and character, it was not everywhere interpreted in the same way. In the Low Countries, the malady was usually regarded as a form of demoniacal possession and was frequently treated by exorcism. The same method was also sometimes employed by the priests in Italy. But here, as its local name — tarantism — indicates, it was thought to be caused by the poisonous bite of the tarantula spider rather than to be due to possession by the Devil. As elsewhere, those suffering from the disease showed extreme sensitivity to music and, at the sound of the appropriate air, would dance themselves into a state of trance after which they would collapse exhausted and, for the time being at least, cured. Once the tune to which the patient responded had been discovered, a single application of this dance and music therapy was often sufficient to lift the affliction for a whole year.

In the fifteenth century it was generally believed in Italy that dancing to the music of fifes, clarinets, and drums, and especially to the brisk rhythm of the tarantella (named after the spider), caused the poison from the tarantula's bite to be dispersed round the body of the victim, whence it was expelled harmlessly through the skin as perspiration. Indeed, as late as the seventeenth century, it was still customary for bands of musicians to traverse the country in the summer months, when the malady was at its height, treating the *taranti* in different villages and towns at large rallies. Because of the marked predominance of female victims, these gatherings were usually known as the 'Little Carnivals of Women'. Although the incidence of tarantism has greatly declined since, it still survives today in an attenuated form in the more remote and backward villages of southern Italy (de Martino, 1966).

I shall examine this interesting phenomenon more fully in a later chapter. My present concern is simply to emphasize that, in contrast to St John's and St Vitus's Dance, tarantism was long considered by many to be a disease caused by the toxic bite of the tarantula spider and not involving any mystical aetiology. More recent research has established that there are two types of tarantula spider, and that only one of these is actually venomous with a poisonous bite capable of producing the symptoms encountered in tarantism. Paradoxically, it is not this toxic spider, but the other completely harmless variety of tarantula, which is larger and looks more threatening, that figures predominantly in tarantism. We shall return to the implications of this discovery later.

Finally, even in cultures where trance is regularly and indeed normally interpreted mystically, some cases may be explained in non-mystical terms. Among the Tungus reindeer herders of Siberia, who provide the *locus classicus* of shamanism (since *shaman* is a Tungus word), hysterical states, involving trembling and the compulsive imitation of words and gestures, are not necessarily always attributed to the action of spirits. In fact the term *olon* (from a verb meaning to be frightened) is used to describe such persons who exhibit this behaviour but are not considered to be possessed by spirits. Those concerned here are sometimes young women uncontrollably repeating taboo'd obscene expressions in the presence of old women and men. Such demure maidens are then employing language normally reserved for their elders and betters; and adding insult to injury by doing this in the company of those whom they should respect and honour. There is thus involved an element of rebellious, flaunting behaviour which is clearly present in my favourite example of this phenomenon. This concerns the scandalous affair of the Third (Tungus) Battalion of the TransBaikal Cossacks. The battalion was being harangued by its irascible Russian colonel, and suddenly began to repeat after him all his commands and gestures, and, as these were not obeyed, the flood of obscene curses which followed. What happened afterwards is not recorded and is in any case irrelevant here. We should note, however, the behaviour of this kind, which is not interpreted as mystically caused, rapidly shades amongst the Tungus into states where a mystical aetiology is invoked.

II

The altered state of consciousness (which may vary very considerably in degree) and which for convenience we call trance is, in the circumstances in which it occurs, open to different cultural controls and to various cultural interpretations. Indeed, as with adolescence, trance is subject to both physiological and cultural definition. Some cultures follow our own medical practice in spirit if not in detail in seeing this condition as a state of mental aberration where no mystical factors are involved. Other cultures see trance as mystically caused; and others again interpret the same physiological phenomenon in different ways in different contexts. The existence of rival and apparently mutually opposed interpretations of trance occurs of course today in our own society. With the advance of medical science, the incidence of trance states interpreted by the Church as signs of possession has progressively decreased since the Middle Ages. Yet outside this rigid framework of established religion, fringe cults have increasingly taken over a mystical interpretation of trance as the sign of divine inspiration. This is certainly the manner in which trance is overwhelmingly understood in revivalist movements like those of the 'Bible Belt' of the USA, and seems also to be growing in significance in the newer protest cult groups which employ drugs such as LSD and other psychedelic stimulants.

The ideological leap from a non-mystical to a mystical evaluation of trance may be illustrated by the Indian Shaker cult founded by John Slocum in Washington state at the end of the last century (Barnett, 1957). Here, uncontrollable bodily agitation and trance states achieved in emotionally charged church services, are referred to as 'shaking', in the manner we have already seen amongst the Samburu tribe of Kenya. But whereas for the Samburu this condition has no mystical implications, amongst the Shakers (as with the early Quakers) each seizure represents a manifestation of the Holy Spirit. Trance indeed is both personalized and objectified, so that an Indian speaks of 'his shake' as a distinctive vital force, or power, and people will say in support of their convictions: 'So-and-so is true, because my shake told me so.' Here trance has become divine possession.

If, however, possession by an external agency or spirit may be one explanation of trance, it does not follow that all conditions in which spirit possession is postulated necessarily involve trance. Much confusion in the literature on spirit possession results directly from assuming that these two states are necessarily and always equivalent. As we shall increasingly see, in many cultures where possession by a spirit is the main or sole interpretation of trance, possession may be diagnosed long before an actual state of trance has been reached.

Frequently, for example, illness is seen as a form of possession; yet the possessed patient is far from being in trance. Indeed it is regularly only in the actual treatment of possession, either by exorcism, or by a procedure which aims at achieving a viable accommodation between victim and possessing agency, that trance in the full sense is induced. As the great German medical student of possession, T.K. Oesterreich, noticed of medieval treatments, it was frequently only in the full throes of clerical exorcism that 'possession' (i.e. trance) in the clinical sense really occurred. This penetrating observation corresponds very well with the evidence of Charcot's experiences at the Salpêtière mental hospital in Paris in the second half of the nineteenth century. There, as now seems clear, it was the great physician himself who often induced the more extravagant manifestations of 'grand hysteria' in his patients!

Spirit possession thus embraces a wider range of phenomena than trance, and is regularly attributed to people who are far from being mentally disassociated, although they may become so in the treatments which they subsequently undergo. It is a cultural evaluation of a person's condition, and means precisely what it says: an invasion of the individual by a spirit. It is not thus for us to judge who is and who is not *really* 'possessed'. If someone is, in his own cultural milieu, generally considered to be in a state of spirit possession, then he (or she) is possessed. This is the simple definition which we shall follow in this book. This, of course, is not to deny that there are degrees of possession. As we shall see, this is widely recognized in those cultures which employ this mystical aetiology.

Spirit possession, then, is one of the main, widely distributed mystical interpretations of trance and of other associated conditions. The other major mystical theory is that which attributes these states to the temporary absence of the victim's soul, and is consequently usually known in anthropology as 'soul-loss'. The Belgian anthropologist Luc de Heusch has argued that these two mystical explanations are mutually necessary (de Heusch, 1962; 1971). Possession can only occur if at the same time there is a 'depossession' of the self, such as is implied in the doctrine of soul-loss. At first sight this seems to make excellent sense. But in practice we find empirically that while these explanations may co-exist in some cultures, or in some contexts of trance in a particular society, other people, if they even explicitly draw this logical inference, do not trouble to stress it. The picture is also further complicated by the fact that in many cultures man is considered to possess not one but several souls. A few examples will show the complexity of the situation.

The Yaruro Indians of Venezuela evidently follow de Heusch's logic. They believe that when their shamans journey to the spirit land they leave behind them a mere husk of their personality. This residuum serves as a link in the channel of communication which in trance they establish with the spirit powers. In this state of depossession they are possessed by visiting helper spirits. Here clearly, and fairly explicitly, soul-loss is seen as a necessary pre-condition for spirit possession. The Akawaio Caribs of British Guiana take a rather similar view which they express in a very imaginative way. They believe that in trance, which is induced by chewing tobacco, the shaman's spirit (or soul) becomes very small and light and is able to detach itself from his body and fly with the aid of 'ladder spirits' into the skies. The swallow-tailed kite, known colloquially as 'clairvoyant woman', helps the shaman's spirit to soar aloft to commune with other spirits. At the same time, his body, which is left behind as an empty receptacle, is filled by various forest spirits. It is these which now possess his body and speak through it. However, to complicate matters, the Akawaio also believe that the shaman's body can be concurrently occupied by several ghosts or spirits as well as by his own spirit or soul. Indeed a successful shaman's helping familiars stay with him all the time. Thus he may be in a constant state of latent possession, but only occasionally, at séances, in full trance (Butt, 1967).

In Haitian voodoo, likewise, at least according to the doctrines of the shamanistic priests themselves, when a *loa* spirit moves into the head of an individual it does so by first displacing his *gros bon ange*, one of the two souls which each person carries in himself. This temporary eviction of the 'good angel' soul, causes trembling and convulsions which are characteristic of the opening stages of possession and trance. Similarly among the Saora tribesmen of Orissa, in India, when a shaman goes into trance and the spirit comes upon him, his own soul is temporarily expelled and the spirit takes its place in his heart or Adam's apple. Finally, in this vein, the Arctic Tungus believe that each man has two or three souls. The first soul may leave the body causing unconsciousness, but nothing more serious. Prolonged absence of the second soul, however, leads to death; and after death this soul goes to the world of the dead. The third soul remains with the body until it has decomposed and then leaves the body to live on with the dead man's relatives. Tungus shamanism which, as we shall see, involves possession may be accompanied by a displacement of one of these three souls.

Amongst numerous other peoples with whom we shall be concerned in this study, however, the implication that possession by an external agent can only occur if the subject's own soul is temporarily displaced is not emphasized, and sometimes receives no explicit recognition. This, for example, is the position amongst the Muslim Somali nomads of north-east Africa, where possession is conceived of as an 'entering' by a spirit without any doctrine that this entails the absence of the person's own soul. The latter, in any case, is believed to leave the human body only on death. And even where, as in some of the cases which we shall exmaine later, one person is believed to possess another — so that the possessing agency is in some sense an emanation of a living person — this is not necessarily viewed as involving the displacement of either participant's soul. This lack of explicit concern with the inner mechanism of possession is, in fact, a general feature of a great many cultures where the doctrine of possession is stressed.

Conversely, in many other societies, where little emphasis is given to possession in the interpretation of trance and illness, soul-loss is the primary idiom in which these phenomena are described. In Africa, this pattern of explanation involving soul-loss without possession seems generally rare. One good example, however, which will serve to illustrate the distinction, concerns the hunting and gathering Bushmen of the Kalahari desert in South Africa. In this culture trance states are a monopoly of men. They are used therapeutically to release the power of the spirit in the human body to fight the evil powers which cause illness, and to cure sickness in the afflicted. In healing dance ceremonies to the accompaniment of singing and hand-clapping, adult men work themselves into a state of trance. In this stimulating atmosphere the spirit (or soul) boils up in a man's body and goes to his head. Perception is altered. Things appear to be smaller than usual and to fly about. Eventually the spirit temporarily leaves the body, and sets out to fight those powers which the Bushmen fear as the cause of sickness and death. In this spiritually active condition, men lay their hands on the sick patient and rub sweat into his body until he is believed to be cured. Soul-loss trance sometimes also occurs spontaneously in response to a sudden fright or terrifying experience. The presence of a marauding lion, for instance, may trigger off trance states. As amongst the Samburu, whose non-mystical conception of trance we considered earlier, the Bushmen associate soul-loss trance with the expression of fear and aggression (Marshall, 1969, pp. 347–81; see also Katz, 1982).

This culturally determined emphasis on soul-loss, rather than on spirit possession, is a strongly developed religious motif in many North American Indian societies. Outside that area, possession is either the dominant element or co-exists, in varying degrees of emphasis, with soul-loss as the explanation of trance and associated phenomena. It is with this possession ideology, that we are mainly concerned in this book.

III

We have already made free use of the originally Tungus term 'shaman', and its convenient anthropological derivative 'shamanism'. 'Shaman' is widely employed by American anthropologists, but rarely by their British colleagues, to denote a variety of social roles, the lowest common denominator of which is that of inspired priest (see Lewis, 1986, pp. 94–107). We are now in a position to examine more closely the connections between the shaman so conceived and possession.

According to Mircea Eliade, the diagnostic features of shamanism in the classical Arctic sense are quite specific. The shaman is an inspired priest who, in ecstatic trance, ascends to the heavens on 'trips'. In the course of these journeys he persuades or even fights with the gods in order to secure benefits for his fellow men. Here, in the opinion of Eliade, spirit possession is not an essential characteristic and is not always present. As he himself puts it:

> The specific element of shamanism is not the incorporation of spirits by the shaman, but the ecstasy provoked by the ascension to the sky or by the descent to Hell: the incorporation of spirits and possession by them are universally distributed phenomena, but they do not belong necessarily to shamanism in the strict sense (Eliade, 1951, p. 434).

Moreover, in Eliade's view, different elements in the shamanistic complex can be assigned to different stages of historical development:

> It is beyond doubt that the celestial ascension of the shaman is a survival, profoundly modified and sometimes degraded, of the archaic religious ideology which was centred on faith in a

Supreme Celestial Being and the belief in concrete communications between the sky and earth . . . The descent to Hell, the
fight against the evil spirits, and also the increasingly familiar
relations with spirits which aim at their incorporation or at the
possession of the shaman by them, are all innovations, for the
most part recent enough, and to be imputed to the general
transformation of the religious complex (Eliade, 1951, p. 438).

As with other religious phenomena, shamanism is obviously subject
to historical development and change. That is not in dispute. But
anyone who cares to examine the data will be impressed by the slender
and ambiguous character of the evidence on the basis of which this
particular interpretation is so confidently asserted. It is not necessary
for our purposes, however, to enter into any detailed discussion of the
probability of this particular evolutionary theory of the development
of Asiatic shamanism. Our concern is to see whether Eliade is correct
in seeking to drive a wedge between spirit possession and shamanism.
Other writers on the subject clearly accept his judgement. Thus, in
his stimulating comparative study, Luc de Heusch has sought to
develop these ideas into an ambitious, formalistic theory of religious
phenomena. Here shamanism (in Eliade's sense) and spirit possession
are treated as antithetical processes. The first is an ascent of man to
the gods: the second the descent of the gods on man. Shamanism, in
de Heusch's view, is thus an 'ascensual metaphysic' — a movement
of 'pride' in which man sees himself as the equal of the gods.
Possession, on the other hand, is an incarnation. This, and other
alleged distinctions, are developed by de Heusch into an elaborate
complex of structural antitheses which he somewhat grandiloquently
describes as the 'geometry of the soul'. However logically satisfying
these Hegelian contrasts may seem, the crucial question here is whether
the empirical evidence supports, or refutes, the distinction which Eliade
and de Heusch seek to make between shamanism and spirit possession.

To settle this issue we must go back to the main primary accounts
of Arctic shamanism utilized by Eliade and also by de Heusch. When
we examine these sources carefully we find that this distinction is in
fact untenable. Shamanism and spirit possession regularly occur
together and this is true particularly in the Arctic *locus classicus* of
shamanism. Thus, amongst both the Eskimos and the East Siberian
Chukchee, shamans are possessed by spirits. More significantly still,
this is also true of the Arctic Tungus from whose language the word

shaman derives, and whom, therefore, we may take to epitomize the phenomena under discussion. Let us start at the beginning. The Tungus word *shaman* (pronounced *saman* among the adjacent Manchus) means literally 'one who is excited, moved, or raised' (and this, incidentally, is very similar to the connotations of other words in other languages employed to describe possession). More specifically, a shaman is a person of either sex who has mastered spirits and who can at will introduce them into his own body. Often, in fact, he permanently incarnates these spirits and can control their manifestations, going into controlled states of trance in appropriate circumstances. As Shirokogoroff, the great Russion authority on the Tungus, puts it, the shaman's body is a 'placing', or receptacle, for the spirits. It is in fact by his power over the spirits which he incarnates that the shaman is able to treat and control afflictions caused by pathogenic spirits in others.

Shamanism is tied to the Tungus clan structure of which, indeed, it is an essential component. Tungus clans are small, scattered patrilineal units, rarely boasting more than a thousand members. As well as family and lineage heads, or elders, and politically significant 'big-men' who are primarily concerned with directing the secular life of the group, each clan normally has at least one generally recognized shaman. This 'master of spirits' is essential to the well-being of the clan, for he controls the clan's own ancestral spirits and other foreign spirits which have been adopted into its spirit hierarchy. In the free state, these spirits are extremely dangerous to man. Most are hostile and pathogenic and are regarded as the sources of the many diseases which affect the Tungus.

Most diseases, thus, are seen as having a mystical basis in the action of these noxious spirits. As long as the clan shaman is doing his job properly, however, in incarnating these spirits and thus controlling them by containing them, all is well. Indeed with the inducement of regular offerings, these tamed spirits are considered to protect the clan from attack by other alien spirits and also to ensure the fertility and prosperity of its members. These 'mastered' spirits can thus be applied to fight off, or overcome, other hostile spirits which have not yet been rendered harmless by human incarnation. With the aid of the tamed spirits, the clan shaman can divine and treat such sickness and affliction as does strike his kinsmen. The shaman is thus in a sense a hostage to the spirits, and Shirokogoroff lays particular stress on the strenuous and demanding character of his calling.

Although the shaman acts in other contexts also, the main centre of his activity is the séance. Séances may be held to make contact with the spirits of the upper or lower worlds. For instance, the shaman may be consulted by his clansmen to reveal the causes of an outbreak of disease, or to discover the reason for a run of bad luck in hunting. This requires him to call up the spirits into himself and, having established the cause of the misfortune, to take appropriate action. He may, for example, consider it necessary to take a sacrificial reindeer to the spirits of the lower world and seek to persuade them to remove the difficulties his kin are experiencing.

Other séances are concerned with the spirits of the upper world, or with spirits living in this world. Shamanistic rites addressed to spirits in the latter category may involve the liberation of a person or clan from the spirits of a hostile shaman, or clan, or other foreign source; sacrifice to benevolent or malevolent spirits; and divination of a wide range of afflictions with the aid of the shaman's spirits. Sometimes the shaman may practise his art much more informally, concentrating his power with the aid of the brass mirror which is one of the commonest incarnations of a Tungus shaman's familiars. In this case ecstasy is likely to be limited to shaking. Nevertheless, the séance remains the main ritual drama of shamanism and includes possession. Shirokogoroff gives a vivid description of the atmosphere in which it is conducted, which coincides closely with accounts of séances in many of the other possession cults which we discuss in this book.

> The rhythmic music and singing, and later the dancing of the shaman, gradually involve every participant more and more in a collective action. When the audience begins to repeat the refrains together with the assistants, only those who are defective fail to join the chorus. The tempo of the action increases, the shaman with a spirit is no more an ordinary man or relative, but is a 'placing' (i.e. incarnation) of the spirit; the spirit acts together with the audience, and this is felt by everyone. The state of many participants is now near to that of the shaman himself, and only a strong belief that when the shaman is there the spirit may only enter him, restrains the participants from being possessed in mass by the spirit. This is a very important condition of shamanizing which does not however reduce mass susceptibility to the suggestion, hallucinations, and unconscious acts produced in a state of mass ecstasy. When the shaman

feels that the audience is with him and follows him he becomes still more active and this effect is transmitted to his audience. After shamanizing, the audience recollects various moments of the performance, their great psychophysiological emotion and the hallucinations of sight and hearing which they have experienced. They then have a deep satisfaction — much greater than that from emotions produced by theatrical and musical performances, literature and general artistic phenomena of the European complex, because in shamanizing the audience at the same time acts and participates (Shirokogoroff, 1935).

This psychologically highly charged atmosphere of the séance makes it, when it is applied to curing the sick, no doubt highly effective in the treatment of certain neurotic or psychosomatic disturbances. And as Shirokogoroff also points out, even in the case of organic illnesses, it probably also has considerable significance in strengthening the patient's will to recover. Thus, both from this point of view and from its purely ritual aspects, shamanism plays a highly significant role in Tungus clan life. No clan is secure without its shaman. Consequently when the shaman's powers of control over the spirits are waning an urgent search begins for a successor. Should the old shaman lose his powers completely, or die before he can be replaced, the spirits will be freed to wreak havoc in the clan. This must be avoided at all costs. The position may in fact be inherited, or it may be acquired by an unrelated young shaman who has given ample proof of his command of the ecstatic technique and control over spirits. The extent to which this institution is linked with clanship is seen in the fact that when a clan grows large and splits into two new exogamic groups, each nascent new clan must have its own shaman. Shamanship and spirits are part of the clan patrimony.

Among the Tungus, then, possession by pathogenic spirits is a common explanation of illness (though not the only one), and at the same time the normal road to the assumption of the shaman's calling. The stock indication of a person's initial seizure by a spirit is culturally stereotyped 'hysterical' behaviour (although such behaviour, as we have seen, may also be interpreted non-mystically). The signs of this 'Arctic hysteria', as it is usually known in the literature, are: hiding from the light, hysterically exaggerated crying and singing, sitting passively in a withdrawn state on a bed or on the ground, racing off hysterically (inviting pursuit), hiding in rocks, climbing up trees, etc. Unless there are contra-indications, people who exhibit these symptoms of hysterical flight are likely to be regarded as possessed by a spirit, and may, or may not, be encouraged to become shamans. If they do receive support and encouragement, they quickly learn to cultivate the power of experiencing demonstrable ecstasy. And when in response to such appropriate stimuli as drumming and singing they can produce this state at will, they are well on the road to public recognition as 'masters of spirits'. The controlled production of trance is taken as evidence of controlled possession by spirits. Here we should note, although as we shall see the distinction is not unambiguous, that the Tungus distinguish between a person possessed (involuntarily) by a spirit, and a spirit possessed (voluntarily) by a person. The first is uncontrolled trance interpreted as illness; the second is controlled trance, the essential requirement for the exercise of the shamanistic vocation. The accuracy of Shirokogoroff's interpretation here is amply confirmed in exhaustive modern re-appraisals of the Tungus and Arctic shamanism by such leading specialists as Delaby, 1976, Siikala, 1978, and Basilov, 1984.

We can see now that, contrary to the views of Eliade and de Heusch, in its Tungus form shamanism involves controlled spirit possession; and that, according to the social context, the shaman incarnates spirits in both a latent and an active form, but always in a controlled fashion. His body is a vehicle for the spirits. We can also see that the shaman's vocation is normally announced by an initially uncontrolled state of possession: a traumatic experience associated with hysteroid, ecstatic behaviour. This, I think, is a universal feature in the assumption of shamanistic roles and is even present, though in muted form, when these pass by inheritance from one kinsman to another. Thus, in the case of those who persist in the shamanistic calling, the uncontrolled, unsolicited, initial possession seizure leads to a state where possession can be controlled and can be turned on and off at will in shamanistic séances. This is the controlled phase of possession, where as the Tungus say, the shaman 'possesses' his spirits (although they also possess him).

Luc de Heusch has sought to distinguish between these two phases in terms of a much more thorough-going and wide-reaching distinction between what he calls 'inauthentic' and 'authentic' possession. The first of these he sees as an undesired illness, a baneful spirit intrusion, which can only be treated by the expulsion, or exorcism, of the intrusive agency. The second, in contrast, is the very stuff of religious experience: a 'joyous Dionysian epiphany'. This desired state of exaltation is realized by what is in effect a 'sacred theatre'. Thus for de Heusch, these are not merely separate phases, as I have distinguished them, within the assumption of the mystical calling; but, on the contrary, totally opposed experiences belonging to two separate types of cult. In his view the first cult is based on exorcism, the second on the deliberate cultivation of ecstatic states. Erica Bourguignon, who in contrast realizes correctly that these are not necessarily totally opposed experiences characteristic of different kinds of religious cult, calls them 'negative' and 'positive' possession (Bourguignon, 1967). I prefer the more neutral analytical terms 'uncontrolled' and 'controlled' possession, or 'unsolicited' and 'solicited' possession which, as I hope will become increasingly clear, have greater explanatory utility. Finally, we may note here how as Anna-Leena Siikala (1978) has emphasized, beliefs in pathogenic demonic possession on the one hand and spirit-inspired shamanizing on the other, far from belonging to separate cultic or religious traditions, regularly reinforce each other within the same religion.

It will be evident, then that the Tungus evidence makes nonsense of the assumption that shamanism and spirit possession are totally separate phenomena, belonging necessarily to different cosmological systems and to separate historical stages of development. Without wishing to wander too far from the present argument, we might note parenthetically that this misleading misunderstanding has been applied quite widely in other contexts. Thus in his discussion of Greek religion, E. R. Dodds takes soul-loss as the definitive characteristic of shamanism. On this basis he treats the rise of shamans, amongst whom he numbers Pythagoras, as an ideologically distinct later development of Greek religion replacing the earlier spirit-inspired world of the Apollonian oracles and the cult of Dionysus (Dodds, 1951). Classical scholars will know whether the cosmological changes Dodds infers are justified. But since at least the conceptual distinction in terms of which they are described is not, it seems possible that the imposition of a misleading model may have skewed his interpretation.

We can see now that we are perfectly justified in applying the term shaman to mean, as Raymond Firth (Firth, 1959, pp. 129–48; 1967) rightly stresses, a 'master of spirits', with the implication that this inspired priest incarnates spirits, becoming possessed voluntarily in controlled circumstances. The evocative Polynesian expression 'god-box' expresses the relationship between the shaman and the power he incarnates very exactly. All shamans are thus mediums and, as the Black Caribs of British Honduras so expressively put it, tend to function as a 'telephone exchange' between man and god. It does not follow, of course, that all mediums are necessarily shamans, although as will be shown in the next chapter the two are usually linked. People who regularly experience possession by a particular spirit may be said to act as mediums for that divinity. Some, but not all such mediums are likely to graduate in time to become controllers of spirits, and once they 'master' these powers in a controlling fashion they are properly shamans. Thus, what so often begins as a hostile spirit intrusion, may be later evaluated as the first sign of grace in the assumption of the shamanistic calling. Not all such traumatic experiences necessarily have this outcome. But all shamans seem to have experienced something of this initial trauma. These are thus, very frequently, phases in a forward-going process, rather than sign-posts to totally distinct types of cult. Perhaps the reader will accept this for the moment and, if unconvinced, suspend final judgement until the problem is explored more fully in later chapters.

IV

We must now examine the sorts of relationship which people of different cultures conceive to exist between shamans and mediums and their possessing familiars. Amongst the Tungus, some emphasis is given to the idea that a contractual relationship binds the shaman and the spirits which he incarnates. This conception of an agreement of compact, sometimes involving the surrender of the shaman's own soul (as in the Faust legend), is stressed amongst the Eskimos. There, the shaman-to-be who has received a spiritual call gives up his soul to those spirits which are henceforth bound to him as familiars. Thus Rasmussen reports that the first thing which the neophyte's instructor has to do is to withdraw the soul from the pupil's eyes, brain and entrails, and to hand it over to the helping spirits which then become his familiars. The apprentice shaman must also learn how to attain enlightenment or 'light', that mysterious luminous fire which the shaman suddenly feels in his body and which enables him to see all that is otherwise hidden from mortal eyes.

This gift of illumination, in return for a surrendering of the self or part of the self, described in the classical language of mysticism as gnosis — a fusing of man and divinity — is part of controlled spirit possession everywhere. In some cases the immediate relationship may initially be with minor powers or tutelary spirits — the 'controls' or 'guides' of western Spiritualism, through whose help the shaman is able to incarnate and communicate with higher divinities or powers. In other cases, there may be a more direct relationship, without such intermediaries, with a more central divinity, or 'refraction' of that divinity, and very frequently, as the shaman's power grows, his repertoire of incarnable spirits increases in the same measure. Whatever the conceptual details involved, shamanism includes a special relationship with a divinity or divinities, a relationship which, of course, is most dramatically realized in full incarnation when the personality of the possesed is totally effaced. Ecstatic communion is thus essentially a mystical union; and, as the Song of Solomon and other mystical poetry so abundantly illustrate, experiences of this kind are frequently described in terms borrowed from erotic love. Indeed, as Ernest Jones (1949) has justly observed, the notion that 'sexual intercourse can occur between mortals and supernatural beings is one of the most widespread of human beliefs'.

This imagery is by no means absent in that widespread symbolism for possession according to which the spirit, when incarnated in its earthly host, is said to ride its 'horse'. Thus, for instance, in the richly dramatic *bori* spirit possession cult of the Hausa-speaking peoples of west Africa (which we shall investigate more fully later) possessed women are described as the 'Mares of the Gods'. The spirits 'mount' them; but they also 'mount' the spirits. Amongst the Sidamo tribes of southern Ethiopia, this idiom is even extended to differentiate between the possession of men and of women. Men are 'horses' for the spirits, and women are 'mules'. Such fine distinctions are not made everywhere.

This expressive language of the stables, which is widely employed in possession cults and often contains sexual innuendoes, may have several components. Thus in many cultures we find the notion that in a state of latent or incipient possession prior to actual trance the spirit is perched on the shoulders or neck of its host. It mounts into his head, or some other centre of the body, assuming full possession of its receptacle only when complete trance occurs. Thus the Greek oracle at Delphi was mounted by the God Apollo who rode on the nape of her neck; and the same imagery appears in Haitian voodoo and elsewhere. Full possession itself is widely perceived as a form of temporary death, sometimes called 'half-death', or 'little death'. At the same time, though by no means universally, ecstatic possession seizures are sometimes explicitly interpreted as acts of mystical sexual intercourse between the subject and his or her possessing spirit. Among the Dayaks of southern Borneo, in public rituals in which the priests and priestesses of the community become possessed by the two supreme deities of the cosmos — the Hornbill of the upper world, and the Watersnake of the lower world — this is represented as a divine coition. This theme is directly evoked in the accompanying chants, and reproduced in acts of intercourse amongst the congregation. As the hymns sung express it: 'The journey of Jata (the Watersnake) in her golden boat is ended; Mahatala (the Hornbill) has arrived in his boat of jewels. They let down the pole into the vagina of the Watersnake; they lower the staff of the Hornbill into the open gong.' (Scharer, 1963, p. 135). The relationship between the devotee and the spirit, which he or she regularly incarnates, is often represented directly in terms either of marriage or of kinship. To some extent, which of these idioms is chosen seems to depend upon the sexual identity and character both of the subject and of the spirit involved. Thus, male shamans who incarnate their own ancestor spirits are hardly likely to conceive of their mutual relationship other than in terms of descent. Conversely, the idiom of marriage seems to be favoured where stress is laid on the contractual rather than the biologically determined nature of the relationship, and where the possessed subject and possessing spirit are of opposite sex. 'Marriage' between men and masculine divinities is not, however, absolutely excluded. Nor should we ignore the potential importance of the theme of incest here. For the two separate ideologies of marriage and descent may be combined as in the case of effeminate male Burmese shamans, possessed by female *nat* spirits, who are represented as their 'mothers' or 'sisters' (Spiro, 1967). More explicitly and dramatically, among the Tukano Amazonian Indians of Colombo with the aid of a local hallucinogenic preparation, shamans experience ecstatic visions of an incestuous return to the cosmic womb (Reichel-Dolmatoff, 1971).

The metaphor of spiritual marriage is familiar to us from our own Christian tradition. This is the relationship traditionally postulated between the Church and Christ; and, as we know, nuns are specifically bound in spiritual union to the Sacred Bridegroom. Many Christian mystics have used the same idiom, for example St Bernard, who wrote of Christ as his soul's Bridegroom; and this imagery has often been employed by Islamic mystics both in relation to the Prophet Muhammad, and even to Allah. This usage, however, is by no means a monopoly of these religions. All over the world, we find this conception of a spiritual union, parallelling human marriage, used to image the relationship between a spirit and its regular devotee. Such unions, as with their human counterparts, are moreover often blessed with issue. Few anthropologists have been privileged to discover this quite as directly as Professor Raymond Firth did on the Polynesian island of Tikopia. There, following an illness which was taken by the Tikopians to signify that he had been 'overcome' by the powerful female spirit Pufine-i-Vaisiku, Firth was surprised to discover that he had inadvertently begotten several spirit sons. This occurred during his first work in the island in 1929. When he returned twenty-three years later, he found that the incident was still remembered. He was asked about his spirit sons (who presumably had grown up in the interval) and eventually arranged to make contact with them through a friendly medium (Firth, 1967, p. 319). In Muslim Malaysia in 1986, on the other hand, a woman who claimed to have had a child by a spirit to which she was 'married' was fined by an Islamic court for committing adultery.

This uxorial imagery is also employed in Haitian voodoo; amongst the Akawaio Carib-speaking Indians of British Guiana where the shaman, the 'one who perceives', has the swallow-tailed kite as his spiritual partner; in Buddhist Burma; in Bali with its highly theatrical possession cults; in the elaborate possession cults of Dahomey and Songhay in west Africa; in Ethiopia; and in many other African possession cults elsewhere. With this widespread distribution, a detailed enumeration of examples here would make dull reading and serve little purpose. Several cases, however, raise points of wider significance and are therefore worth discussion briefly.

Amongst the Saora tribesmen of Orissa, living on the fringes of Hindu caste society, a shaman is often chosen by the direct intervention of a female spirit, marriage with which effects the new priest's dedication. Thus, as one shaman plaintively put it. 'I too had much trouble before I married, for several tutelary (i.e. spirit) girls were after me . . .' And another man happily wedded to his spirit partner told Verrier Elwin how, on the advice of an established shaman, he had married a spirit girl (Elwin, 1955). The marriage proved fruitful and the shaman had thus acquired three fine spirit boys, the celestial counterparts of his earthly family of three sons and a daughter. Significantly, such spiritual wives are considered to be Hindus, in distinction to their earthly partners, and exact a strict code of behaviour from their spouses. Before any important sacrifice, for example, the shaman must fast and abstain from earthly sexual intercourse. When he dies, he is 'taken away' by his tutelary partner and joins her in the underworld. In the process he himself becomes a spirit and a Hindu, and is thus separated from his mortal spouse who, when she in turn dies, may not join him.

Thus the shaman's spiritual union not only defines his dedication to a particular spirit, but also sets him apart from other members of his society and imposes a barrier in his relations with mortal women. This is most marked in the case of women who become shamans. The spirit partners of such women regularly come to lie with them and tend to monopolize their affections. Since, moreover, the spirit husband is a Hindu, this represents a step up for his mortal wife. As can readily be imagined, while giving the woman increased status and freedom, this also renders her a formidable marriage partner to ordinary men. We shall examine these implications of this common situation more fully in the following chapter.

Amongst the Arctic Chukchee there are further complications within the same theme. Here the sexually normal male shaman often has a spirit wife who is considered to take part in the everyday life of the family in which she is thus incorporated. Women shamans, however, are disadvantageously placed, since their spirit familiars recoil from any contact with the birth of children. Thus women with shamanistic vocations find that their powers wane when they have children, and they do not recover them fully until they have stopped bearing. This opposition between mundane and celestial maternity occurs frequently in spirit possession cults and has significant implications, as we shall see later. Its effect among the Chukchee is of course to strengthen men's control of the shamanistic profession which, however, is equally open to homosexual and to heterosexual males. The former, known as 'soft-men', fall into various categories according to the degree of feminine behaviour which they exhibit. Some extreme homosexual shamans, who are greatly feared for their mystical power, have spirit 'husbands' as well as the human husbands with whom they live. These latter, however, are not in a very enviable position, since they are kept in order by the spirit spouse who is regarded as the true head of the family (Bogoras, 1907). Thus spiritual liaisons are evidently adapted to all tastes, and exhibit as much variety as those of the mortal partnerships which they mirror. As Milton reminds us in *Paradise Lost*: 'Spirits when they please, can either sex assume, or both!'

A voodoo marriage certificate recording the mystical union of a woman with her spirit (DAMBALLAH) LIBERTÉ, ÉGALITÉ, FRATERNITÉ

Republic of Haiti, 5.847 — The year 1949 and sixth day of the month of January at 3 o'clock in the afternoon. We, Jean Jumeau, Registrar of Port-au-Prince, certifies (sic) that citizens Damballah Toquan Miroissé and Madame Andrémise Cétoute appeared before us to be united by the indissoluble bond of the marriage sacrament. Inasmuch as Madame Cétoute must consecrate Tuesday and Thursday to her husband Damballah without ever a blemish on herself, it being understood Monsieur Damballah's duty is to load his wife with good luck so that Madame Cétoute will never know a day's poverty: the husband Monsieur Damballah is accountable to his wife and owes her all necessary protection as set down in the contract. It is with work that spiritual and material property is amassed. In execution of article 15.1 of the Haitian Code. They hereto agreed in the affirmative before qualified witnesses whose names are given. [Signatures.]
(From Métraux, 1959, p. 215)

Finally, let us look briefly at the very explicit use made in Ethiopian *zar* possession and in Haitian voodoo of celestial marriage as the regular means of induction into the ranks of the chronically possessed. In Ethiopia, the new acolyte, far from yet being a shaman, is referred to as a 'bride' and is assigned two human protectors or 'best-men', just as in mortal unions the bride is attended by two supporters to whom she may afterwards turn for help if she has difficulties with her husband. She thus takes as spiritual partner a spirit of opposite sex.

This marital theme is even more elaborately developed in the voodoo cults of Haiti. There a person who wishes to secure the permanent protection of one of the *loa* or 'mysteries' may make a formal proposal of marriage, and so may the god. Ezili, the patron goddess of lovers, is particularly uxorious and regularly offers her hand to any man who serves her zealously, especially if he is about to take a mortal wife! She then insists on marrying her devotee first, in case he should forget her. Such marriages are celebrated with elaborate ceremonies which Métraux has recorded in detail (Métraux, 1959). Mortal unions are exactly paralleled even to the extent of the issuing of a wedding certificate (see above). In spiritual unions the marriage vows apply particularly strongly. When the god, and his or her mortal partner, have pronounced the ritual phrases and exchanged rings (by proxy) as a sign of plighted troth, they share a common destiny. The *loa's* duty is to watch over his spouse, but he must be given presents in return. The night of the day consecrated to his worship must also be reserved for him and not shared with mortal partners. Some human spouses make up a separate bed for their spirit and sleep on it on the allotted night.

As in other cases, both men and women contract such unions which are much more binding and strongly sanctioned than those in mortal society. The extent of their solidary character is particularly evident in those special cases which have a more sinister quality involving as they do a compact with a spirit made specifically to gain success and riches. Here the Faustian theme is strongly emphasized, and the person who seeks to advance his fortunes through such a 'commitment' may be allowed only a specified span of years before he is 'taken' by the evil spirit, or 'hot point' (*point chaud*), to whom he is engaged. Paradoxically, after his death, such a spirit force may enter the deceased's family estate and pass to his heirs as a transformed benevolent *loa* (Larose, 1977).

As I said earlier, although this marital imagery is very widely used to represent the relationship between man and spirits, the bond of mystical union may also be expressed in terms of a direct blood-relationship. Here the shaman or devotee is described as a child (a son or daughter, according to sex), or occasionally, as a younger sibling of the spirit. This filial idiom is employed in parts of South America. It is prominent in the possession societies known as *candomblés* in Brazil and in the linked syncretic religion of Umbanda (compounding Amerindian, African, and European elements) which is sweeping from the great Brazilian urban centres into the interior of the country in the wake of socio-economic change and modern communications (Pressel, 1977). Sometimes this genetic symbolism occurs together with the marriage imagery which we have just discussed, cult devotees being collectively called 'the children' of the spirits, but each individual having his or her own spirit partner. Both these images, of course, are present in Christianity where the shaman Jesus is the 'Son' of God, direct issue of the mystical union of the 'Virgin Mary' with God; and the traditional Church itself, incarnating the Holy Spirit, is further united to its spiritual Bridegroom, Christ. We need not pursue these intricate familial relationships further here. Sufficient has been said to illustrate the character of the two principal metaphors in which the link between man and spirit is figured.

V

We began this chapter by noting the universality of states of altered consciousness and dissociation, and saw that these may be explained in different cultures either mystically or non-mystically (and sometimes in both ways in different contexts). Spirit possession and soul-loss (sometimes more accurately described by Linton's term 'soul-projection') are the two principal mystical explanations. Although they may exist side by side, usually emphasis is placed on one rather than the other, and it is of course the possession aetiology that chiefly concerns us. Possession is believed to be both involuntary (or uncontrolled), and voluntary (or controlled). Those who practise controlled possession, 'mastering' spirits, are in the Arctic context known as 'shamans'. I retain this term for men or women who play a wide repertoire of social roles on this basis.

The attainment of the shaman's calling is normally the climax of a series of traumatic experiences and 'cures' in the course of which the extent of his control of trance progressively increases. Ultimately he achieves a stable relationship with a spirit which is formulated, either in terms of marriage, or of direct kinship.

Finally, however bizarre or eccentric possession may seem to us, it cannot be too strongly emphasized that in the religions which we explore in this book, possession is a culturally normative experience. For our purposes whether or not people are actually in trance, they are only 'possessed' when they consider they are, and when other members of their society endorse this claim or indeed initiate it. Thus as Stewart has put it:

> It matters little whether manifestations of possession are in reality due to physical or pyschical abnormalities or whether they are artificially induced by auto-suggestion. The essential factor in possession is the belief that a person has been invaded by a supernatural being and is thus temporarily beyond self-control, his ego being subordinated to that of the intruder (Stewart, 1946, p. 325).

The subjective experience of possession in this sense, although it occurs in a western Spiritualist[1] context which is only marginally normative in our secular culture, has been very well described by the Genevese

[1]For an intriguing anthropological account of contemporary spiritualism in Wales, see Skultans, 1974.

medium Hélène Smith to her investigator Flournoy. The latter gives the following account in his interesting book, *Des Indes à la planète Mars* (Paris, 1900):

> Hélène has more than once described to me that she had the impression of becoming and momentarily being Leopold (Leopold Cagliostro, the eighteenth-century magician). This happens to her during the night or particularly on waking in the morning; she first has a fugitive vision of her cavalier, and then he seems to pass gradually into her: she feels him as it were invade and penetrate her whole organic substance as if he became herself or she him. It is in short a spontaneous incarnation . . .

In the cults with which we deal next, personal interpretation of this kind are culturally standardized and form part of orthodox, everyday belief.

Chapter Three

AFFLICTION AND ITS APOTHEOSIS

I

Possession by an intrusive spirit is by no means invariably as warmly welcomed as it evidently was in the case of Hélène Smith. The initial experience of possession, particularly, is often a disturbing, even traumatic experience, and not uncommonly a response to personal affliction and adversity. Up to a point, this is even the case in those societies where the position of shaman-priest has become firmly instituted and passes more or less automatically to the appropriate heir by title rather than by personal attainment. In the first place, in such circumstances not every heir is as keen to succeed to his predecessor's position as the spirits are anxious to effect this transition. Where the successor shows reluctance in assuming his onerous duties, the spirits remind him forcefully of his obligations by badgering him with trials and tribulations until he acknowledges defeat and accepts their insistent prodding. We find examples of this spiritual blackmail in all those societies where, as among the Tungus, the position of shaman is regarded as an inherited office. An instance from the Macha Galla of Ethiopia will serve to illustrate the general situation. The old shaman of one of the Macha clans sent his son to Addis Ababa to be educated. There the Emperor helped him and he acquired a good schooling. While he was still at Addis Ababa under the Emperor's protection, his father died and he immediately fell ill. He had no strength, and did not want to return to his home there to succeed to his father's position as clan shaman. After a long period of illness, however, the Emperor advised him: 'You will not get well here and your education affords you no joy. Return to your father's land and live as your custom bids you.' Then the son returned home and became a shaman and soon recovered (Knutsson, 1967, p. 74).

Moreover, in such societies where in theory the position of inspired priest is an inherited endowment, in practice it can also be achieved, even if only in exceptional cases, by individual initiative. And the less well-qualified by birthright the aspiring shaman is, the more violent and dramatic will be the possessions by which he seeks to demonstrate the efficacy of his calling. As is recognized in Haitian voodoo, in such cases the new devotee is like an unbroken horse, throwing himself and his spirit rider about with violent, wild plungings.

Thus while some shamans slip without fuss into the mantles of their predecessors, or are summoned by dreams and visions to their calling, this is by no means the universal pattern of recruitment. Very commonly, as with St Paul, the road to the assumption of the shaman's vocation lies through affliction valiantly endured and, in the end, transformed into spiritual grace. In Bali many of the temple mediums are recruited following an illness which is later reinterpreted as a benign inspiration. In Haiti, similarly, possession and initiation into the cults of the *loa* mysteries often follow a serious illness or other affliction. And here it is very noticeable that those whose lives flow smoothly without much difficulty or distress are rarely summoned by the spirits. For the less fortunate, it is only by induction into the *loa* cult group that protection and security are ensured. Hence-forward those who have been severely tried find comfort and solace in the ever-present care of their guardian spirit. If they are hungry, the *loa* appears to them saying 'Take courage; you will have money.' And the promised help comes (Métraux, 1959, p. 95).

Here, clearly, initiation into the ranks of the chronically possessed is in the nature of a cure. Moreover, as elsewhere, the devotee is prone to experience possession in difficult, stressful situations, from which there is otherwise no satisfactory escape. Thus Métraux reports that the Haitian patient undergoing a painful operation may achieve, through becoming possessed, a fuller anaesthesis than that provided by the medical authorities. Shock following traffic accidents similarly sometimes manifests itself as possession by a *loa*. And even shipwrecked sailors, helplessly floundering in the sea, have sometimes been visited by the spirits and thus carried in safety to the shore. In exactly the same way, possession by spirits of the Shango cult conveniently supervenes in Trinidad in situations of difficulty and conflict and is not unknown in the hearing of a case in court (Mischel, 1958, pp. 249–60).

Likewise, in the Arctic, there are many similar reports of the same ambiguous association between affliction, or illness, and divine inspiration. The Chukchee, for example, compare the preparatory period in the assumption of the shaman's calling to a long and severe illness, and in fact the call of the spirits is often a direct consequence of an actual illness, misfortune, or danger. One Chukchee out harpooning seal on an ice-flow slipped into the water and would, as he later said, certainly have drowned but for the miraculous appearance of a friendly walrus which comforted him and helped him to regain a foothold on the ice, so that he was able to scramble to safety. Afterwards, full of gratitude for his safe deliverance, he made offerings to the walrus and became a shaman with that creature as his helping spirit.

The biography of the Chukchee shaman called 'Scratching-Woman' reported by Bogoras illustrates the same theme (Bogoras, 1907, p. 424). This shaman's father was a small sickly fellow with a few reindeer which he finally lost in a thick fog. He died of starvation in the search for the missing herd, but his wife and son survived, being cared for by relatives. Then followed many years of privation and misery for the son. As a boy, he hauled fuel on a sledge for richer folk and was paid with a little meat and blood. What he could thus earn was, however, far from adequate and he remained weak and sickly. Then one day he began to beat the drum (used by the Chukchee for summoning spirits), and to call for spirits. One by one all the supernatural beings appeared before him, and he became a shaman. The spirit of the Motionless Star visited him in a dream and said: 'Cease being such a weakling. Be a shaman and be strong, and you will have plenty of food!' With this inspirational guidance and exhortation, Scratching-Woman soon found luck had changed in his favour. He quickly amassed a large reindeer herd and married into a well-to-do family. When his father-in-law died, he became head of the family, his wife being the eldest child. Thus from his lowly orphan beginnings, the spirits made him a successful shaman and herder.

Amongst the Eskimo there are many similar accounts of the rise to fame and fortune of shamans whose origins were full of misery and privation. Indeed, among the Iglulik Eskimo, Rasmussen was told how the primeval shaman had first appeared at a time of desperate affliction and adversity. And in many of the biographies he collected, the helping spirits made their first appearance by molesting the person they were later to befriend and make a shaman. Thus the most dreaded of all helping spirits, the sea-ermine, would attack men while they were out in their kayaks, slipping up the sleeves of their clothes and running over their bodies filling them with 'shuddering horror'. Such dangerous and terrifying encounters frequently figured as the prelude to the assumption of the shamanistic vocation (Rasmussen, 1929, p. 122).

Similar motifs, of course, abound in our own culture. The New Testament traditions emphasize the lowly origins of the Carpenter of Nazareth and His early spiritual travails, particularly His temptation by the Devil on the mountain; and such themes recur in the inspirational biographies of a host of later and lesser Christian figures. If it was only after her death at the stake that final authenticity was granted to the ambiguous 'voices' of Joan of Arc, some other more recent Christian mystics of similar background have sometimes been more fortunate.

One of the less well known, but not least interesting, of these was the Swedish tailor's daughter, Catharina Fagerberg, who was born in 1700. After a period of employment as a domestic, she learnt to weave linen and, while following this trade, rejected the advances of a leather-worker who wished to marry her. Then followed seven years of severe mental and physical torment in the course of which she was frequently visited by a 'good spirit', who explained that the cause of her anguish lay in her possession by devils which had been sent to trouble her by a black magician at the behest of her slighted suitor. Gradually however, inspired — as she believed — by God, Catharina acquired the power to contain her affliction and to diagnose and cure disease in others. Her reputation as a faith-healer soon spread and she inevitably came into conflict with the ecclesiastical authorities. But, in a century in which witch-trials were outmoded, she was acquitted, leaving her spiritual manifestations to be dismissed by her sceptical opponents as morbid fantasies. However, in a world where many still believed in evil spirits and witchcraft, as well as in divine inspiration, Catharina enjoyed wide success as a local shamanistic healer. She was supposed to incarnate 'good' and 'evil' spirits, and, by sending out her own 'life-spirit', to divine distant events (Edsman, 1967).

These examples remind us how, frequently, those whom the gods call they first humble with affliction and despair. Moreover, as we saw amongst the Tungus, the powers involved are often, either directly or indirectly, both the causes of misfortune and the means of its cure. Those who become shamans thus commonly act, in effect, on the basis of the crude slogan: if you can't beat them, join them. It is, furthermore, precisely by demonstrating his own successful mastery of the grounds of affliction that the shaman establishes the validity of his power to heal. This conception of the shaman as the 'wounded surgeon', to borrow T.S. Eliot's memorable phrase, will be examined more fully later. For the moment, all we need to note is that, while there is a real sense in which all religions are essentially cults of affliction, in the inspirational calling this association has a particular and poignant significance. In the language of theology, the shaman's initial crisis represents the healer's passion, or, as the Akawaio Indians themselves put it, 'a man must die before he becomes a shaman'.

II

The link between affliction and its cure as the royal road to the assumption of the shamanistic vocation is thus plain enough in those societies where shamans play the main or major role in religion and where possession is highly valued as a religious experience. Here what begins as an illness, or otherwise deeply disturbing experience, ends in ecstasy; and the pain and suffering of the initial crisis are obliterated in its subsequent re-evaluation as a uniquely efficacious sign of divine favour. In other societies, however, where shamans play only a minor role and are concerned with disease-bearing spirits which are not central to the religious life of the community this apotheosis, although it still occurs, is thrust into the background. Indeed, in these circumstances, the connection between suffering and possession is so overwhelming that at first sight it seems to constitute an end in itself, rather than an end and a beginning.

Here, ostensibly at least, possession connotes misfortunes and sickness, and cult activity is primarily concerned to alleviate distress rather than to attain ecstasy. The emphasis is on disease and its cure, and not, overtly at least, on affliction as a means to the achievement of mystical exaltation. It is this feature, as we saw in the last chapter, which has led some writers to characterize such healing cults as being concerned only with 'inauthentic', or 'negative' possession, and to contrast these with religions where 'authentic' possession is realized as a divine ecstasy. To elucidate this misleading, and ultimately false, antithesis we must look more closely at such apparently 'negative' cults.

This negative aspect is strongly reflected in the character of the spirits involved. For by those who believe in them, but actually worship other gods, these malign pathogenic spirits are regarded as being extremely captious and capricious. They strike without rhyme or reason; or at least without any substantial cause which can be referred to social conduct. They are not concerned with man's behaviour to man. They have no interest in defending the moral code of society, and those who succumb to their unwelcome attentions are morally blameless. At the same time they are always on the look-out for a convenient excuse to harass their victims, and they are inordinately sensitive to human encroachment. To step on one inadvertently, or otherwise unwittingly annoy it, is sufficient to so inflame the spirit's wrath that it attacks at once, possessing its trespasser, and making him ill or causing him misfortune. These unattractive characteristics are displayed by all these hostile spirits, whether they are conceived of as anthropomorphic powers, or as puckish nature sprites.

Since they are so pointedly indifferent to human conduct, it would be reasonable to suppose that these unpleasant spirits would be quite indiscriminate in their selection of human prey. This, however, is far from being the case. Contrary to what might be expected, they show a special predilection for the weak and oppressed. We should be wrong, however, to leap immediately to a pessimistic assessment of the workings of providence in these cases. For as we shall see, it is often precisely through succumbing to these seemingly wanton visitations that people in such adverse circumstances secure a measure of help and succour. Thus, in complete contrast to the sublime indifference to the human condition which they are supposed to display, such spirits are in fact acutely sensitive to the plight of the under-privileged and oppressed. These assertions, fortunately, can easily be confirmed. All we have to do is to look closely at a number of societies where illness is interpreted as malignant possession, paying particular attention to the categories of person most at risk and to the circumstances in which they most frequently succumb to possession. Since we are here primarily concerned with the incidence of disease, we shall in fact be following what in medical parlance would be called an epidemiological approach.

Let me begin with data on the Somali pastoralists of north-east Africa which I collected in the course of field-work in what is now the Somali Republic (Lewis, 1969). In this strongly patrilineal Muslim society, witchcraft and sorcery as these phenomena are known elsewhere do not figure prominently in the interpretation of illness and misfortune. Their main religious life is concerned with the cult of Allah whom Somalis approach through the mediation of the Prophet Muhammad and a host of more immediate lineage ancestors and other figures of real or imputed piety who, as in Roman Catholicism, play a vital role as mediating saints. As in other Muslim countries, this public cult is almost exclusively dominated by men, who hold all the major positions of religious authority and prestige. Women are in fact excluded from the mosques in which men worship and their role in religion tends to be little more than that of passive spectators. More generally, in the Somali scheme of things, women are regarded as weak, submissive creatures. This is the case despite the exacting nature of their nomadic life, and the arduous character of their herding tasks in managing the flocks of sheep and goats, and the draught camels, which carry their tents and effects from camping-ground to camping-ground.

In this male-dominated and highly puritanical culture, spirit possession, which is regarded as one cause among others of a wide range of complaints (ranging from slight malaise to acute organic diseases such as tuberculosis), occurs in a few well-defined contexts. The first of these which I shall discuss here concerns cases of frustrated love and passion, and involves emotions which, especially on the part of men, are not traditionally recognized or overtly acknowledged. The stiff-lipped traditional view is that the open display of affection and love between men and women is unmanly and sentimental and must be suppressed. The expression of love towards God, in contrast, is a highly approved emotion which is widely encouraged and rapturously phrased in Somali mystical poetry. But the direct acknowledgement of similar feelings between men and women is totally out of place. Thus, if a girl who has been jilted by a boy she loved and who privately undertook to marry her exhibits symptoms of extreme lassitude, withdrawal, or even more distinct signs of physical illness, her condition is likely to be attributed to possession by the object of her affections. Here, as in all other cases of Somali possession, the victim is described as having been 'entered'. (Although in this case it is strictly the personality of her former lover which is supposed to have 'seized' her, rather than a free spirit entity, I make no apology for mentioning this type of possession here since it serves as a useful prologue to what follows.)

This interpretation of the disappointed girl's state is consistent with the traditional sex morality where the conception of romantic attachment was, as I have indicated, excluded. Only within the last twenty years or so has this rigid attitude begun to change — especially in the towns which, as elsewhere in Africa, are the foci of social change and modernity. There today, among the younger generation, the explicit recognition and acceptance of romantic love is a popular theme given wide currency in contemporary Somali verse and radio 'pop' songs which scandalize men of the older generation. With these enlightened views, young western-educated Somalis today describe such cases of young women's possession, in the Shakesperian idiom of 'lovesickness'. The traditional attitude, on the other hand, is much more in keeping with that exhibited by seventeenth-century French Catholic ecclesiastics in their handling of the celebrated case of the hysterical Sister Jeanne des Anges, prioress of the convent school at Loudon, and her frustrated infatuation for the notoriously amorous Canon Urbain Grandier. As readers of Aldous Huxley's lively evocation in _The Devils of Loudon_ will recall, this poor nun's condition was attributed to possession by malevolent spirits and Grandier was held responsible. He was convicted of witchcraft and burned at the stake in 1634.

In the Somali Republic these matters are dealt with less drastically, and no legal action can be taken against the man involved. The interpretation which these facts suggest is virtually that given by young educated Somalis themselves. For a jilted girl no other institutionalized means are traditionally available to express her outraged feelings. For it is only where a formal engagement has been contracted, with the consent of the two parties of kin, that a suit can be filed for breach of promise. The disappointed girl's private emotions and feelings are of little moment in the jural world of men. Hence illness, and the care and solicitude which it brings, at least offer some solace for her wounded pride. Of the treatment administered to the possessed girl, all that need be said here is that, as with Sister Jeanne des Anges, the invading familiar may be exorcized by a cleric — in this case a Muslim man of religion.

The other context of Somali possession is similarly regarded as an illness and involves parallel symptoms ranging from mild hysteria or light depression to actual organic disorders. In this case, however, these disturbances are unequivocally attributed to the ingress of a hostile spirit or demon. As elsewhere in Islam, Somalis believe that anthropomorphic _jinns_ lurk in every dark and empty corner, poised ready to strike capriciously and without warning at the unsuspecting passerby. These malevolent sprites are thought to be consumed by envy and greed, and to hunger especially after dainty foods, luxurious clothing, jewellery, perfume, and other finery. In the context which I am about to describe, they are known generally as _sar_, a word which describes both the spirits themselves and the illness attributed to them. The smitten victim is said to have been 'entered', 'seized' or 'possessed' by the *sar*.

The prime targets for the unwelcome attentions of these malign spirits are women, and particularly married women. The stock epidemiological situation is that of the hard-pressed wife, struggling to survive and feed her children in this harsh environment, and liable to some degree of neglect, real or imagined, on the part of her husband. Subject to frequent, sudden and often prolonged absences by her husband as he follows his manly pastoral pursuits, to the jealousies and tensions of polygyny which are not ventilated in accusations of sorcery and witchcraft, and always menaced by the precariousness of marriage in a society where divorce is frequent and easily obtained by men, the Somali woman's lot offers little stability or security. These, I hasten to add, are not ethnocentric judgements read into the data by a tender-minded western anthropologist, but, as I know from my own direct experience, evaluations which spring readily to the lips of Somali women and which I have frequently heard discussed. Somali tribeswomen are far from being as naïve as those anthropologists (see e.g. Wilson, 1967, pp. 67–78) who suppose that tribal life conditions its womenfolk to an unflinching acceptance of hardship and to an unquestioning endorsement of the position accorded them by men. My interpretation here is further corroborated from a modern woman's perspective by Raqiya Abdalla's (1982) study of female circumcision and infibulation and, more impressionistically perhaps, in Nuruddin Farah's early novel, *From a Crooked Rib* (1970).

In these circumstances, it is hardly surprising that many women's ailments, whether accompanied by definable physical symptoms or not, should so readily be interpreted by them as possession by *sar* spirits which demand luxurious clothes, perfume, and exotic dainties from their menfolk. These requests are voiced in no uncertain fashion by the spirits speaking through the lips of the afflicted women, and uttered with an authority which their passive receptacles can rarely achieve themselves. The spirits, of course, have their own language but this is readily interpreted (for a suitable fee) by female shamans who know how to handle them. It is only when such costly demands have been met, as well as all the expense involved in the mounting of a cathartic dance ('beating the *sar*') attended by other women and directed by the shaman, that the patient can be expected to recover. Even after such outlays, relief from the *sar* affliction may be only temporary.

Significantly, in some cases the onset of this spirit illness coincides with a husband's opening moves to marry an additional spouse; and in every example which I encountered some grudge against her partner was borne by the woman involved. It scarcely requires any elaborate forensic technique to reach some understanding of what is involved here; certainly, Somali men draw their own conclusions. What the women call *sar* possession, their husbands call malingering, and they interpret this affliction as yet another device in the repertoire of deceitful tricks which they consider women regularly employ against men. This ungallant charge men support by alleging that the incidence of the disease is markedly higher amongst the wives of the wealthy than amongst those of the poor. Women in their turn counter this insinuation with the ingenious sophistry that there are some *sar* spirits which only attack the wealthy while others molest the poor. Not surprisingly, *sar* spirits are said to hate men.

Despite their essentially sociological view of the situation, men's attitudes are in fact ambivalent. They believe in the existence of these *sar* spirits (for which the Quran provides scriptural warrant, since they are assimilated to *jinn*), but with typical Somali pragmatism they are sceptical when their own womenfolk and pockets are directly affected. Depending upon the marital circumstances and the value placed upon the wife concerned, the normal reaction is for the husband to accept reluctantly a few bouts of this kind, especially if they are not too frequent. But if the affliction becomes chronic, as it is apt to, and the wife becomes a more or less regular member of a circle of *sar* devotees, then, save in exceptional circumstances, the husband's patience is liable to wear thin. If a good beating will not do the trick (and it often seems very effective), there is always the threat of divorce and, unless the wife actually wants this (as she may), or is genuinely physically ill (as she may very well be) or severely psychologically disturbed, this threat usually works. Leaving aside for the moment the wider implications of membership of a regular association of *sar* devotees, it is evident that this characteristically female affliction operates amongst the Somali as a limited deterrent against the abuses of neglect and injury in a conjugal relationship which is heavily biased in favour of men. Where they are given little domestic security and are otherwise ill-protected from the pressures and exactions of men, women may thus resort to spirit possession as a means both of airing their grievances obliquely, and of gaining some satisfaction.

Somali women have a strong and explicit sense of sexual solidarity and feelings of grievance and antagonism towards men who, in their turn, regard the opposite sex as possessing a unique endowment of guile and treachery. Of course, both these sexual stereotypes are mutually reinforcing. It might even be argued, without stretching the facts too far, that here, as in other societies where sexual differentiation is equally strongly engrained, there are in effect two cultures — the officially dominant world of men, and the subordinate sphere of women. It is certainly in terms of such a wide-ranging dichotomy that Somali men see women's possession as a specialized strategy designed to forward feminine interests at their expense. This 'sex-war' view of the situation is very evident in the following folk-tale which, whether it records a true episode or not, has a very clear moral.

The wife of a well-to-do official was feeling out of sorts one morning and sitting morosely in her house, where there happened to be fifty pounds of ready cash belonging to her husband. An old woman (a *sar* specialist) came to visit the dejected wife and soon convinced her that she was possessed by a *sar* spirit and would need to pay a lot of money for the mounting of a cathartic dance ceremony, if she were to recover. The necessary *sar* expert was quickly engaged, food bought, and neighbouring women summoned to join in the party. When the husband returned from his work at midday for his lunch, he was surprised to find the door of his house tightly barred and to hear a great hubbub inside. The shaman ordered his wife not to let him in, on pain of serious illness, and after knocking angrily for some time the husband lost patience and went away to eat his lunch in a tea-shop. When, in the evening, the husband finally got back from work the party was over. The wife, who had recovered remarkably quickly, met him and explained that she had been suddenly taken ill. *Sar* possession had been diagnosed, and in consequence she had unfortunately to spend all her husband's ready cash to pay for the curing ceremony. The husband accepted this disturbing news with surprising restraint.

On the following day, which was a holiday, while his wife was out shopping in the market, the husband took all her gold and silver jewellery and her cherished sewing-machine to a money-lender from whom he received a susbtantial advance. With this money he assembled a party of holy men and sheikhs and feasted them royally in his house. When his wife returned later in the day, she found the door firmly closed and heard sounds of exuberant hymn-singing within. After trying unsuccessfully to get in, she in her turn went off puzzled to inquire from neighbours what was going on. When she finally returned home later, she found her husband sitting quietly by himself and asked what had happened. 'Oh', said the husband, 'I was suddenly taken ill, and to recover I had to summon a group of holy men to say prayers and sing hymns on my behalf. Now, mercifully, I am better; but, unfortunately, since there was no ready cash in the house I had to pawn all your jewels and even your sewing-machine in order to entertain my guests.' At these words, as can be imagined, the woman raised a loud lament. But after a short period of reflection her anger subsided, as she perceived the reasons for her husband's action. She promised fervently never again to 'beat the *sar*'. Her husband in his turn undertook never again to entertain holy men at his wife's expense and later redeemed her riches. And so, we presume, the couple lived on afterwards in amity.

The use by women of *sar* spirit possession, which this simple tale so well illustrates, is not confined only to the Muslim Somali. This pattern of possession exists also in Ethiopia (under the name *zar*), where it appears to have originated, and in the Muslim Sudan, Egypt, parts of North Africa, and the Arabian Gulf where it has even penetrated the sacred city of Mecca. In Christian Ethiopia, its psychological and dramatic aspects have been explored by the French surrealist poet and ethnographer, Michel Leiris (Leiris, 1958; see also Tubiana, 1983). Further light on its social significance there has been shed by subsequent anthropological research by Messing (1958), Young (1975), and Morton (1977). Messing records how wives use the cult in Somali fashion to extort economic sacrifices from their husbands by threatening a relapse when their demands are ignored — a process which the husbands seek to check by advocating Christian exorcism as the most appropriate treatment. Although more expensive initially, this latter procedure is theoretically efficacious as a single treatment. This avoids the unattractive prospect, following the initial initiatory illness, of the wife drifting into a *zar* coterie which would damage the husband's reputation as a respectable Ethiopian Christian. It is thus, perhaps, not inappropriate that the *zar* spirit and initiatory illness should also be known as 'creditor' (*kureyna*) — creating onerous debts which extend through the spirit-possessed victim to burden her male kin. Much the same appears to be the case with economically depressed women in Cairo, although *zar* possession seems to have an appeal for some rich women too, and *zar* ceremonies have become folkloric events and even made the basis for a distinctive 'Oriental' ballet dance style (*Arabesque*, 1978; 1983). To the extent that *zar* possession offers one explanation of illness, improved medical facilities and other aspects of modernization seem to have a somewhat ambiguous impact on the phenomenon. In the Egyptian countryside where village women are less secluded than their bourgeois sisters — cherished by their husbands as symbols of Islamic respectability — they are reported to be less intensively involved in the cult than the latter (Saunders, 1977). In some villages such possession is known as the 'excuse' and the possessed victim referred to literally as 'excused' — as indeed she is from her routine tasks (Morsy, 1977; 1978). These themes are very explicitly displayed in the suburbs of Khartoum, capital of the Sudan republic. There researchers report that *zar* spirits possessing wives may not only demand gifts, including in one case several gold teeth, but also roundly upbraid the husbands in terms which would not be tolerated were they expressed directly by the women themselves (Constantinides, 1977, 1985; al-Shahi, 1984).

III

As an explanation of a wide range of *symptoms*, *zar* possession provides women patients (acting consciously or unconsciously) with an opportunity to pursue their interests and demands in a context of male dominance. Sometimes they are clearly competing with other women (e.g. co-wives) for a fuller share of their husband's attentions and regard. This may be related to difficulties or inabilities in fulfilling and sustaining men's ideal female roles as, for instance, with fertility problems. In other cases, they may be directly striving for more consideration and respect and sometimes actually competing with the head of the family for a larger slice of the domestic budget. These 'sex-war' aspects are by no means restricted to the *zar* complex. Without attempting any comprehensive survey of all similar cults elsewhere, let us look briefly at a few selected examples which are illuminating in various respects.

In African ethnography, one of the earliest and most vivid descriptions is given by Lindblom in his study of the Kamba of East Africa (Lindblom, 1920). In this society a sharp distinction is made between the local ancestral spirits which uphold morality and represent the ongoing interests of their descendants, and other, capricious spirits. These latter demons are typically spirit representations of neighbouring peoples — Masai, Galla and other tribes — including Europeans. These external or 'peripheral' spirits of foreign origin are not worshipped directly as the ancestors are, but regularly plague Kamba women. As elsewhere, the afflicted women 'speak with tongues' in a foreign dialect in accordance with the provenance of the invasive spirit. The spirits' demands, however, are quite clear. What they seek are gifts and attention from the menfolk, usually from the husbands, each spirit requesting things which reflect its tribal identity. Swahili spirits thus demand richly embroidered Arab-style hats, and European spirits articles which the Kamba take to symbolize European identity. Women's clothes are a popular request, so that the spirits help to enlarge the wardrobes of those they possess. That conscious deception is sometimes involved here is clearly indicated in a poignant little case history recorded by Lindblom. A woman with a craving for meat could only gain her husband's consent to the slaughter of an animal by resort to possession in which her hunger was voiced by the spirit. Unfortunately, however, once her desires were satisfied she made the serious mistake of boasting her successful deception so openly that it came to the ears of the husband who, outraged, sent her packing to her father.

Parallel cases are reported from Tanzania, where, some thirty years ago, Koritschoner described the high incidence in women of an affliction popularly called 'devil's disease' in Swahili. Again the possessing spirit, which manifests its presence by hysterical and other symptoms, demands gifts which reflect its origin. Treatment here is often a lengthy business; and involves not only the usual costly cathartic dances but also the presence for some time of the therapist within the family of the afflicted woman. In this enlightened therapy, the sick wife is made to feel the centre of attention and her husband may even be constrained to modify his behaviour towards his spouse (Koritschoner, 1936, pp. 209–217). Among the Swahili of southern Kenya, similar possession illnesses in wives, expressing conjugal strife, are treated by expensive exorcisms controlled by men. In the exorcism a sort of bargaining from a position of weakness ensues in which: 'demands made by women in marriage (for money, clothes and consumer goods) and refused, are made in the voice of a male spirit and granted. Husbands are publicly bound to provide the goods which will be used by the wife in the name of the spirit after "cure" has been effected.' (Gomm, 1975, p. 534: on patterns of Swahili possession more generally see Giles, 1987.)

Again, among the Luo of Kenya another account describes a similar cult of amoral, malevolent spirits of external origin, existing alongside the ancestor cult which sustains local morality. The Luo ancestors cause sickness and misfortune amongst their descendants when people, neglecting customary rules, commit sins. But the foreign non-ancestral spirits, which particularly single out women for their attentions, are not concerned with administering the social code. They cause a wide range of afflictions ranging from organic illnesses to such minor troubles as constipation. Treatment, which as usual is expensive and involves dancing and feasting, is undertaken by a female shaman who summons the spirit possessing the patient and finds out what it wants. Often a victim has to be temporarily 'hospitalized' in the shaman's home, thus enjoying a pleasant respite from the work-a-day world of the hard-pressed Luo housewife. In the course of the therapy, the spirit agency involved is not so much permanently expelled as brought under control. And once pronounced fit, and restored to the bosom of her family, the wife must henceforth be treated with respect and consideration lest the dreaded affliction recur (Whisson, 1964).

Finally from East Africa, among the Taita, Grace Harris has described a similar woman's possession affliction caused by spirits other than those which sanction morality, and functioning in much the same way to exert pressure on men. Here an element which is present in many of these cathartic rituals and which is in this case particularly stressed is the assumption by possessed women of male postures and dress. Here too there is direct evidence, which is not always so well elucidated, that women actually envy men and resent the male domination which, according to some anthropologists, they should be conditioned to endure with equanimity and passive acceptance (Harris, 1957, pp. 1046-66).

The number of cults of this type in Africa is legion and we shall have space here for only one further example, from West Africa, which is particularly elaborate and well developed. Like its eastern analogue *zar*, the Hausa *bori* spirit cult of Nigeria and Niger has spread to North Africa and has a wide distribution (see e.g. Tremearne, 1914; Dermenghem, 1954; Monfouga-Nicolas, 1972; Echard, 1978; Besmer, 1983). The cult is based upon an imposing pantheon of some two hundred individually named divinities which are related amongst themselves in a manner reminiscent of the gods of ancient Greece. These spirits range in descending order of grandeur from the mighty 'King of the *jinns*' to a tiny cluster of sprites known familiarly as 'the little spots' which, despite their innocent-sounding name, are held responsible not only for a number of minor ailments but also for smallpox. As with many of its less expansive counterparts, this *bori* galaxy is thus not merely a census of spiritual forces, but equally a medical dictionary. Each spirit is associated with a particular group of symptoms, although there is inevitably some overlap. Both amongst the Muslim Hausa in West Africa proper, and in its northern extension in North Africa this cult is again predominantly one of women. Women are the regular devotees in shamanistic exercises designed to cure and control the grounds of their ailments. Here, as elsewhere, in the polygynous family, women succumb to afflictions caused by these pathogenic spirits in situations of domestic conflict and strife. It is thus most significant that amongst the residual, pagan Hausa, when a man turns to embrace Islam, his wife is apt to join the *bori* cult (Last, 1979). When possessed, such wives are treated with a deference and respect which they are not otherwise accorded. Thus, as a Nigerian anthropologist has put it, wives

manipulate *bori* episodes in such a way as to reduce their husbands to social and economic straits. Hence *bori* is not only a symbolic but also a real way of defying the male dominance which pervades Hausa society. In *bori* women find an escape from a world dominated by men; and through *bori* the world of women temporarily subdues and humiliates the world of men (Onwuejeogwu, 1969).

It is not my intention to prolong this recital of women's complaints indefinitely. A few brief examples outside Africa must, however, be given if only to indicate that what we are discussing is far from being a uniquely African syndrome. In the Polar regions, women are especially prone to contract 'Arctic hysteria' which may be diagnosed as possession by a spirit. The incidence of this affliction is highest in the harsh winter months when the struggle to survive is most acute. Gussow, who has interpreted this condition in Freudian terms, refers to the hysterical flights, to which those affected are prone, as unconscious seductive manoeuvres and invitations to male pursuit. It is, he argues, the refuge of those women who in circumstances of adversity and frustration seek loving reassurance. Stripped of its Freudian cadences, this interpretation closely parallels the line of analysis which we have been following (Gussow, 1960).

Similarly, in parts of South America, where traditional deities still uphold customary morality and are monopolized by men, we find women prone to attack by peripheral spirits of the sort we have come to anticipate. This is the case, for instance, amongst the Mapuche of Chile, where such afflicted women may in the course of time graduate to become female shamans. The Black Carib women of British Honduras are likewise plagued by a variety of evil spirits which have no connection with the ancestors who, within a Christian framework, uphold morality. One such is a demon bush-sprite which lurks in shady places, and is particularly attracted to pregnant or menstruating women. It woos women in their dreams and inflicts sickness upon them. But the most feared of all such spirits in this culture is that described as the 'devourer', which is claimed to be known in English by the outlandish title of 'belzing-bug'. This terrifying creature can assume such various forms as a crab, snake, hen, armadillo, or iguana, and possesses girls, making them dance. The treatment of these afflictions is, as we have now learnt to expect, as rewarding to the women molested as it is economically damaging to their husbands and menfolk (Taylor, 1951).

This sex-linked possession syndrome we are tracing seems to be equally prevalent in India and in South East Asia generally. In Uttar Pradesh disaffiliated malevolent spirits, or ghosts, haunt the weak and vulnerable and those whose social circumstances are precarious. Thus the young bride 'beset by homesickness, fearful that she may not be able to present sons to her husband and his family may label her woes a form of ghost possession'. And, 'if she has been ignored and subordinated, the spirit possession may take an even more dramatic and strident form as a compensation for the obscurity under which she has laboured' (Opler, 1958, Dube, 1970). Amongst the Havik Brahmins of Mysore, where as many as twenty per cent of all women are likely to experience peripheral possession at some point in their lives, the pattern is similar. Here it is again mainly insecure young brides (or older, infertile women) who are most exposed to this form of possession. More generally, women as a class are considered weak and vulnerable and thus easily overcome by spirits which, flatteringly, are believed to be attracted by their beauty. In possession, the spirit conveys 'its' demands, causing the husband and his family to mount an expensive ceremony designed to placate it and to persuade it to leave the sick host. Until wives have gained more secure positions in their families of marriage and have given birth to heirs, the illness is liable to recur, thus granting the sick woman all the attention and influence which she is otherwise denied (Harper, 1963, pp. 165–177).

Reports from Muslim Malaysia have, likewise, tended to focus attention on the dramatic diagnostic and healing seances of the inspired shaman (*bomoh*). More recently, however, as well as presenting a subtle analysis of the symbolism of the séance, Clive Kessler (1977) has carefully analysed the epidemiology of possession afflictions which principally affect women. There are three main categories of female victim: reluctant young brides in arranged marriages; older wives caught in the stresses of polygynous marriage with the threat of divorce; and widows and divorcees. The insidence of possession in all three cases, as Kessler (1977, p. 316) shows, 'derives from and also quite openly expresses the problematic relation between the sexes in Kelantanese peasant society'. The evidence thus confirms 'the connexion', we are tracing between 'stress, illness and possession', and 'the sexual politics involved here are, moreover, largely understood by *bomoh* and expressed . . . in the ritual therapy they employ'.

In rural Sri Lanka, the same possession pattern recurs; subordinate women are frequently beset by demons which cause sickness and voice the demands of the afflicted host very clearly. Here, as we have seen in some previous examples, there is also explicit evidence that women resent the position granted them by men: the partial alleviation which they achieve by possession does not exhaust their antagonism. Thus women frequently pray to be reborn as men and give other indications of their dissatisfaction with their lot as a sex (Obeyesekere, 1970, 1981; see also Kapferer, 1983). Again in Burma, as Spiro has shown, the cult of amoral *nat* spirits which is led by possessed women complements the official Buddhist religion dominated by men, and permits the former sex to protect and advance their interests (Spiro, 1967). Similarly, in one of the very rare sociological analyses of these phenomena in Indonesia, Freeman has reported the same patterns of married women's spirit ailments, among the Iban of western Borneo, which are attributed in this case to possession by lustful male incubi (Freeman, 1965).

In traditional Chinese culture also, women are, as ever, especially liable to possession by disaffiliated spirits and, as is well known, play an important part as mediums and shamans. Thus, in a psychiatric study in Hong Kong (to which I shall be referring again later), women in situations of domestic stress and conflict are shown to employ the same feminist strategy with similar results (Yap, 1960, pp. 114–37).

Finally, in the profusely syncretic Japanese religious tradition where a perennial shamanic current has flowed from the earliest times to the present, possessed women have figured prominently. According to Hori (1968), the leading authority on Japanese folk religion, the generic term for shaman, or possessed medium — *miko* — implies that the role is primarily a feminine one. Historians of the ancient 'theocratic' period describe possessed female shamans acting as court oracles and, in some traditions, such inspired female shamans figure as dynastic founders. In the Heian period (784–1185), contemporary sources recount cases of aristocratic women possessed by gods and spirits in contexts of domestic strife of the kind with which we are now familiar. The eleventh-century *Tale of Genji* contains a number of striking episodes of jealous women possessed by aggressive spirits in contexts of polygynous and concubinal conflict, with the usual sex-war over-tones (Bargen, 1986). This tradition of female spirit possession has persisted to the present (Blacker, 1975) and in contemporary Japan spirit possession is one of the commonest problems bringing women to seek refuge in the exorcistic Japanese 'New Religions' — whose founders are frequently possessed women (Davis, 1980). The linkage between women's spirit afflictions, and domestic conflict is, perhaps, today even more directly and pervasively evident in South Korea (see e.g. Harvey, 1979; and Kendall, 1985).

IV

It will now be clear, I think, that we are dealing with a widespread spiritual interpretation of female problems common to many cultures, whose diagnosis and treatment gives women the opportunity to gain ends (material and non-material) which they cannot readily secure more directly. Women are, in effect, making a special virtue of adversity and affliction, and, often quite literally, capitalizing on their distress. This cult of feminine frailty which, in its aetiolated form, is familiar enough to us from the swooning attacks experienced by Victorian women in similar circumstances, is admirably well adapted to the life situation of those who employ it. By being overcome involuntarily by an arbitrary affliction for which they cannot be held accountable, these possessed women gain attention and consideration and, within variously defined limits, successfully manoeuvre their husbands and menfolk.

Since the illnesses which they suffer are interpreted as malign posses-sions in which their personality and volition are effaced by those of the spirits, it is obviously not the women themselves who make these wearisome and costly demands on men. Although the spirits speaking in various tongues, all monotonously voice the same (to male ears) irksome requests, their enunciation in this oblique fashion makes it possible for men to give into them without ostensibly deferring to their wives or jeopardizing their position of dominance. And if, in the possession rituals, as they often do, women (no doubt often in mockery) assume men's clothing and accoutrements and behave at least as aggressively as their partners, is not imitation the sincerest form of flattery?

Hence, within bounds which are not infinitely elastic, both men and women are more or less satisfied: neither sex loses face and the official ideology of male supremacy is preserved. From this perspective, the tolerance by men of periodic, but always temporary, assaults on their authority by women appears as the price they have to pay to maintain their enviable position. The concessions women extract can be regarded, in turn, as 'rewards for colluding in their own oppression' (Gomm, 1975, p. 541).

In this connection the actual conceptual identity of the spirits generally involved seems highly significant. In most cases these spirits are either unwelcome aliens originating among hostile neighbouring peoples, or mischievous nature sprites existing outside society and culture. In other cases where this salient characteristic of externality is more narrowly defined, they are either restive, disaffiliated ghosts, or ancestors belonging to groups other than those where they cause so much havoc. In a word, they are other peoples' spirits. They are thus officially dissociated, as we have seen, from the overt social norms of the communities in which they figure so frequently as sources of affliction. This ostensibly amoral, rather than immoral quality makes them particularly appropriate as the carriers of disease for which those who succumb to them cannot possibly be blamed. Again, both women and men can have a clear conscience on this score.[1]

At the same time, the special predilection which these peripheral spirits display for women seems also peculiarly fitting. For whether or not they be regarded as pawns in the marriage games which Lévi-Strauss and other alliance theory enthusiasts insist men are always

---

[1] To appreciate the full significance of this evasive action we have to go back to Job in the Old Testament. Like him, most tribal communities assume that a high proportion of misfortunes and illnesses are to be interpreted as punishments for sins. Possession by a peripheral spirit thus provides an explanation of sickness which does not carry this implication of guilt.

playing, there is no doubt that in many, if not most societies women are in fact treated as peripheral creatures. The peripherality of women in this sense is, irrespective of the system of descent followed, a general feature of all those societies in which men hold a secure monopoly of the major power positions and deny their partners effective jural equality. Here, of course, there is in one sense an obvious and vital contradiction since, whatever their legal position, women are equally essential to the perpetuation of life and of men. It is they who produce and rear children, and play a major part in their early training and education. Thus the treatment of women as marginal persons denies, or at least ignores, their fundamental bio-social importance and in social terms clashes with their deep commitment to a particular culture and society.

Returning now to our previous argument, if, to a significant degree, it is in terms of the marginalization of women from full participation in social and political affairs and their final subjection to men that we should seek to understand their marked prominence in peripheral possession we must also remember that these cults which express sexual and domestic tensions are yet permitted to exist by men. It seems possible that this tolerance by men of these cults, as well as the ritual licence and blessing also accorded to women more generally, may reflect a shadowy recognition of the injustice of this contradiction between the official status of women and their actual importance to society. If, in short, women are sometimes, even in traditional societies, explicitly envious of men, the dominant sex in turn also acts in ways which suggest that it recognizes that women may have some ground for complaint. This is not the only factor affecting men's interests and behaviour however. As Roger Gomm (1975) shrewdly observes, the redefinition of a problem of discipline (of the husband over the wife) as a problem of possession enables men to maintain 'a stance of competence in the face of conflicting evidence — although at a financial cost'. Moreover, the translation of a marital problem 'into one of possession' enables all parties to co-operate in effecting a 'cure'.

These aspects are perhaps more evident when we consider the wider elaborations of women's peripheral possession. Although I have repeatedly used the term 'cult', so far I have concentrated on the use made by women in their domestic situation of possession afflictions as an oblique protest strategy against husbands and menfolk. Their possession is diagnosed and treated as an illness. The primary emphasis is sometimes initially on the casting out, or exorcism of the intrusive pathogenic spirit. But since such complaints tend to be habit-forming, what is eventually achieved is often more in the nature of an accommodation between the chronically possessed patient and her familiar. The patient learns, in effect, to live with her spirit. The spirit is thus finally 'tamed' and brought under control, but usually only at the cost of recurrent ceremonies in its honour. This process is normally realized by the woman concerned joining a club, or group of other similarly placed women under the direction of a female shaman. Such societies meet periodically to hold dances and feasts for the spirits in which their members incarnate their familiars and perform rituals in their honour.

As long as we maintain the external view — which men endorse — that all these activities are designed to combat sickness and disease, we can consider them as directly therapeutic in intention. They are essentially cures, and in psychiatric terms, the cult meetings assume much of the character of group therapy sessions. (This is an aspect of their character which we shall discuss more fully later.) However, from reports of the elaborate, if furtive, ritual procedures involved — and from which men are rigorously excluded — it is abundantly clear that such occasions are for the women themselves more in the nature of religious services. Thus the healing cult is, for its participants, a clandestine religion, and women are for once exercising a double standard. What men reluctantly accept at face value as illness and cure, the weaker sex enjoys as a religious drama. What is for both initially an illness, thus becomes for women a traumatic induction into a cult group. Consequently, we have here a feminist sub-culture, with an ecstatic religion restricted to women and protected from male attack through its representation as a therapy for illness. Just as with those other possession cults involving men, which occupy a central position in society and where the royal road to divine election lies through affliction, so also here what begins in suffering ends in religious ecstasy.

These apparently contradictory, but in reality highly compatible, elements are all present in tarantism as it survives today in southern Italy and Sardinia. This, as we saw in the previous chapter, is officially an illness caused by the bite of the dreaded tarantula spider. But since, of the two tarantula spiders, the one whose bite is actually harmless is that selected as the ostensible cause of this disease, there is clearly more to tarantism than at first appears. Other considerations fully confirm this suspicion. Those who have been 'bitten' once, re-experience the effects of the 'bite' at regular, often annual, intervals.

The bite can also even run in families. Its first occurrence coincides with the experience of stress and conflict by the victim. And women, though they are actually less likely to be in contact with the real tarantula which could cause their symptoms, are much more prone to contract this disease than men. That we are concerned here with something much more exalted and arcane than the effects of a real spider bite, is further indicated by the rich mythology and ritual which, contrary to the apparently non-mystical aetiology of the affliction, lies at the heart of tarantism.

In the first place, the spider involved is no ordinary insect but a macabre cultural construct ambiguously connected with St Paul. Following the celebrated incident with the serpents in Malta, it is this saint who alone is credited with the gift of curing the bite; and what he cures, he also causes. So the Apostle Paul is ambivalently assimilated to the mystical spider, and in Apulia the rites of exorcism now take place mainly at shrines dedicated to him. In the province of Salente, where tarantism has been studied on the spot by the Italian scholar, de Martino, the main ceremonies take place in St Paul's chapel in the church at Galatina. Here the participants assemble annually on the saint's feast-day in June and dance and sing to the accompaniment of rhythmic clapping. Those who seek a cure and those who come to celebrate their recovery, summon the saint with the invocation: 'My St Paul of the Tarantists who pricks the girls in their vaginas: My St Paul of the Serpents who pricks the boys in their testicles.'

This strangely incongruous identification of the libertine spider with the ascetic Apostle is not as wayward as it appears. For in earlier centuries, the revelries of the tarantists certainly had a highly erotic character, echoing the frenzied dancing of the maenads of Dionysus from which there is some reason to suppose they may actually have developed. And since tarantism today involves possession by the hybrid spider-saint (for that is what the 'bite' really signifies), the expression of this in the language of physical love is, as we have now so often seen, far from unusual. The recognition of the saint's special power to cure the affliction has thus enabled what was probably, in origin, a pre-Christian and possibly once Dionysian popular cult to be accommodated within the local practice of Christianity.

What is clearly involved here today is a loosely Christianized peripheral cult practised mainly by peasant women. As in the other examples we have considered, entry to the cult is achieved by succumbing to an illness for which the mythical tarantula is held responsible. Treatment consists of the usual cathartic dance rituals conducted traditionally in the patient's own home to the tune of the tarantella, but held increasingly today in the saint's chapel. As elsewhere, all this is a costly business for, while the church profits (as well as the patient), heavy expenses fall upon the victim's husband and male kin. Once bitten, the subject is normally bound to the spider-saint for life. The symptoms reappear at regular intervals, being interpreted as further bites by the original spider, and abate only after the dance in its honour has been celebrated. The association of the spider with St Paul, and of the principal curing ceremonies with his feast day, incorporates the cult within the church calendar.

A typical example of the onset and subsequent treatment of the bite will show how everything that has been said previously of these cults applies equally here (de Martino, 1966, pp. 75 ff). A girl, whose father had died when she was thirteen, was brought up in poor circumstances by an aunt and uncle. At the age of eighteen Maria fell in love with a boy who, since his family disapproved of the match because of the girl's poverty, subsequently abandoned her. Maria suffered much from this. One Sunday while gazing listlessly out of her window, she was 'bitten' by the spider and felt constrained to dance. About the same time, a woman of the district began to think of Maria as a possible spouse for her son. When a suitable occasion presented itself, the mother asked Maria to accept her boy in marriage. To gain time, Maria, who was not attracted by the proposal, pleaded that she had not sufficient money to make a trousseau, because of her outlays to musicians for her tarantist dance treatment.

At this point, St Paul providentially appeared, ordering Maria not to marry, and summoning her in mystical union with himself. Shortly afterwards, however, the son and his mother succeeded in luring Maria out to a deserted farm and forced her to live there in shame. After a little time, a quarrel occurred when her mortal spouse brusquely ordered her to iron his clothes. And as she went out to return the iron she had borrowed from a neighbour, she met St Peter and St Paul who said to her: 'Leave the iron and come with us.' When Maria replied, 'And my husband, what of him?' she was told not to worry on that account. This incident occurred on a Sunday, exactly at the time of day when she had been bitten before. After hearing the saint's words, Maria was absent for three days, wandering through the fields. When she returned, she danced, as a result of the second bite, for nine days. With this curious love-bite the saint sought to remind Maria of her holy tryst. Finally, Maria achieved a compromise between the rival interests of her human and spiritual spouses. She agreed to a formal marriage with her human seducer while continuing to celebrate her spiritual union by an annual recrudescence of her affliction in time to participate in the ceremonies on the saint's feast-day.

Thus, constrained by circumstances to marry a man she did not want, Maria continued to pay periodical tribute to the tarantula and to the saint, reviving on each occasion, in the symbolism of the rite, the original adventure of the bite of love and being cured at the same time through the grace of her celestial husband. What had begun as an affliction attributed to the demonic spider, had found its apotheosis in a peculiarly intimate communion with St Paul. And while Maria was thus able to control her illness through her annual participation in the Pauline rites at Galatina, this whole pattern of action was highly expressive of her plight. Through these recurrent outbreaks, followed by treatment at the shrine, Maria was able to sustain her condemnation of her forced marriage, making conjugal life difficult, imposing severe economic stress on the family which she did not love, and flagrantly calling public attention to her problems. If she could not radically remedy her situation, at least she could continue to protest at it in a religious idiom which men could condone as a divinely sanctioned therapy.

V

To understand fully the dynamics of this and other peripheral healing cults, we have to distinguish clearly between a 'primary' and 'secondary' phase in the onset and treatment of possession. In the primary phase, women become ill in contexts of domestic strife and their complaints are diagnosed as possession. The secondary phase is inaugurated when possession bouts become chronic, and the afflicted wife is inducted into what may become permanent membership of the possession cult group. In the course of time, she may then graduate to the position of female shaman, diagnosing the same condition in other women, and thus perpetuating what men tend to regard, uncharitably, as a vicious circle of female extortion. Thus what is considered to begin with as an uncontrolled, unsolicited, involuntary possession illness readily develops into an increasingly controlled, and voluntary religious exercise. The climax in this cycle occurs when the role of shaman is assumed by those women who, in full control of their own spirits, are considered to be capable of controlling and healing spirit afflictions in others. Like the Tungus shaman, they 'master' their own spirits and use them for the public good, or at least for the good of that public which consists of women.

This characteristic sequence of events has been particularly well described amongst the Venda tribe of Southern Africa. Stayt, who studied the situation there in the late 1920s, records that alongside the central morality ancestor cult, an influx of intrusive foreign spirits from the neighbouring Shona peoples of Southern Rhodesia (Zimbabwe) had developed about 1914. These invasive powers possessed women and spoke through them in the Shona dialect. Full of mischief and causing illness, these sprites were believed to lurk in the crevices of trees where they made weird unnatural noises. Their presence in sick married women whom they regularly tormented was diagnosed and treated by female shamans. In the course of treatment directed by the shaman and consisting of drumming and dancing, the spirit possessing the patient would reveal its presence by a deep, bull-like grunt and then announce its demands. In response to the shaman's interrogation, the spirit would typically declare: 'I am so-and-so, and I entered you when you were walking in a certain place. You did not treat me well; I want a present, some clothes or ornaments.' The spirit might also demand such symbols of male authority as a spear, an ancestral axe, a tail-whisk, or a kerrie-stick. Such gifts were formally offered to the spirit who would then allow the patient to recover.

As usual, however, relief was only temporary. Following her first possession, a married woman regularly succumbed at times of difficulty and distress to further attacks, and when seized by the spirits donned the spirit's clothes and danced to its beat. Such a woman had now in fact become a novitiate member of a circle of recurrently possessed women, holding regular dances, and might in time graduate to the position of shaman herself.

In one recorded case, the impetus to assume this position came from a forced marriage from which, unlike the tarantist Maria, the woman concerned succeeded in escaping. The Venda girl in question left her new husband and returned to her own family where her father, angered at this rejection of his authority, beat her. The reluctant bride then ran away into the bush and disappeared completely for six days. After this alarming absence, she returned home looking very ill and complaining bitterly. Her father sent for a shaman diviner who diagnosed that the unhappy bride was now possessed by a spirit.

That night, to her father's astonishment, the girl rose up and commanded him to follow her. The father protested, but since his daughter spoke in a strange voice he was afraid and obeyed. This initial episode was in fact the beginning of this woman's assumption of the career of mistress of spirits. After becoming a full-time member of a women's possession club, she eventually became one of the best-known shamans in Vendaland (Stayt, 1937).

The transition from what I have called the primary phase of peripheral possession to the secondary phase may thus be provoked by an unacceptable marriage, or by an unhappy love-affair — as the ancient physician Galen of Pergamon saw in relation to the onset of hysteria in women. Clearly there are various degrees of protest here. What, in company with many other women, Maria found supportable as long as she also belonged to a cult group, others have rejected completely to assume positions of greater authority and commitment within what might almost be called the protest sub-culture or counter-culture. To some extent, obviously, idiosyncratic personal psychological factors, as well as situational ones, play their part here: some women feel a greater desire than others to play the dominant role of the shaman. Others again, have difficulties in their relations with men and find permanent and devoted attachment to the cult group easier and more rewarding than matrimony.

Such cults, and especially those like the Hausa *bori* cult, which are associated with prostitution, also afford a convenient refuge for divorced wives who are 'between husbands'. Often, though not always, the sort of women who make flighty wives and whose marriages are unsuccessful are precisely those drawn into these movements. In other cases, divorced wives who have failed through no fault of their own may also temporarily attach themselves to these groups. More generally, undoubtedly the commonest spur to the final degree of involvement and professionalization is infertility in women. A high proportion of those who become shamans are in fact either women past the menopause, or their barren younger sisters. Thus those women to whom marriage can offer little, and those who have already enjoyed its fruits as wives and mothers find in the shaman's role an exciting new career. That this position of mastery over spirits and of leadership of rebellious wives should be assumed by those whom society regards as half-men (since they are not fully women) is of course highly appropriate. Thus what we might call the infertility syndrome underlies the androgynous character which is frequently attributed to the leaders of these peripheral cults (cf. Echard, 1978; Constantinides, 1985).

All this of course corresponds very well to the ancient Greek conception of hysteria as a possession affliction relating directly to the womb (*hystera* is the Greek word for womb). One of the earliest recorded writers to have correctly diagnosed this theme was in fact Plato, who expressed his views as follows;

> The womb is an animal which longs to generate children. When it remains barren too long after puberty it is distressed and sorely disturbed: and straying about in the body and cutting off the passages of breath, it impedes respiration and brings the sufferer into the extremest anguish and provokes all manner of diseases besides (quoted in Veith, 1965, p. 7).

It would be pleasant to leave the last word for the moment to Plato. But, before we conclude this chapter there is a wider aspect of the dynamics of these cults to which we must call attention — their historical setting. Although, for the most part, I have written as though these cults were somehow suspended in a timeless eternity, this is of course very far from being the case. As with other religious phenomena, they rise, change, and decline in response to variations in the external circumstances which play upon them. And by considering the cults in this wider context we learn more about them. Often, for example, these comtemporary marginal movements turn out to be the mainline religions of earlier ages which have been eclipsed by new faiths. They are then anachronisms in which historians may be tempted to see a rather specialized illustration of Collingwood's well-known remark about the persistence of the past, 'encapsulated' — as he put it — in the present.

Thus, for instance, in the contemporary Burmese *nat*-spirit possession cult, which is so popular with women, we see much of what survives today of the old pre-Buddhist religion. Or so historians assure us. In the same fashion, most authorities agree in regarding the West African *bori* cult of today as containing elements of the old religion of the Hausa displaced by Islam and thrust into a shadowy, peripheral existence in a Muslim society dominated by men. In its pre-Islamic setting, *bori* spirits were tied to the traditional Hausa clan structure and did not involve possession. And in those halcyon days women enjoyed higher status than they now do as Muslims. Thus with the rise of Islam, the old clan deities 'fell into the public domain' as

Jacqueline Nicolas has put it; though 'public' here has to be understood in the limited sense of referring to women rather than men. Women became possessed by the old gods which their men had discarded. *Bori*, thus, represents a syncretic transformation as much as a 'survival' from pre-Islamic culture (cf. G. Nicolas, 1975; Besmer, 1983; Echard, 1978). Possession is probably a new, post-Islamic element.

A parallel sequence of events is postulated, rather more hypothetically in the case of the *zar* cult in Ethiopia, which, on this view, was an indigenous religion displaced this time by Christianity and thus relegated to the margins of society to be seized upon by peripherally placed people (mainly women). In much the same way and much more recently, amongst the newly Islamized and traditionally matrilineal Zaramo people of the Tanzanian coast, women have been forced into a more subordinate position than they formerly held. In these circumstances they seem to have sought to recover something of their former position by developing a spirit possession cult centring round the old deities, and having all the features we have seen elsewhere.

In many of the other examples we have discussed, however, there is evidence that women are not so much striving to regain a lost paradise as aspiring to achieve entirely new positions of independence and power. Frequently it seems that social changes which have swept their men forward have left them struggling behind, desperately seeking to catch up. Up to a point something of this sort appears to have occurred in the tarantist cult in southern Italy which, formerly, had a wider social catchment, and included a higher proportion of socially disadvantaged men than it does today. In other more exotic cases, unfortunately our historical perspective is drastically shortened by the sheer lack of secure knowledge of the past in any depth. Yet despite this barrier to understanding, there is certainly much to suggest that where these peripheral cults are not (as with *bori*) the residues, however transformed, of old displaced religions, they have often arisen comparatively recently. In Africa, at any rate, it frequently seems that cults of this kind are in part a side-product of the wider contacts and interaction of tribes which the colonial situation encouraged. They may also reflect a response to European conceptions of the status of women. Certainly, at least, such cults are acutely sensitive to changing economic and social conditions, as indeed, we should anticipate from their effects and symbolism.

This is very clearly seen in an impressive study by Elizabeth Colson (Colson, 1969, pp. 69–103) which contrasts the conservative, traditionalist Tonga of the Zambesi valley with their more sophisticated go-ahead countrymen living in the adjoining plateau-land. Amongst these Plateau Tonga, increasingly involved in the modern market economy of Zambia since the 1930s, and with local opportunities for earning cash wages which did not require their menfolk to work extensively as migrant labourers far from home, men and women have been subject to a virtually parallel acculturation. Moreover, the traditional pattern of relations between the sexes was one of unusual equality for an African society. Thus, whether unmarried or not, Plateau Tonga women participated freely in men's social activities and were not strictly hedged about with a barrage of mystical restraints. In this situation, possession by peripheral, non-ancestral spirits called *masabe* is today rare, and, in so far as it occurs at all, affects men and women equally.

Amongst the Valley Tonga the position is quite different. Here men have long participated through labour migration in the wider European-orientated world. Women in contrast have remained at home fascinated by the town delights and mysteries from which they have been excluded. It is these secluded and constrained wives who are regularly subject to possession by spirits that today characteristically demand gifts which these women directly associate with their alluring urban counterparts. As well as for gay clothes and luxury foods, one of the commonest requests is for soap. This change in spirit appetites reflects a growing male sophistication and repugnance for the oil and ochre cosmetics with which Valley women traditionally bedecked their bodies, and a distinct preference by men for freshly bathed and fragrantly scented partners. It is in this glamorous idiom of the beautician's salon that, through their possessing spirits, these rural women today call attention to their exclusion and neglect and seek to alleviate or overcome it. In the past, as so often elsewhere, these same spirits hankered after men's garments and possessions. Matthew Schoffeleers (1985) records a similar outburst of women's spirit-possession in southern Malawi in a context where the collapse of local cotton production and consequent upsurge in male labour migration made women more dependent on and subservient to their husbands.

Whatever may have been the case in the past, these ambitions and longings are today no longer static. Women's aspirations are constantly changing with variations in their circumstances and experience. The demands which the cults express alter accordingly as women, like Oliver Twist, continually ask for more. To be a fully-fledged *bori* woman in Niger, for instance, is synonymous with being a 'with-it' emancipated woman (*zawara*), fully versed in the sophistications of town life and deeply involved in urban politics and other men's activities. Much the same applies, I suspect, to similarly, permanently possessed, women in other urban surroundings, especially where this involves increased domestic confinement and frustration. We shall return to this theme of protest carried to the point of emancipation in the next chapter. For the moment, let us also note how the changing character and imagery of the possessing spirits mirrors the wider varying landscape of social experience. To the former tribal and animal spirits which everywhere figure so prominently in these traditional spirit pantheons are added, while they are still novel and mysterious, such other alien powers as those manifest in telephones, cars, trains, and aeroplanes. Much the same occurs generally with spiritual forces of Christian and Islamic origin. These powers are as readily assimilated in peripheral cults in the third world as was St Paul in southern Italy. With the arrival of these new spirit accretions, reflecting new contacts and new experiences, some of the old spirits become otiose and drop out.

This experiential and explanatory function, as old religious forms stretch out their arms to embrace and come to terms with new experience, is strikingly indicated in the Sudan Republic. There, when the first national football team was formed and public enthusiasm for the sport was high among men, women began to be preyed upon by footballer *zar* spirits. Similarly, during the military régime of General Aboud, a rash of military spirits appeared; and significantly in political circumstances which were widely felt to be oppressive, a new category of anarchist spirits also entered the lists. These novel spirit presentations were a great trial to women amongst whom they faithfully reproduced the main play of events in the greater world of men. Thus, where they may not succeed in doing so more directly, on the spiritual plane at least, women strive to keep in step with men. Again we see clearly that what I have called the subordinate female sub-culture, if only in fantasy, marches forward in pace with the dominant culture of men.

Chapter Four

STRATEGIES OF MYSTICAL ATTACK: PROTEST AND ITS CONTAINMENT

I

It would no doubt be satisfying to male vanity to interpret the marked prominence of women in the possession of cults which we have just discussed as the reflection of an inherent, and biologically grounded female disposition to hysteria. Unfortunately, however, this conclusion is untenable because in practice these movements are not entirely restricted to women. Notwithstanding my emphasis in the previous chapter, several of the cults which we have already examined do in fact also include men, and not only those with obvious personality disorders. Italian tarantism, this 'religion of remorse', as de Martino punningly labels it, which still today attracts a few downtrodden male peasants, had in earlier periods a wider catchment among men. Seventeenth- and eighteenth-century accounts reveal a considerably higher proportion of men tormented by the spider's bite than is the case today. These statistics correspond well with other historical data which show how, in previous centuries, tarantism had a particular appeal for men whose social circumstances were unusually oppressive or constricting.

With its formerly more richly endowed symbolism in which the dancers acted as swaggering captains, grandiose governors, muscle-flexing boxers, and hectoring public orators, the cult gave such men the opportunity of playing a range of roles far removed from those they held in real life. The most wretched beggar could temporarily assume the airs and graces of high society, and command respectful and sympathetic attention for his posturing. The cult also attracted priests who found difficulty in enduring the rigours of their celibate calling as well as nuns who chafed against the discipline and constriction of the religious

90

vocation. Such maladjusted individuals from monastery or convent found some measure of relief through participating periodically in the lusty rites of the Women's Carnival. Today all this is changed. The spider's bite is almost entirely restricted in its incidence to poor peasant women in the remote and more backward parts of southern Italy.

Although we are much less well-provided with detailed information on the social background of its devotees, the cult of Dionysus seems to have exercised a similar appeal not only for women but also for men of low social status. As Jeanmaire has phrased it, Dionysus was the 'least political' of the Greek gods (Jeanmaire, 1951, p. 8). He was essentially a god of the people, offering freedom and joy to all, including slaves as well as freemen excluded from the old lineage cults. Apollo, in contrast, as E.R. Dodds has it, 'moved only in the best society'. Thus it seems that here we have another of these peripheral cults involving spirits of foreign (here supposedly Thracian) origin which inflicted 'illness' on downtrodden men and women, and at the same time offered a means of escape and cure in the associated cathartic rituals.

All this applies equally well to both the *zar* and *bori* cults in Africa which, previously, we have discussed only in relation to women. In Christian Ethiopia, *zar* possession is not in fact a monopoly of the fair sex. The disease also affects and the cult equally embraces men of subordinate social status, particularly people of such marginal social categories as half-Sudanese Muslims and ex-slaves. Indeed in the interval between 1932, when it was observed by Michel Leiris, and more recent descriptions, it is clear that the composition of the cult groups has to some extent changed. Some of the earlier higher class Amhara women adherents seem to have dropped out to be replaced by a wider spectrum of marginalized men — particularly, but not exclusively, non-Christians. Membership of the local *zar* club and participation in its dramatic rituals offer these otherwise under-privileged persons some degree of emancipation from frustrating tradi-tional confinements. Within these clubs, which may also function as savings societies and credit associations, members of low class minority groups have the opportunity of striking up useful associations with people who, though Amhara, are handicapped in other ways. And, in keeping with what is happening on the wider Ethiopian scene, a new aspiration towards upward social mobility is evident in the increasingly exalted status of the spirits which now possess people of humble origins.

Whereas in Ethiopia low class men (often Muslims) may in the *zar* clubs thus rub shoulders with Christian Amhara women of higher status, in southern Somalia each sex has its own cult. Here freeborn women are involved in a possession society called *mingis* (from the Amharic for 'government', 'power', etc.) which is a local variant of *zar* incorporating some Oromo influence (for a musicological account see Giannattasio, 1983). This cult rigorously excludes ex-slaves, who, in this fertile part of the Somali Republic, were formerly employed as agricultural serfs. They have their own possession club known as *numbi*, and meet regularly each week to hold a dance ritual in which they become possessed by the spirit.

Significantly, when these ex-slaves dance in the possession rites they carry as insignia whips which, though they are of course no longer used today, enable them to present themselves not as slaves, but as masters of slaves. This striking role reversal is a crucial element in the ritual.

Again, although in rural districts of northern Nigeria the Hausa *bori* cult is essentially a women's protest movement, in towns — where it is associated with prostitution and also with trade and markets in general — men are also involved, and not merely as customers. Thus in the Republic of Niger, as Madame Nicolas (Nicolas, 1967; Monfouga-Nicolas, 1972) has reported, townsmen become possessed and join the cult. But, significantly, they are foreigners, not local men, who as outsiders may be presumed to be in a position of insecurity and subordination. In the Ader and Kurfey regions of the northern Nigerian Sahel, Nicole Echard (1978) has sketched out historically how the *bori* cult registers external pressures as they are experienced locally. Reacting to the privations of drought and Islamic domination, rebellious men are increasingly attracted to the cult which, in these circumstances, is correspondingly 'masculinized'.

Of greater significance, perhaps, in its inclusion of men is the great extension of *bori* (and to a lesser extent also of *zar*) in north-west Africa. Here in a region dominated by Islamic mysticism, where the profession of the faith is virtually synonymous with being attached to one or other of the Sufi brotherhoods, the *bori* cult has found a new and unexpected home. *Bori* brotherhoods, whose membership consists primarily of ex-slaves and other servile classes of men and women, exist alongside the more orthodox orders of freeborn and higher society. These former slaves are in fact of West African origin, and belong ethnically to such groups as the Hausa, Songhay, and Bambara, etc., and thus in effect continue their old pre-Islamic cults within a Muslim framework. But the significant point for us here is that in this new Islamic setting, these traditional cults assume a peripheral position. And since their rites incorporate many Islamic elements and mingle them freely with the worship of *bori* and other non-Muslim spirits in an unholy alliance, to the disapproving eyes of the pious North African Arabs and Berbers, these rituals have almost the character of 'Black Masses' — if the pun will be forgiven.

Initiation into these 'Black Brotherhoods', as they are known in the French literature, normally follows a possession illness, and the cults are essentially healing in character. (Women of noble Arab birth also seek cures for their complaints through the same ritual, which, of course, usually proves an expensive business for their husbands.) More to the point, although the position is not entirely clear in the existing literature, I think we may infer that, in the case of slaves, the bulk of the expenses involved in such *bori* therapy fell upon their masters, and thus gave the former a lever with which to manipulate the latter. In a more general sense too, these *bori* brotherhoods protected the interests of their members, providing food and lodging for the temporarily indigent, and while slavery still existed would sometimes buy a slave his freedom. With the abolition of slavery, these organizations, more than any others, came to provide the primary focus of allegiance and social identification for the ex-slave community. They championed their members' rights and protected them against harassment or abuse from their Arab and Berber superiors. Here the Black Brotherhoods acted as pressure groups enjoying a special ritual cachet through their association with the widely feared *bori* spirits. On this basis too, some of the cult devotees also still enjoy a lucrative practice as diviners and healers, and play a particularly important role in treating sterility amongst the population at large. Thus an Arab woman who has lost all her children, or one who has not borne any, may summon the *bori* adepts to her aid. They make a secret mark on her leg and bless her; and if she subsequently bears a child this 'belongs' to the cult group and contributes handsomely to its periodic offerings and rituals (Tremearne, 1914; Dermenghem, 1954; Paques, 1964).

Almost everything that has been said about *bori* in north-west Africa applies with equal force to the analogous Christianized slave cults of the Caribbean and South America. In all these areas today we find flourishing possession cults built round a cosmological substratum of the old gods of Africa, which the slaves brought with them, and to which they have clung tenaciously throughout their long period of subjection and oppression. Africa, here, has great force as a symbolic focus of authenticity and beneficent power (cf. Larose, 1977). Now, of course, these cults have in fact become the unofficial religions of the local peasantry, and exist in an uneasy tension with the more orthodox Christianity of élitist society. From our point of view, these cults again centre on spiritual forces which are peripheral to the Christian establishments of the countries concerned and appeal most strongly to the subordinate segments of society. To these they offer a consummate religious experience, lifting up downtrodden men and women to heights of exaltation which, whatever else they do, certainly serve to underscore the lowly secular position of the possessed devotees.

Thus, for example, as has been clearly shown in Trinidad (Mischel and Mischel, 1958), as well as appealing strongly to women, the Shango cult generally also attracts such male adherents as domestic servants and unemployed labourers. Such lowly figures are regularly mounted by powerful, aggressive spirits, and when they incarnate these gods they command the attention of large audiences in what is evidently a highly satisfying fashion. Women similarly are often possessed by domineering male divinities and these allow their 'horses' to express aspects of their personalities which in other circumstances are strongly suppressed. Indeed, it is clear that the Shango cult enables a discordant mass of humanity to achieve a highly dramatic psychic 'work-out', the possessed giving vent in the rituals to emotions and feelings which in other contexts are held in check. And as elsewhere, whatever the possessed person does is done with impunity since he is considered to act as the unconscious and involuntry vehicle of the gods.

All these elements are equally well represented in Haitian voodoo, which embraces over 90 per cent of the island's population and is regarded with contempt and disdain by the small westernized ruling élite. This minority establishment, which is mainly of mulatto stock, clings desperately to western values and to the orthodox Catholic church. From its point of view, as Métraux has so well put it, voodoo is an insidious rural paganism (Métraux, 1959). For the peasants, however, it is a populist religion from which the freedom-fighting ex-slave heroes of the past drew inspiration in the nationalist struggle prior to independence in 1804.

Much of the voodoo ritual and liturgy is of Christian origin; and the *loa* 'mysteries', which are also called 'saints' or even 'angels', although largely of West African derivation, are viewed as part of the

Christian cosmology. When a *loa* 'comes out' in a new devotee it usually has to be baptized, and many spirits, incarnated in their mounts, take holy communion. From the other direction, many Christian saints and even the Virgin Mary are incorporated among the *dramatis personae* of the *loa*. With this degree of syncretism between traditional African powers and those of Catholicism, it is scarcely surprising that the two religious calendars should be closely synchronized (as is also the case with *zar* in Ethiopia and the Sudan). Throughout Lent, the voodoo sanctuaries are closed and no service is celebrated. In Holy Week the cult accessories are covered with sheets, as are the images in the Catholic churches; and on Christmas night voodoo ritual 'takes wing in its full plumage' as Métraux eloquently puts it. Equally, possession by the *loa* is explicitly compared with 'the entering of the Holy Ghost into the curé when he sings mass'. With this degree of congruence, it is only to be expected that the Haitian peasantry who evidently experience no embarrassment or confusion in combining the two faiths should claim that 'to serve the *loa* you have to be a Catholic'.

For their part, the *loa* enter very fully into the lives of their servants. In essence, they play a protective role, and only withdraw their benevolent patronage when they are neglected. Some 'mysteries' even seek employment for the protégés. In the middle of a voodoo service at one of the shrines, a trader or official may be suddenly accosted by a *loa* which demands work for his mount. And who can reject such a divine appeal, particularly when the *loa* making the request vouches for the honesty and industry of its candidate? So deeply in fact do the spirits immerse themselves in the lives of those who dance in their honour, that there are even banker and creditor gods which offer credit facilities for those attending the ceremonies. Their business acumen and taste for speculation indeed drive some 'mysteries' to invest money with merchants from whom good dividends can be expected. Such investments carry with them the blessing of the gods and bring good luck. But since the *loa*, like their human agents, are pitiless in financial matters those who borrow from them do so at their own risk.

The cult groups which arise round an influential *loa* priest or *hungan* bearing such nostalgic African names as 'Gold Coast', 'God First', 'The Flower of Guinea Society' etc., fulfil a similar range of functions in towns to those served by the *bori* societies in north-west Africa. They act also as welfare and betterment associations and play a highly significant role in defining the social identity of their members. Above all, while in the regular danced rituals the possessed devotees are enabled to give free rein to their suppressed desires and ambitions — which the gods gleefully and freely express on their behalf — the cult also gives great psychic satisfaction to 'poor souls ground down by life'. Usually, as we would expect, downtrodden men and women are possessed by gods which, in fantasy, express their hopes and fears and bespeak upward social mobility.

In addition to the obvious enjoyment which, like its analogues elsewhere, this 'danced religion' affords its devotees, opportunities for status enhancement of a more direct and tangible kind are also present. We have already seen how the gods may solicit jobs for their followers from those who are in a position to grant such favours. At the same time, the career of voodoo priest or priestess, which may be gradually assumed as a cult member's control over and knowledge (*connaissance*) of the 'mysteries' (*loa* spirits) increases, can be both lucrative and rewarding. A successful *hungan* is at once priest, healer, soothsayer, exorcizer, and organizer of public entertainments — this last representing the theatrical and recreational aspect of the cult which is not to be dismissed lightly. In addition, such a figure is regarded as an influential political guide, and frequently acts as an electoral agent for whose services senators and deputies pay handsomely. Thus to assume this role of leader of a cult group is to climb the social ladder and to acquire a prominent place in the public gaze. Competition, however, is fierce, and rival priests vying with one another for larger congregations of adherents will do their utmost to discredit their adversaries. Here the standard allegation, which coincides with that generally levelled by the Catholic élite at voodoo as a whole, is that one's opponents are sorcerers or witches, working, as the Haitians say, 'with both hands'. Such judgements here, as elsewhere, turn on whether mystical power is employed for the general, public good, or for narrow, private advantage (cf. Larose, 1977; Lewis, 1986, pp. 51ff). Under the regimes of the notorious Dr Duvalier ('Papa Doc') and his son, voodoo was elevated virtually to the status of a state religion, with cult groups, serving to underpin the dictators' power at the local level (Courlander and Bastien, 1966; Larose, 1977). Implicitly, if not explicitly, voodoo had moved to the centre of the stage.

II

Since, as well as women more generally, these cults evidently also attract men of servile origin and of other oppressed categories, we should expect to find further examples in highly stratified, inegalitarian polities elsewhere. The Swahili-speaking inhabitants of Mafia island, off the coast of Tanzania, provide a well-documented example of such a case.

The island's Muslim population consists of various tribal elements arranged in a definite order of precedence with the Pokomo, the most African and least Arabian in ethnic affiliation, occupying (in the 1960s) the lowest rung on the status ladder. The Pokomo are traditionally excluded from full participation in the official political and ritual life of this Islamic society, and find their fulfilment in a highly developed spirit possession cult, through membership of which they exert influence and power in the wider community. These despised islanders are subject to possession by 'land spirits' of the bush classified as 'devils' (*shaitani*) which cause illness either through their own malevolence or because they have been sent by a person with power over them (i.e. by a witch). As usual, these spirits are not concerned with morality, and the illnesses which they inflict on the unwary are not viewed as punishments for infringements of the social code.

Such afflictions are diagnosed and treated by Pokomo shamans who control the spirits concerned and initiate their victims into the possession clubs which meet regularly to hold dance rituals. The cult is open to both men and women of the Pokomo group, and ambitious recruits can in time graduate to the position of shaman and diviner. Since shamans are paid for their services as medical advisers, which are not restricted to patients of their own tribe, they can become wealthy and influential in this mixed society. Thus through these land-spirit cults which, with their flamboyant rites (including blood-drinking), are condemned by pious Muslims of higher social standing, Pokomo men can achieve *de facto* positions in the island which would otherwise be beyond their grasp.

Parallel to this Pokomo cult, a separate possession cult of sea-spirits exists amongst the higher status groups, but is restricted to women. Such higher class women are prone to possession afflictions by these spirits which come from over the sea, in fact from Arabia, and which cause those they possess to speak in Arabic. These ennobling 'Arab' spirits are flatteringly attracted by the beauty of their female hosts. The incidence of the afflictions they cause is exactly similar to what we have found in so many other cases. In stress situations in the domestic family, women succumb to them, and they are especially concerned with such feminine conditions as frigidity, infertility, and pregnancy. Treatment requires costly outlays by the husband and his kin, and eventually usually leads to initiation into the possession cult group. This meets regularly on Fridays and its ritual is in effect a parody of the Islamic religious services which men dominate and from which women are excluded. Since in Mafia, men's worship is largely organized through the mystical brotherhoods or *tariqas*, this women's possession society, like its *bori* analogue in North Africa, follows the same model. At their possession meetings women sing the same hymns as men do in the services of the Muslim brotherhoods.

Clearly while gaining protection from the exactions of their menfolk whom they influence through possession illnesses, women also thus participate vicariously in the male-dominated culture of the island. Although there are here two parallel possession cults — one for the low status Pokomo, and another for women of high status — the spirits of the former are considered generally to be more powerful, and the leading Pokomo shaman in fact controls both cults (Caplan, 1975).

In two other African examples which are worth mentioning briefly, men in low social positions and women generally are not separately served by distinct possession cults as in Mafia or southern Somalia, but collected together in the same cult. This is the situation which has been admirably described amongst the Muslim Songhay of the Niger bend by Jean Rouch (Rouch, 1960; Olivier de Sardan, 1984). In this officially Muslim society, non-ancestral spirits called *holey* have an analogous role to the *bori* among the neighbouring Hausa. In this stratified society, *holey* spirits, which include both nature sprites and foreign powers expressive of Songhay's wider geo-social environment, plague women and men of low caste. Here illness, diagnosed as possession by these spirits, appears to function amongst these peripheral social categories as a strategy of oblique redress in the manner we have explored in other cases. Ultimately, recurrent possession is interpreted as an unchallengeable call by the spirits and requires formal initiation into the cult.

Such initiated 'children of the spirits' as they are called, are directed in their ritual activities by men of low occupational castes, and particularly by the Sorko fishing people of the Niger valley. Elderly men of this group, which may represent an autochthonous element in the population, are considered to be 'married to female spirits and incapable of being interested in other women'. Such Sorko priests often abandon their traditional riverine pursuits and devote themselves entirely to the *holey* cult. In the wider society their main ritual tasks concern rain-making, the organization of hunting dances to secure river game, and the direction of rituals designed to alleviate the effects of disasters caused by thunderstorms during the rainy season. Here their primary role is that of intermediaries with Dongo, the thunder god. Thus amongst the Songhay, the two most marginal elements in society — women of all groups and men of low caste — are brought together in a common cult of affliction which is integrated in the total religious and officially Muslim life of this complex West African people.

A similar synthesis under different circumstances has taken place amongst the Gurage, a Semitic-speaking people of central Ethiopia (Shack, 1966). Here, with those Gurage who have not yet converted to Islam or Christianity, there are two main religious cults. The first, which is restricted to freeborn men, concerns the sky god *Waka* which is worshipped as the guardian of general morality. This deity receives annual sacrifices at his shrine, which is the centre of Gurage political and religious life and where he is represented by a female priestess. This position is vested in a particular clan, but the office is only potential. It becomes active by the marriage of a woman of the appropriate descent group to a male ritual consort who must again be drawn from another designated clan. However, it is this woman, human 'wife' to the deity, who, assisted by women of the despised class of Fuga carpenters, leads this cult of men. Spirit possession is not involved here.

In contrast, possession is the dominant motif in the parallel women's cult addressed to the female deity *Damwamwit*. Through possession by this spirit, Gurage women in general and downtrodden Fuga men (who are attached as clients to freeborn Gurage families) are allowed special licence and a degree of status enhancement otherwise denied to them. Thus, as can be imagined, women when in trouble with their husbands, or Fuga dependants in difficulties with their Gurage masters, readily become possessed. Moreover, as though to drive the point home further, their protecting spirit is liable to attack anyone who wantonly molests them (see Woldetsadik, 1967; Knutsson, 1975; Todd, 1980).

I see this combined women's and Fuga movement as an essentially peripheral cult which has become institutionalized to the point where it is integrated in the total Gurage religious system alongside the male cult of the masculine spirit, *Waka*. Here possession has not been permitted to intrude within the male-dominated main morality cult, but has been allowed to exist and persist amongst women under male leadership — apparently at the price of granting female direction in the former cult. Unfortunately we know nothing of the historical circumstances underlying this synthesis; and whether or not this balancing of roles between the sexes represents a fair compromise between men and women in a society where there is reported to be much explicit sexual antagonism is equally debatable. With respect to the downtrodden Fuga, however, it appears that the licence allowed to them in possession can be viewed as, in effect, an acknowledgement in ritual terms of their oppressed condition.

In thus touching on the theme of ritualized rebellion which, here as elsewhere, is undoubtedly present in these cults of the underprivileged, we must be careful not to assume that such canalized expressions of insubordination necessarily represent a completely satisfying catharsis which totally exhausts pent-up resentment and frustration. Here my last African example, that of the *kubandwa* possession cult in the kingdom of Rwanda, provides a salutary warning against the over-ready acceptance of this 'establishment' view of the general situation. Traditional Rwanda provided an extreme example of a mixed conquest state, organized into rigid caste-like divisions. The system was dominated by the proud Tutsi who, as intrusive pastoral aristocrats, ruled a society in which they formed only some 10 per cent of the total population. The bulk of the kingdom's inhabitants consisted in fact of Hutu cultivators who could not marry Tutsi and were attached to the latter as clients, producing grain for them and helping to look after their cattle. This symbiotic arrangement freed the noble Tutsi from many of the humdrum tasks of daily life and permitted them to devote their energies to governing and conquering. At the same time, it also allowed the despised Hutu to participate vicariously in the dominant pastoral culture of their masters. Finally at the bottom of the social pyramid lay the pygmy hunters called Twa who, like the aristocratic Tutsi, formed a very small proportion of the population.

The 'premise of inequality', as Maquet (1961) calls it, under which the Hutu and Twa laboured was to some extent alleviated by their participation in the *kubandwa* spirit possession cult. This cult, which was quite separate from that of the ancestors sustaining customary morality, centred round the god *Ryangombe* and his assistant spirits. *Ryangombe* like Dionysus, was essentially a god of the people, uniting in his worship subordinate Twa and Hutu as well as the lordly Tutsi. The anti-establishment tone of the cult was plainly evident in the unflattering and obscene names for many subsidiary spirits and the ironic slogan: 'I love the Tutsi' (Berger, 1976). Initiation into the cult followed a spirit illness and involved, as so often elsewhere, a mystical union with the deity and his attendant spirits. Once this was achieved, the initiate was protected from the power of the ancestor cults which, as we should expect, strove hard to uphold caste morality. Significantly, *Ryangombe* is depicted in myth as the victorious rival of King Ruganzu, the most celebrated Tutsi conqueror of the court traditions.

Although the existing accounts of this cult do not make clear whether or not Twa and Hutu used possession, as we should anticipate, to press their interests in their relations with their Tutsi patrons, our sources on this movement strongly emphasize its role as a safety valve for the ventilation of suppressed aggression on the part of the subordinate groups in the kingdom (de Heusch 1966; Berger, 1981). That this was only a partially successful palliative, however, is clearly evident from the more recent sequence of events in this troubled area to the east of the Congo. In the last days of Belgian rule the Tutsi, in the same spirit as the white settlers in Rhodesia, pressed for early independence in order to stamp out any further erosion of their traditional authority. And shortly before independence, the suppressed Hutu turned from such relief as they may have found in the *kubandwa* cult to precipitate a bloody revolution in which they seized power from the Tutsi and massacred thousands of their former masters.

III

As we saw in the case of women's cults where, however ambivalent male attitudes to such troublesome spirits may be, men at least believe in them in general, so here too it is obviously essential that both superior and subordinate should share a common faith in the existence and efficacy of these mutinous powers. This basic necessity for a mutual trust in the symbolism of such peripheral possession is required, since otherwise clearly the voice of protest loses its authority. This aspect of the situation is readily emphasized if we compare for a moment European 1960s manifestations of 'Flower-Power' with that interesting nineteenth-century Fijian precursor, usually known as the Water Baby Cult. Whatever messages of peace they may have borne in earlier centuries and despite the efforts of Interflora, in our secular society flowers are no longer deeply evocative symbols charged with esoteric meaning. Not so in nineteenth-century Fiji. There, in the context of the first impact of modern social change, young people and minor chiefs excluded from high positions in the traditional authority structure rallied together to form the Water Baby Cult, being possessed by forest and water spirits, and taking new personal names — usually those of flowers. Unlike our own Flower-People, these Fijian counterparts achieved through possession and their participation in the cult a measure of attention and respect which they had previously been denied (Worsley, 1957). The symbolism selected was appropriate to the task to which it was applied.

All the elements we have so far discussed are particularly well displayed in the context of the Hindu caste system. Several recent writers on Indian communities comment upon the predilection which peripheral spirits (often those of the unquiet and untimely dead) show for men of low caste. In some cases this may lead to dramatic and lasting revolutionary changes in status. Thus, in a lower Himalayan village, Gerald Berreman (1972) recounts in detail the life history of a remarkable young blacksmith who, following a series of calamities, was possessed by a deity and performed many miracles to become venerated himself as a living god. More commonly, through possession, such lowly orders are allowed a limited franchise to protest against their menial circumstances. One of the best analyses of this pattern of ritualized mutiny is that provided for the Nayars of Malabar by Kathleen Gough (Gough, 1958).

This high caste of warriors and land-owners is traditionally divided into a number of matrilineages, the functionally most significant units of which are matri-segments known as *taravads*, each with its own estate, and led by the senior male in the group. As we should expect, within the local practice of Hinduism the ancestors of these groups are largely concerned with the morals and obedience to caste rules of their descendants. These essentially family spirits are carefully tended by the head of each *taravad*. Sickness and affliction are interpreted as manifestations of their wrath at some act of unfitting behaviour within the group.

There are, however, other options. Some instances of disease and injury are referred not to the ancestors but to alien ghosts. These latter are typically the spirits of low caste menials and dependants of Nayars who have died following a quarrel with their masters, or who were actually killed by them. Such spirits, as can be imagined, haunt and harass their former superiors, causing much malicious misfortune and sickness. To cope with this, shrines are erected to these demanding spirits and they are regularly propitiated — not by the head of the Nayar group himself, but by an attached low caste servant. Through this priest, offerings of toddy and chickens are made annually by the Nayar family concerned to keep the spirit contented. Propitiatory sacrifices are also made on other occasions in response to afflictions for which these peripheral spirits (in our terminology) are held responsible. Here diagnosis is provided by a low caste diviner.

In the propitiation rites, the low caste officiant usually becomes possessed by the spirit. While in this condition, he may make further demands on his Nayar masters as well as taking the opportunity of voicing any grievances held at the time by the low caste dependants of the Nayar group concerned. These representations are made of course by the spirit and are therefore not to be dismissed lightly. Similarly, in the actual appeasement rituals, these low caste ritual experts (described as professional exorcists) in defiance of normal convention act very aggressively towards their Nayar masters. In this ritual context, however, they must be treated with great respect by the Nayars and given gifts and such other presents as they request.

In the light of the foregoing, it is no surprise to find that the incidence of actual afflictions laid at the door of these spirits tends to coincide with with episodes of tension and unjust treatment in the relations between master and servant. Thus, as so often elsewhere, from an objective view-point, these spirits can be seen to function as a sort of 'conscience of the rich'. Their malevolent power reflects the feelings of envy and resentment which, people of high caste assume the less fortunate lower castes must harbour in relation to their superiors. Moreover, these aggressive ghosts are in this case no longer used only by the weak and downtrodden through the oblique strategy of self-possession. They also take the offensive and directly attack Nayars, causing possession afflictions which can only be cured by low caste exorcists. The Nayars have thus good grounds for taking these capricious spirits seriously. Again, these powers can also be directly employed in witchcraft and sorcery. Those who control them are credited with the power of sending them against an enemy. And here it is precisely their low caste dependants, who specialize in dealing with these unclean spirits, that the Nayars regard as potential witches and sorcerers.

This brings us to the theme of the next section of this chapter — the relationship between peripheral possession and witchcraft. But before we embark on that, let us note that in the case we have just examined these low caste spirits which the Nayars treat as aliens are of course ancestral to the subordinate groups concerned. For what are external to the Nayars, are kith and kin to their servants. Thus it is not here a question of a single ethnic-group being plagued by forces from hostile neighbouring peoples. On the contrary, the situation is that spirits which are central to one sub-group in a plural society are marginal to other units within the same system. The enemy in short is not at the gates, but within the heart of the composite society. Externality or peripherality is thus highly relative and in the Nayar case defined, as one would expect, by caste barriers. The case is similar in other culturally and ethnically heterogeneous systems where the gods of subordinate segments of the wider society are feared as capricious malcontent powers by their superiors. This is in fact the position with the *bori* slave cults of north-west Africa.

Again externality may be even more narrowly defined. It may be considered that, where women are married exogamously by men of other lineages, each wife brings her own ancestor spirits with her and these are alien to her husband's family and kin. Or, alternatively, a wife may be thought to have privileged access to her husband's ancestral spirits which are foreign to her. In either case, women are concerned with spirits which have a degree of externality or marginality in the situation in which they are operative. In many societies, and particularly among the South African Bantu peoples, such affinal ancestor spirits regularly cause possession afflictions in the women concerned, but once these are mastered their victims become socially approved anti-witchcraft diviners (see e.g. O'Connell, 1982). Here, exactly as with more thoroughly foreign peripheral spirits, women employ these 'extra-descent' spirits to advance their aims and interests in the manner we have now come to expect.

Thus, however narrowly or broadly conceived the peripherality of the spirits involved may be, the effect is always the same. What we find over and over again in a wide range of different cultures and places is the special endowment of mystical power given to the weak. If they do not quite inherit the earth, at least they are provided with means which enable them to offset their otherwise crushing jural disabilities. With the authority which the voice of the gods alone gives, they find a way to manipulate their superiors with impunity — at least within certain limits. And, as we saw in the last chapter, to an extent that is hard to gauge precisely, this is broadly satisfactory to all concerned, subordinate as well as superior. Yet, as I have repeatedly emphasized, this is not to say that such limited expressions of protest exhaust the store of revolutionary fervour. However seemingly satisfying the play of such cults, the potentiality for deeper and more radical outbursts of pent-up resentment is always there.

Sartre, in his preface to Frantz Fanon's *The Wretched of the Earth*, clearly views the matter differently. Speaking of the last days of colonialism in Algeria he says:

> In certain districts they make use of that last resort — possession by spirits. Formerly this was a religious experience in all its simplicity, a certain communion of the faithful with sacred things; now they make of it a weapon against humiliation and despair; Mumbo-jumbo and all the idols of the tribe come down among them, rule over their violence and waste it in trances until it is exhausted (Sartre, 1967, pp. 16–17).

Few will want to challenge Sartre's view that bullets are more effective weapons than spirits in the struggle against foreign colonizers. But his nostalgic picture of the pristinely innocent character of possession in its traditional, pre-colonial setting shows remarkable ignorance of the true sociological significance of the Black Brotherhoods. And certainly this innocuous assessment is not shared — outside the colonial situation — by those against whom such cults are aimed. As we shall see, the protest cults we have described are only tolerated within defined limits, and are regularly contained by defence mechanisms which seem designed to check excessive insubordination.

IV

In the foregoing pages, as in the previous chapter, we have traced the widespread ascription of misfortune and illness to amoral peripheral spirits which plague the weak and downtrodden. Those men and women who experience these afflictions do so regularly in situations of stress and conflict with their superiors, and, in the attention and respect which they temporarily attract, influence their masters. Thus adversity is turned to advantage, and spirit possession of this type can be seen to provide an oblique strategy of attack. This aspect of such possession immediately ranks it with witchcraft and sorcery accusations which, as is well known, are similarly employed to explain distress and disease in situations of strife and tension. If we now proceed to compare these two ways of reacting to misfortune, it will be obvious that they represent very different styles of attack. Let us first be clear, however, that although in witchcraft (or sorcery) it is always the bewitched subject who thrusts himself forward to catch our attention and sympathy as the innocent 'victim' of evil machinations, the real victim in any objective sense is the accused 'witch'. It is of course in this sense that we speak of 'witch-hunts', such as those employed in America to hunt down communists, and where there is no doubt as to the identity of the real victims. Thus where people believe in the reality of witchcraft, the victim of affliction who pins responsibility for his difficulties on an enemy by accusing him of witchcraft is pursuing (however unconsciously) a direct strategy of mystical assault.

On the other hand, the victim who interprets his problems in terms of possession by malevolent spirits utilizes, as we have amply seen, a devious manoeuvre in which immediate responsibility is pointed not at his fellow men, but upon mysterious and malign forces outside society. Here it is only indirectly that pressure is brought to bear by the 'victim' on the real target which he seeks to reach. It is in the reaction of other members of his community to an affliction for which no one can be blamed that a measure of redress is achieved. From the stand-point of the subject of misfortune the effect, at least in certain respects, may be broadly similar in the two cases. This is true to the extent at least that both strategies immediately rally support and succour to the side of the subject. Yet the fact that the means of achieving this result differ so radically suggests that each strategy might be appropriate to a different set of circumstances from the other. Thus we should expect to find distinct social correlates distinguishing the fields in which these two tactics are applied. We now have ample material to establish whether or not this is actually the case.

Before we do this however, we should dispose of the prior question: if (as I am arguing) peripheral possession and witchcraft both reflect social tensions, although in different ways, are they mutually exclusive? That they are totally dissimilar phenomena was clearly the view taken by a group of eminent French anthropologists at a grand international colloquium on spirit possession. In a curiously old-fashioned manner, these scholars in effect argued that what pertains to God (possession) and what belongs to the dark world of the devil (witchcraft) can scarcely be brought together within the same universe of discourse.

This judgement, which no doubt reflects the time-honoured

distinction so laboriously urged by Frazer and others between religion and magic, is also that reached from a different point of view by some Anglo-Saxon anthropologists. Thus in a well-known paper on shamanism among the Nuba tribes of the Sudan, S.F. Nadel says: 'The Nyima (a Nuba tribe) have no witchcraft. Shamanism absorbs all that is unpredictable and morally indeterminate and saves the conception of an ordered universe from self-contradiction' (Nadel, 1946, p. 34). Here Nadel has in mind the fact that spirit possession offers a means of explaining away unmerited misfortune in a manner which does not question the essential goodness and justice of other celestial powers. Similarly, and more succinctly, in her comparative study of witchcraft, Lucy Mair declares that where people 'believe that their sufferings come from malevolent spirits . . . they are not driven to turn to witchcraft as an explanation . . .' (Mair, 1969, p. 30).

As is so often the way with bold anthropological generalizations, however, these assertions are not borne out by the facts. In many cultures, witchcraft or sorcery (I am not distinguishing between these here) and malevolent spirit possession do occur together. This is true indeed, with very few exceptions, of almost all the cases we have examined in this and the preceding chapter. In addition, the very common association of witchcraft with spirit familiars, often of opposite sex to the possessed witch, is a rather obvious indication of the impossibility of regarding these mystical forces as necessarily mutually exclusive. Nor, of course, does one need to look very far afield to find striking examples of the co-existence of the two phenomena: our own sixteenth- and seventeenth-century Christian culture, to look no further back, offers an abundant record of witches whose malign power depended upon invasive *incubi* and *succubi*.

Hence, evidently, in many cultures these two forces co-exist and often blend into a compound power. This provides us with an excellent opportunity for testing my initial deduction that, since they represent different strategies, they should have distinct contexts of operation.

As in fact we have already seen, peripheral possession is regularly used by the members of subordinate social categories to press home claims on their superiors. Witchcraft (or sorcery) accusations (and I emphasize that I am talking about the incidence of *accusations*) on the other hand, run in different social grooves. Typically, they are launched between equals, or by a superior against a subordinate. The rare exceptions to this generalization prove the rule. For where witchcraft charges are brought against a superior by an inferior, the explicit intention is to question the legitimacy of this status difference and ultimately to assert equality. So it is, for example, amongst the Lugbara tribe of Uganda, where when disaffection amongst his followers reaches a climax, the old village elder finds himself repeatedly accused of witchcraft by his rebellious juniors. Here the aim, clearly evident in its effects, is to discredit the leader's waning claims to legitimacy and finally to thrust him from his pedestal.

An excellent illustration of the separate fields in which possession and witchcraft accusation operate is provided in the polygynous family situation. Where people believe in both these mystical forces, witchcraft accusations are levelled against each other by the co-wives, and by the mutual husband against any of his wives. Spirit-possession, as we have so frequently seen, is, in contrast, the preferred mode of assault employed by each co-wife in her dealings with her husband. A wife usually only accuses her husband of witchcraft when she seeks to sever their marital relationship and to assert her full independence.

Thus we see that peripheral possession expresses insubordination, but usually not to the point where it is desired to immediately rupture the relationship concerned or to subvert it completely. Rather it ventilates aggression and frustration largely within an uneasy acceptance of the established order of things. Witchcraft and sorcery accusations in contrast, representing as they do more drastic and direct lines of attack, often seek to sunder unbearably tense relationships. This is an aspect of the operation of such accusations which has been elegantly demonstrated by Marwick (1952) and others. Thus if possessed subordinates kick against the pricks at regular intervals, those who press witchcraft charges kick over the traces completely. For witchcraft accusations represent a distancing strategy which seeks to discredit, sever, and deny links; and ultimately to assert separate identity.

So far then, I have been arguing that when peripheral possession and witchcraft both occur together in the same culture, they tend to flourish in different social contexts and to exert contrasting effects. However, in many cultures, the situation is in reality more complicated than this since these two powers frequently coalesce in a highly revealing way. Here the situation of the Nayar, and their low caste dependants represents one widely found pattern. Those low castes whom the Nayars allow to protest against their authority periodically through the medium of possession, and whom they employ as exorcists, are also suspected by them of being witches or sorcerers. Thus there is a general association between low caste status, spirit possession, exorcism, and witchcraft — such, in short, that spirit possession and witchcraft represent two inseparable facets of the position held by low caste Indians. Despite their very varied cultural circumstances, we find the same theme running through most of the other instances which we have discussed in this and the previous chapter. Whether it is subordinate men or women in Africa or Asia who voice their protests through possession, it is precisely they who are held to be potential witches. This blanket categorization exists in most cases. But, if we look more closely at the data, we shall see that accusations of witchcraft are particularly frequently directed at those of these social categories who employ possession in what I have called the 'secondary phase' in the development of these cults. It is especially those subordinate men or women who, having graduated to become leading shamans, are singled out for attack and denunciation as witches.

Thus it seems that the irritation aroused by the effects of possession amongst the ranks of the manipulated establishment fastens most securely on those who in assuming a positive, active, and above all, militant role are indeed in danger of exceeding the bounds of tolerance. These leaders of mutinous women or depressed men who, in diagnosing and treating possession afflictions amongst their colleagues, perpetuate the whole system are the most dangerous agents of dissent and potential subversion. Hence it is they who are held in check by accusations of witchcraft which seem designed to discredit them and to diminish their status. Thus, if possession is the means by which the underdog bids for attention, witchcraft accusations provide the countervailing strategy by which such demands are kept within bounds. There is a poetic justice in this. For, in effect, both subordinate and superior are indulging in self-fulfilling prophecies the result of which is to entrench the notion that the weak enjoy a special endowment of mystical power. It is also all admirably logical. If the spirits involved can cause affliction through uncontrolled, involuntary possession, then when they become subject to controlled, voluntary possession in the persons of shamans drawn from the lowest strata of society they can scarcely be expected to have shed completely their capacity to harm. Far from it indeed, for these upstart controllers of spirits are, by their very power over the spirits, suspected of causing what they cure. Thus where witchcraft implies the use of such spirits, he who can cast out malign spirits is *ipso facto* a witch.

V

In the pattern connecting witchcraft with spirit possession which we have just established, three separate contexts of possession can be distinguished. First, we have the case of afflictions which those who suffer them interpret as involuntary possession by an evil spirit. Secondly, there is the state of voluntary, controlled possession which, from being an affliction, has virtually become an addiction, and is celebrated clandestinely as a religious devotion. It is this type, or context, of possession which is most forcefully realized by the shaman. The latter, as a master (or mistress) of spirits, is considered capable of taming these malevolent powers, and thus of treating those afflicted by them. But, by the same token, he can also send them out to attack his enemies, thus inflicting involuntary possession illnesses upon his adversaries. This gives us our third context of possession.

Here, unlike the position in the first context, a possession illness is diagnosed as being due to possession by a spirit which is not deemed to be acting on its own account, but to have been sent by an ill-disposed shaman. This is regarded as witchcraft and the treatment consists in exorcising, rather than taming, or domesticating, the spirit involved. By casting it forth, rather than by reaching an understanding with it, the victim is enabled to recover. Thus, this interpretation of primary phase possession as witchcraft does not lead the affected victim to join a possession cult group through membership of which he can then proceed to the secondary phase. On the contrary, the spirit is cast out, and the victim is not inducted into a cult group.

This distinction between these alternative diagnoses and treatments of the same external symptoms (for these remain constant), is consistent with the social status of the victims involved. Subordinates see primary phase possession as due entirely to the intrinsic malice of the spirits. But their superiors, when they in turn fall victim to the same spirit-caused afflictions, see in them the malicious envy of their inferiors. Thus the mystical explanation selected by the entrenched establishment enables its members to denounce their subordinates as spirit-ridden witches. By this manoeuvre they reassert their superiority and strengthen the gap which separates them from their lowly subordinates, whose despised, though feared, esoteric possession cult there is no question of their entering. Figure 4.1 attempts to clarify this tangled pattern.

In this configuration, then, possession illnesses among subordinates are not regarded as witchcraft. This equation only arises when the same

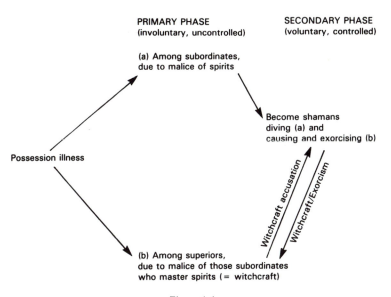

Figure 4.1

afflictions, with identical symptoms, are experienced by members of the superior strata of society against whom the whole apparatus of peripheral possession is directed. In all these contexts of possession, although the extent to which they are held to be subject to human control varies, the spirits involved are identical. They are without exception amoral, peripheral spirits with a special relationship with the lower classes. These dark powers, as I have repeatedly emphasized, have no direct part to play in maintaining or enforcing social morality. Their victims, who sustain possession involuntarily, are presumed to be morally guiltless. The possessed, and therefore bewitched, rich man is as innocent as his possessed (but not bewitched) inferior.

This, however, is not the only fashion in which possession and witchcraft are associated. Another configuration occurs in other cases, and in fact applies in some of the examples — such as the South African Bantu — which we have already discussed. In this second possession-witchcraft complex, the spirits which cause and cure sickness do not fall in the same category. On the contrary, they are divided into two opposed groups, one causing illness, and the other healing it, and these are embraced within a dualistic cosmology which distinguishes sharply between the powers of darkness and those of light. Let me illustrate. Amongst such patrilineal tribes as the Zulu and Pondo of southern Africa, married women regularly succumb to possession afflictions caused by their own paternal ancestors. Such illnesses, ascribed to the action of these ancestor spirits, may, as we have already noted, be employed to precisely the same effect as other more extraneous powers elsewhere. Similarly, in the long term, repeated possession by these spirits leads the wives concerned to assume the roles of diviners, diagnosing and treating witchcraft afflictions in others.

As we would now anticipate, such women who play this thrusting social role are a ready target for witchcraft accusations. But, in distinction to our first pattern, here these women are no longer considered to be inspired by the same spirits as those they utilize when they act as diviners. Whereas in that benevolent role, their familiars are their own (or their husbands') ancestors, when they are credited with acting as witches they are thought to have as their agents hideously obscene sprites, such as the *tokoloshe*. These are hirsute, anthropomorphic dwarfs, armed with such grotesquely long penises that they have to be carried over the shoulder. Other familiars with whom witches also have liaisons are spirits of Indian or European origin, an attribution which, at least in fantasy, defies the harsh laws of South African *apartheid* (cf. Ngubane, 1977). Witches are believed to send out these demons to execute their fell designs against their enemies.

Here, in distinction to the first pattern which we traced, there are two opposed types of spirit which possess people. Only one of these, that comprising the evil, non-ancestral spirits, is definitely associated with witchcraft. Again there are three contexts of possession. First, married women suffer illnesses which are interpreted as involuntary possession by their own (or their husbands') ancestors. Secondly, repeated possession by these spirits leads women to join cult groups whose leaders practise the controlled, voluntary, incarnation of the same spirits as a religious exercise. Such female shamans, however, operating vicariously with the ancestors whose main cult is directed by men, run the risk of being accused of witchcraft. No longer acting with the same spirits, but now inspired by evil demons, such women are considered capable of plaguing men with possession afflictions which can only be treated by exorcism. This gives us our third context of possession where, in contrast to the other two contexts, the spirits involved are the malign counterparts of those benign ancestors who inspire divination and combat witchcraft.

I interpret the different alignments involved here as follows. Having got one foot in the door, as it were, of the world of power and of men, women and other subordinates obviously cannot be discredited and thus held in check by reference to spirits which are essentially moral in character. Hence they can only be exposed as witches by presumed association with an alternative, and unambiguously evil, category of mystical forces. There are further aspects to be considered here. Wyllie (1973) has perceptively shown how another type of witchcraft —'introspective witchcraft', where the self-confessed witch is held to act involuntarily, against her will — corresponds closely to our concept of peripheral possession. The self-declared witch, typically a mother filled with destructive impulses towards her children, is treated as a sick patient who needs help and attention for an affliction for which she cannot be blamed. The treatment — removing the affected mother from her domestic role until she has recovered — is similar in nature and effect to that accorded peripheral possession illnesses. Thus, in its epidemiology and consequences, this form of self-confessed witchcraft is closer to peripheral possession than to the more familiar 'extrovert' witchcraft and sorcery discussed above (cf. Lewis, 1986, chapter 3). We may conclude, I think, that the gamut of connections between possession and witchcraft is wider than might be supposed and merits further research and analysis.

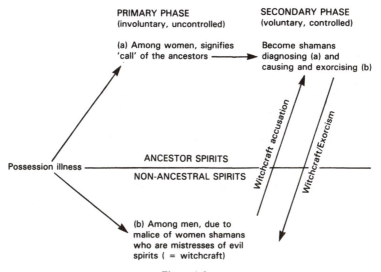

Figure 4.2

Chapter Five

POSSESSION AND PUBLIC MORALITY —
I ANCESTOR CULTS

I

In the circumstances which we have just discussed, possession plays a significant part in the enhancement of status. One result of possession by those spirits which we have classed as 'peripheral' is to enable people who lack other means of protection and self-promotion to advance their interests and improve their lot by escaping, even if only temporarily, from the confining bonds of their allotted stations in society. Onerous duties and obligations are cast aside as those concerned find refuge in clandestine cults which, since they are represented as cures, can be reluctantly tolerated by the established authorities.

These protest cults, which to a certain extent are indeed ritual rebellions, do not, however, detach their followers completely from the societies and cultures in which they originate. Although they may have this potential, in the cases we have examined it is not realized fully; for these movements are ultimately contained within the wider, and in reality often pluralistic, worlds of which they are part. Here clearly, escape is only partial and incomplete. And a crucial aspect of their containment lies in the general acceptance that the spirits concerned are malign pathogenic powers which lack any direct and explicit moral significance in the total society. Yet, as we have seen, these powers are in fact ambivalent, providing in most cases both the grounds of illness and the means to its cure. Consequently, their evaluation as amoral evil forces is inevitably highly relativistic. As I have suggested, while their malevolence is emphasized by the official establishment, for those who surreptitiously pay cult to them they appear in a very different guise. Those powers which the conservative

114

establishment holds at arm's length, so to speak, and regards as evil demons causing sickness and misfortune, can be tamed, and are then venerated as gods of another hue by their actual victims. Thus the moral status of the spirits is by no means absolute, but on the contrary depends upon the position from which they are viewed.

In fact, peripheral cults of the sort we have examined are only a few steps removed from those thoroughly moralistic and thrusting messianic religions which so often arise in circumstances of acute social disruption and which frequently employ possession as a supreme religious experience. With these we move from a partial to a fuller escape into new pastures. Here the adherents of such innovating religious movements, well represented by the so-called separatist churches of Africa and the Caribbean and most of those cults which Lanternari lumps together as 'religions of the oppressed, (Lanternari, 1965), endeavour to detach themselves much more radically from their traditional social setting. Now protest has become much more strident in tone, and has progressed from a merely repetitive kicking against the pricks to the formulation of separatist aspirations which completely reject the established order. Initially, such movements may appear in the guise of cures. But in their eventual development they transcend the status of covert cults to become fully fledged religions. Possession by the divinity is then an explicit and openly encouraged aim, an ecstatic communion which represents the summit of religious experience, and is also, of course, the idiom in which those who aspire to positions of religious leadership compete for power and authority. The conception of religion as a mere therapy for illness is then transformed into the worship of powers whose competence extends into all aspects of life.

The boundaries between such movements and those we have examined previously are not absolute. They remain ill-defined and shifting, and it is often extremely difficult to assess with confidence the precise placement of a particular instance in its temporal and social setting. An obvious case in point is Haitian voodoo. If, in many respects, voodoo seems to fall squarely within the peripheral cult class, in other respects it might more appropriately be characterized as a separatist ecstatic religion. Here, and in other parallel cases, the difficulty of making the most appropriate classification is further compounded by the attempts of the rejected establishment to discredit such would-be separatist religions as mere peripheral cults, tolerable as long as they are presented as cures, but intolerable when they claim to be religions in their own right. Our own Christian history, of course, affords innumerable examples of separatist sects of this kind struggling to achieve an independent existence but held in check through their persecution as heresies.

II

A revealing anthropological report on the Giriama tribe of Kenya provides a splendid example of this transitional situation, where what, in its local context, appears initially as a peripheral possession cult is in fact, for its adherents, the gate of entry to a highly moralistic religion and a means of legitimately escaping from irksome traditional responsibilities. The circumstances are as follows. From the 1920s onwards, the Giriama, who were traditionally subsistence cultivators trading with the Muslim Swahili and Arabs of the coast, began to grow cash crops and with this increasing economic specialization there arose an entrepreneurial class of traders and progressive farmers. The emergence of this new local élite was accompanied by a marked increase in sorcery accusations directed by a successful minority at their jealous kin and neighbours, who formed the majority of the population, and continued to live as subsistence farmers. In keeping with the overall status hierarchy of the colony, the most powerful and successful entrepreneurs tended to become Christians while the bulk of this new class adopted Islam. Their mode of Islamization was circuitous but very revealing. Members of this stratum of society were plagued by Muslim spirits which caused them to succumb to sicknesses for which the only secure remedy was to adopt this faith. In the immediate local context and in relation to traditional Giriama beliefs, these spirits appeared in the guise of malign peripheral demons with no moral relevance to the old social order. Those who were attacked capriciously by them were ill without having committed any moral misdemeanour.

Conversion to Islam is thus in the local context evaluated as cure, and such converts are in fact described by the Giriama most appropriately as 'therapeutic Muslims'. Conversion, however, obliges the new Muslim adherent to observe the Islamic requirements in diet and to abstain from traditional intoxicants, thus isolating him from his neighbours and enabling him to escape from customary commensual obligations. At the same time, the risk of being offered ensorcelled food at parties by jealous neighbours or kin is also reduced.

Clearly, for the ambitious progressive Giriama who seeks to curtail his traditional responsibilities, conversion to Islam (which in the pre-independence setting, also represented the assumption of a higher status in the wider society) is a most rewarding path to follow. At one blow, he legitimizes his anti-social ambitions of personal aggrandizement and protects himself from the malicious envy of the less successful. And all this is done in the form of a cure for a possession illness for which he cannot be held accountable. Stricken by an amoral spirit, the path to recovery leads him into the sheltering arms of a prestigious world religion and a new and more individualistic morality.

Here we see in miniature one of the most revealing patterns of conversion from traditionalist tribal religions to the universalistic religions of Islam and Christianity. In the present context, however, the point I want to emphasize is that in this instance we find possession beginning as an illness and ending, not merely as a cure in a clandestine cult, but moving forward into an overt and increasingly accepted morally endowed religion. Islam cannot be contained by the traditional society which, in fact, is itself becoming increasingly Islamized. Here the tail is wagging the dog; and what was once merely a peripheral cult may yet become the central morality of the Giriama. In this case, of course, it is not the lowest stratum of society which turns to possession as a form of escape, but a class of socially mobile people whose ambitions are at odds with their traditional obligations, and well-placed as they are, in circumstances where Islam represents high status, they are in effect succeeding in carrying others of their community with them. Yet, as David Parkin (1979, 1972) — the anthropologist from whom I quoted this material — warns us, the final outcome is still in doubt. For the prestige both of Arabs and of Islam has markedly declined in Kenya since independence.

It is, therefore, perhaps too early to claim this illustration, with its evocative echoes of protestant capitalism, as a success story in the history of what was originally a peripheral cult. Nevertheless, this example helps us to see how in the social circumstances of their formation, Christianity and Islam likewise must have appeared initially as cults of peripheral spirits which the entrenched religious establishments of their times were ultimately unable to destroy or control. Other new cults, in which the gods similarly announce their messianic message through possession illnesses, have not always been so successful. Many of the world's millennarian movements and 'religions of the oppressed' have either been so successfully discredited and contained that they have fizzled out, or have succeeded only in achieving a shadowy unofficial existence, as reluctantly tolerated popular 'superstitions'. Other cults, or the same ones at different points in their history, have turned their backs on the dominant cultures under whose sway they originated, to find a lonely haven as separatist movements on the margins of societies which they could not radically change, and where they could not impose their new faith as the main source of public morality. In such cases, possession by the deities which are worshipped by the faithful, remains a striking feature of religious life. Indeed, the less successful such movements are in securing a dominant position in the cultures in which they originate, the more possession is likely to occupy the centre of the stage as the central drama of religious activity. Where, on the contrary, such peripheral cults succeed in supplanting the old established order and eventually become themselves new establishment religions, possession tends to become relegated to the background and to be treated as a sign of dangerous potential subversion.

So if it is in the nature of new religions to herald their advent with a flourish of ecstatic effervescence it is equally the fate of those which become successfully ensconced at the centre of public morality to lose their inspirational savour. Inspiration then becomes an institutionalized property of the religious establishment which, as the divinely appointed church, incarnates god: the inspired truth is then mediated to the masses through rituals performed by its duly accredited officers. In these circumstances individual possession experiences are discouraged and where necessary discredited. Possession in fact becomes an aberration, even a satanic heresy. This certainly is the pattern which is clearly and deeply inscribed in the long history of Christianity.

Possession, interpreted as divine inspiration, has thus a tendency to become less dramatic and significant as a new cult gains increasing popularity and firmly establishes itself in its cultural milieu. The changing character of Quaker religious services, which have become less possession-orientated as the movement has become more and more successful, illustrates the point very well. Where, however, such cults do not attain a comparable degree of acceptance, or are passively opposed or even actively persecuted, as long as they retain the support of oppressed sections of the community, possessional inspiration is likely to continue with unabated vigour. This is the situation with most Pentecostal movements, and in the independent or separatist churches in Africa and America and elsewhere (Sundkler, 1961).

If generalized possession, enthusiasm in the original sense of the word, signals the rise of new religious cults, and sober ritualistic dogmatism is the mark of religions which have become so thoroughly embedded in society that almost all trace of inspirational spontaneity has departed, the question naturally arises as to what middle ground lies between these two poles of religious expression. In this and the following chapter we shall attempt to answer this question. We shall examine religions which still depend upon possession as the primary source of their authority, and which are neither mere peripheral healing cults, nor ossified ritualistic orthodoxies drained of inspirational vitality.

In these religions the spirits which men incarnate stand at the centre of the stage in the religious life of society and play a crucial, and direct, role in sanctioning customary morality. In these circumstances, as we have seen, possession may initially appear as a form of illness or trauma. Yet ultimately it is regarded as the mark of divine inspiration, the certain proof of a person's fitness for pursuing the religious vocation, and the basis for the assumption of leading ritual roles and positions. Here we are no longer dealing with possession in clandestine cults masquerading as cures, but with the most compelling and conclusive attestation of the presence of the gods in mainline religions whose competence and scope encompass the whole of social life.

Far from simply expressing obliquely the tolerated protests of the underprivileged against the dominion of their earthly masters, possession is now the idiom in which those who contend for leadership in the central religious life of the community press their claims for recognition as the chosen agents of the gods. Shamanism is now no longer a special form of particularistic protest, but, on the contrary, a central religious institution fulfilling, as we shall see, a host of functions which vary with the social structure in which it is embedded. Under these new conditions we should expect to find that whereas previously possession has been monopolized by those seeking an escape from the shackles of traditional confinements, it now acquires a wider and more exalted catchment. Where before our shamans were women, or men drawn from subordinate social strata, here we should expect that such disabilities were no longer necessary for the assumption of the shamanistic vocation. As I shall try to show, this deduction seems empirically well founded.

III

Those moralistic tribal religions which we must now consider assume many different forms. But one of the commonest and most obvious examples of this type is that addressed to the worship of ancestor spirits. So we shall begin our detailed examination of the role of possession in central morality cults with illustrations drawn from societies with ancestor cults. By no means all ancestor cults involve possession, of course, and we shall later have to discuss why some do include shamanism, whereas others do not. For the moment, however, let us concentrate on positive instances. The hunting and gathering Veddas of Ceylon, studied by the Seligmans (Seligman, 1911) in the first decade of this century, provide as good a starting point as any. In this fragmented, matrilineally organized society, based on small bands of related families without any formal apparatus of political authority, shamans who incarnate their ancestors (the *yaku*) play an important role. The ancestor cult here is merged with and includes the worship of a legendary hunter-hero whose assistance is invoked to secure success in the chase. These powers watch over their descendants and, only when they are neglected, show their annoyance by withdrawing their protection, or by becoming actively hostile.

Each small family-based band has at least one shaman with the power to summon the spirits. One of the most important tasks of the shaman is to officiate at funerals. On such occasions the shaman calls to the spirit of the dead kinsman who speaks through his mouth in hoarse guttural accents, declaring that he approves the funerary offering, that he will assist his kinsmen in hunting, and often giving specific advice on the direction which the group should follow in subsequent hunting expeditions. Here, as so widely elsewhere, the shaman's controlled possession trance is achieved by means of dancing and singing which becomes increasingly frenetic as he works himself up to the point of ecstasy. Possession dances directed by the local shaman (whose position is usually inherited matrilineally, but may pass to a son) are also mounted at other times to secure success in hunting and in collecting honey which forms an important part of the Vedda diet. On these occasions the spirit summoned (which possesses the shaman) shows consideration also for the health of those it watches over, inquiring solicitously 'if anyone is sick'.

This central possession cult of the ancestors who are the guardians of customary morality is evidently directly concerned with the basic subsistence activities of this hunting and gathering people, and possession is employed as a means of communication between man and the gods through the medium of the shaman. The office of shaman is perhaps the most clearly defined and specialized position in the society and is held by men. If, however, trance experienced by men is interpreted as inspirational possession by the ancestors, illnesses may also be diagnosed as possession by evil foreign spirits connected with women. Thus amongst the Veddas, as the Seligmans found them, there were apparently two possession cults: one addressed to the ancestors and concerned with public morality and dominated by men; and a subsidiary, peripheral cult centering on foreign spirits which afflict women with illness.

From the information collected by the Seligmans, which is not very detailed on this point, this latter cult appears to have been highly responsive to new external contacts in the manner we have found with other peripheral movements elsewhere. Contrasting their ecstatic religion with that of the neighbouring, more strongly 'Sanskritized' agriculturalists, Brian Morris (1981) reports a somewhat similar pattern of possession among the hunting and gathering Hill Pandaram of the Ghat forests of South India. As we shall often see in the examples which follow, where central and marginal possession religions exist side by side in the same society, the first is primarily reserved for men, while the second is restricted essentially to women, men of low status, or both.

IV

Many of our illustrations of peripheral cults in earlier chapters have been drawn from Africa, and some authorities have even claimed that these marginal cults, rather than the central religions which are our present concern, are an African speciality. Partly to correct this misleading impression, I now turn to examine several well-documented African central possession religions. I begin with the Shona-speaking tribes of Zimbabwe who have a very vigorous shamanistic religion. This religion offers a fruitful field for comparative study, for, since their colonization, various Shona groups have been subject to very different influences. These variations in the wider geopolitical environment of a people who are largely homogeneous in culture are reflected in the beliefs and practices of the different Shona tribes in a fashion which is highly relevant for our analysis. Within the framework of a broadly common culture, we shall thus be able to trace significant changes in the nature and status of their possession cults as these have altered in response to external pressures. In the following pages we shall concentrate on two contrasting groups whose ecstatic cults have been fairly fully studied: the isolated and relatively conservative Korekore Shona of the Zambesi Valley (Garbett, 1969, pp. 104–27; Lan, 1985); and the highly acculturated Zezuru Shona, living round the European capital of Salisbury (Fry, 1969).

The Korekore have an elaborated central shamanistic religion addressed to the ancestors and concerned primarily with the control of natural phenomena which are of direct importance in day-to-day living. This group of Shona cultivators, heirs to the once powerful Monomotapa dynasty, entered their present territory as invaders, and are today organized in widely scattered tiny chiefdoms, grouped round scions of the royal lineage. The density of population is low, communications are poor, and relations between the different chiefdoms are maintained through the cult of the ancestors. At the time of the 1896 rebellion against the white authorities, it was through this channel of communication that Korekore solidarity was mobilized, with shamans playing a crucial role in promoting divinely inspired unity against the foreign intruders. Much the same pattern recurred in the 1970s when traditional shamans legitimated nationalist guerillas fighting for independence against the white unilateral regime in Southern Rhodesia (see Lan, 1985).

Shamans, who are mainly men, incarnate ancestor spirits of the long dead, and these spirits are believed to control the rainfall and fertility in particular tracts of country. The entire Korekore tribal area is in fact divided into provinces, presided over by particular ancestor spirits, each of which is linked with the founding settlers of a given region. Every such provincial guardian spirit has at least one shamanistic medium who regularly acts as its human host, but who is not necessarily a lineal descendant of the spirit. The functions of these essentially religious figures are clearly distinguished by the Korekore from those of their secular chiefs. Shamans are considered to deal with the moral order and with the relations of man to the earth. Natural disasters such as drought or famine are believed to be caused by the anger of the spirit 'owners of the earth', who must be approached and appeased through their shamans. These misfortunes are interpreted as the consequences of breaches of the moral order, so that the spirits communicating through their chosen mediums act as the censors of society.

122

At ritual séances held to honour the spirits, the possessed shaman exhorts the people of his neighbourhood to shun such evils as incest, adultery, sorcery and homicide, and emphasizes the value of harmony in social relations. In this way, through his attendant spirit, the shaman embodies and gives expression to the sentiments and opinions of the people in his area. Disputes are taken to him for settlement, as well as to the official secular courts, and he is also asked to decide issues concerning succession to chieftaincy and quarrels between neighbouring chiefs. In these matters it is the judgement of the guardian spirit, very properly sensitive to public opinion, that is delivered by the shaman.

Those who live together in the same province thus fall directly under the authority of their local guardian spirit, whose human representative exercises a substantial degree of political and legal, as well as ritual power. At the same time, every Korekore is directly bound by descent to his own ancestor spirits which will also figure as guardian spirits in some provinces but not in others. Only where the residents of a province actually trace descent from the local guardian spirit — which is then their ancestor — will these two attachments coincide. Where this is not the case and men of the same lineage live in different parts of the country, they will honour the local guardian spirits and, at the same time, respect their common lineal ancestors elsewhere. Those kinsmen who thus fall under this dual spiritual dispensation will consult their lineal ancestors, through the appropriate shamans, in issues which relate directly to kinship. Lineal ancestors, rather than guardian spirits, are thus consulted over succession to kinship-linked offices, in the inheritance of property (including wives), and in sickness and misfortunes which have been diagnosed as expressions of ancestral wrath.

These two largely separate fields of spirit authority — the first concerned with regional interests, and the second with kinship obligations — finally merge at the national level in the Korekore cult of the founder of the Monomotapa dynasty. Within this tribal cult, the shamans of component provinces are ranked in a rigid hierarchy corresponding to the seniority and size of the regions whose spirits they incarnate. This spiritual organization represents virtually all that survives today of the centralized tradition of the Monomotapa kingdom, which achieved its political zenith in the fifteenth and sixteenth centuries.

In this highly institutionalized possession cult, recruitment to the post of authorized shaman for a particular guardian spirit is strictly controlled by the shamanistic hierarchy. The aspiring shaman who becomes possessed may at first be regarded as troubled by an evil spirit (a *shave*) of foreign origin. If, however, the curative rituals which are then applied to 'bring out' this noxious demon fail, further divination may suggest that the invading agency is a guardian spirit. The patient is then sent to an accredited shaman for observation. If he evinces the true symptoms (experiencing strange dreams, and wandering in the forest where the guardian spirits are believed to roam in the guise of lions), these suggest that his call is genuine. He is then referred to a senior shaman of the hierarchy for further scrutiny. The aspirant has now achieved the status of an apprentice shaman, and is required to furnish final proof of the authenticity of his inspiration. This is established when his possessing spirit reveals the correct historical details of its origin, the location of its shrine, and its precise genealogical links with other spirits of the official spirit hierarchy. As a final proof, the new recruit has to pick the ritual staff used by the spirit's previous human incarnation from among a bundle presented to him by the senior examining shaman.

Admission to the profession is thus strictly controlled by the hierarchy of established mediums, and the position is generally one which is reached by achievement rather than ascribed by birth. Many of those who wish to become shamans, but are not considered suitable, are rejected on the grounds that they are possessed not by guardian spirits, but by *shave* demons. It is in fact essential for the aspirant to be sponsored by an already well-known and powerful shaman if he is to succeed. A further important qualification, although one that is not always honoured in practice, is that the candidate should be a stranger to the people and locality whose guardian spirit he claims to incarnate. This doctrine is clearly in keeping with the shaman's role as an impartial arbitrator, inspired by the spirit of a distant and long-departed ancestor, in the affairs of any particular local community.

Amongst the Korekore Shona, then, there is a clearly defined morality cult in which the spirits that watch over the conduct of men and control their interests make known their wishes through a group of chosen agents who are organized in a clearly structured shamanistic hierarchy. Inspirational possession here is virtually a male mono-poly. Other forms of possession, which are interpreted as illnesses caused by malevolent, intrusive, foreign spirits, regularly afflict women and may be used by them to advance their interests in the way we have seen elsewhere. This pattern thus corresponds closely to that among the Veddas of Ceylon.

Now let us pursue this comparative analysis of Shona religion by turning to the less politically centralized Zezuru. In this Shona tribe, positions of religious leadership and power are similarly obtained through possession by spirits of the dead. Here, however, there are two main classes of spirits: the patrilineal ancestors (the *vadzimu*), and the more powerful *makombwe* spirits which are considered to be closer to God and have no precise genealogical relationship with living Zezuru. Both types of spirit solicitously guard the traditional morality. They allow misfortune and sickness to strike those who flout public opinion by withdrawing their protection, thus leaving their wayward dependants at the mercy of witches, malevolent spirits of foreign origin, and other sources of mystical danger.

To a greater extent than among the Korekore, and without its connecting links, Zezuru society as a whole is fragmented into a number of petty chiefdoms each associated with a small, local ruling dynasty and subdivided into wards, under sub-chiefs, and villages led by headmen. The latter offices are traditionally 'owned' by particular patrilineages; and chiefs and sub-chiefs are appointed and paid by the national administration. The encapsulation of this traditional structure within the colonial system, as so often elsewhere, has imposed a rigidity and fixity which were formerly absent.

The vital structure of Zezuru society is based upon patrilineal kin groups. Each local group of co-resident kin has amongst its members one or more shamanistic mediums who act as the vehicles of its ancestors and express their wishes. When, as a result of growth in population, pressure on land, and internal dissension, such a community splits, each new faction is led by a rival shaman. In the internal life of the society, therefore, one avenue to political advancement is through possession by a powerful ancestor spirit. The authority of a village headman may thus depend upon his being the senior spirit medium in his village. Such shamans are the foci for relations between the living and dead members of their localized kin groups, and also act as arbiters of minor disputes. Ambitious men, who seek a wider sphere of authority, may succeed in gaining public acceptance as the recognized vehicles for more powerful and remote ancestors, or for *makombwe* spirits which are not limited in their appeal to particular lineages. The acknowledgement of claims of this exalted kind depends, of course, upon the popularity of a shaman's divinations and prophetic pronouncements, his success as a healer, and his reputation as a rain-maker.

In contrast to the position among the Korekore, here there is no fixed hierarchy of particular spirits, nor of those who claim to incarnate them. Instead, intense competition exists between contending mediums who seek to establish their reputations as the recognized mouthpieces of the most powerful spirits, and rivals are discredited by belittling the status of their attendant spirits. At the village level, there is apparently some concordance between the colonially-based administrative system and that of popularly inspired shamans. For, as we have seen, shamans may be village headmen. But at higher levels of political grouping, where larger units of population are involved, these two spheres seem to be largely distinct; and there is no single, all-embracing, national dynastic cult knitting the Zezuru together in the same manner as the Korekore.

While the Korekore pattern I have described seems to flow in a virtually continuous line from the past, the situation among the Zezuru is very different. In fact, the Zezuru shamanistic cults I have outlined represent a recent resurgence of their traditional religion. To appreciate the implications of this we have to set the Zezuru in context and review their recent history. Situated as they are close to the main centres of European settlement, the Zezuru are much more fully involved in the modern exchange economy of Rhodesia than the remote and sheltered Korekore, and much more deeply affected by contemporary social and political trends. A large proportion of Zezuru men indeed spend most of their lives working in nearby Salisbury (Harare) or in other urban centres.

With this degree of involvement in the European-dominated world, it was only natural that the Zezuru should have been acutely sensitive to changing political conditions. After the failure of the rebellion of 1896, in which they participated, the Zezuru were subjected to intense missionary endeavour and soon began to abandon their traditional religion in favour of Christianity. European education, and the culture which went with it, were warmly received and accepted with enthusiasm. Spirit mediums dwindled in their numbers and following and lost their power and prestige to the rising new élite of Shona evangelists and teachers. A new morality, validated by the Christian faith, thus gradually replaced the old authority of the ancestor spirits which appear to have been relegated to the status of mere peripheral spirits and left to plague women.

In the early 1960s, however, this picture changed radically. With the growing suppression by the white Rhodesian government of the African Nationalist parties which the sophisticated Zezuru supported, there developed a self-conscious and deliberate rejection of Christianity and of European culture. Endowed with a new and increasingly politicized content, traditional religion burst forth again, filling the vacuum left by the prohibition of nationalist politics. Spirits which in the dominant world of men had become little more than a memory suddenly began to claim new mediums with growing insistence. The idiom of ancestral possession was quickly reinstated as a highly respected and popular vehicle for expressing local interests and ambitions. Many evangelists who had sought advancement through European culture dropped out of the church and became shamans. Teachers, and others who had secured positions within the European-dominated world, were dramatically recalled to the faith of their fathers. And the newly restored traditional religion was now highly expressive of Zezuru (and, in a wider context, of Shona) cultural nationalism.

It would be strange of course if this *volte face* occurred simultaneously throughout Zezuru society. Thus the fact that a considerable number of modern Zezuru shamans, possessed by ancestor spirits, are women suggests that these represent a residue from the earlier situation when the Christianization of Zezuru culture converted the ancestors into peripheral spirits which plagued the weaker sex. What, at an earlier stage, the men had rejected, women clung to. If this hypothesis is correct, the position has now so changed that the powers such women incarnate are again eminently respectable, and they are clearly on to a good thing! For events have changed in such a way that what was abandoned to them as cast-off clothing from the central world of men is once again very much *à la mode*.

If we now leave the Shona and return for a moment to the Tonga of Zambia whose cult of peripheral *masable* spirits we considered in an earlier chapter, we can, I believe, find further support for this interpretation. In discussing peripheral possession among the Tonga it will be recalled that we found very different patterns in the two groups we distinguished — the isolated, conservative Valley Tonga, and the acculturated, progressive Tonga of the Plateau. Similar differences occur today in the incidence of possession by another category of Tonga spirit which we have so far not mentioned.

The spirits involved here are those known as *basungu* which formerly,

127

in both Tonga groups, played an important part in sanctioning morality (Colson, 1969). These central spirits are often derived from the souls of leading 'big men' who, in their own lifetime, have played a significant role as points of political influence in this traditionally uncentralized community. They possess men (again, as with the Shona, not necessarily their own lineal descendants) and enable them to act as prophetic diviners, mediators, rain-makers, and community leaders in their turn. Their shrines become focal points for neighbourhood rituals relating to the rains, the harvests, and the prevention and control of natural disasters. The shamans, incarnating these spirits, act as intermediaries between the world of the spirits and the world of men. They direct a cult which is essentially concerned with public morality, fertility, and prosperity, and which, in a sense, celebrates success since it is the spirits of the successful who in turn inspire those who succeed in subsequent generations.

Whereas the cult of peripheral *masabe* spirits seems, as we saw earlier, to be of recent origin and directly concerned with expressing the reaction of the Tonga to novel cultural experiences, the *basungu* cult is apparently of much longer standing and is today generally declining. There are, however, important differences here between the two Tonga groups. In the case of the conservative Valley Tonga where *masabe* possession flourishes among wives separated from their migrant worker husbands, *basungu* possession is still quite popular. But, significantly, it now involves women rather than men. This suggests that this old central morality religion is now assuming a marginal position in relation to the dominant, acculturated sphere of men. Amongst the go-ahead Plateau Tonga, who have now virtually abandoned the *masabe* cult, this degradation appears to have gone even further. What remains of the attenuated central *basungu* cult in a culture increasingly inspired by western values has been relegated to a very peripheral position.

V

This excursion into Central African ethnography again demonstrates how the peripherality, or centrality, of possession cults can only be adequately assessed when we take into account the total social and political circumstances in which they occur. The extent to which ecstasy is imbued with moral force is a function of the total situation of a given society. And, in keeping with our findings in previous chapters, we see here in detail the process by which cults, which were once central, lose their moral significance and degenerate into amoral peripheral movements. Such changes, however, in the status and importance of possession cults are by no means necessarily final. As the Zezuru case so well shows, new circumstances may give new life to an old cult which has been thrust into a marginal position, bringing it back again into the centre of the stage. This suggests that main and peripheral possession cults should be seen as opposite extremes on a single continuum, rather than as completely different types of religion. This is a point to which we shall return later. At the same time, we may note how changes in the status of a particular possession cult are accompanied by changes in its personnel. In conformity with our findings in earlier chapters, marginal cults appeal to subordinates, and especially women; while those cults which stand at the centre of society and celebrate public morality generally draw their inspired leaders from more exalted strata.

The sentiments of protest which peripheral cults enshrine have in these central possession religions a different significance which I shall discuss more fully in the following chapter. For the moment, I wish to conclude this examination of the role of possession in central morality religions, based on ancestor cults, by considering one of the most elaborate and interesting that has so far been reported from Africa. This concerns the politically centralized Kaffa people of south-western Ethiopia (Orent, 1969). This society, ruled in the nineteenth century by a divine king, is divided into a large number of patrilineal clans and lineages which, to a considerable extent, form local groups. Lineage segments are usually led by a male shaman (*alamo*) who acts as a medium for the spirits of his patrilineal ancestors. In this capacity he functions as a diviner, diagnosing the causes of sickness and misfortune within his group in terms of ancestral wrath incurred by its members when they sin. The ancestors, which are thus approached and appeased through the lineage elder and shaman, are concerned primarily with the maintenance of lineage morality and with the solidarity and cohesion of their groups. A man inherits his father's spirit (his *eqo*), being selected from a group of brothers by the spirit. Once chosen, he must build a shrine for the spirit and he becomes subject to a series of stringent taboos which emphasize his position as a shaman and set him apart from other men.

As in the other cases we have considered, divine calling is highly responsive to the needs of society. When an agnatic group led by one shaman grows large and presses so heavily upon its land resources that a split becomes inevitable, the party which hives off is grouped round a new elder who soon becomes possessed by a spirit in the appropriate manner. Here, clearly, inspiration legitimizes secular authority. Although the Kaffa are mostly nominal Christians, participating in the rites of the Ethiopian Church, they still also hold steadfast to their traditional beliefs in the efficacy of their ancestral spirits. Each Friday, the members of a small local lineage congregate at the shrine to consult the spirit through its human mount. Petitions are answered with inspired judgements and advice on the following morning, while on Sunday, little abashed, they attend mass at the nearest orthodox Ethiopian Church. The spirits are consulted for advice on matters of domestic policy, and for the diagnosis and treatment of the causes of sickness and misfortune. Supplicants are questioned by the shaman to discover whether their complaints can be attributed to moral misdemeanours or negligence. If so, the guilty party will be asked to offer sacrifices to the offended ancestor spirit. Frequently these offerings are made in promissory form, and neglect of such promises, once the desired end is achieved, is believed to bring down the wrath of the ancestors on their ungrateful dependants.

This *eqo* cult clearly caters for the interests both of corporate groups and of individuals who seek positions of leadership based upon their ecstatic relationship with the ancestors. As we might anticipate, it is built into the structure of Kaffa society in a highly formalized fashion. Prior to their conquest by the armies of Emperor Menelik, the creator of modern Ethiopia, Kaffa was ruled by a divine king (the *tato*) who, with the aid of his council, presided over numerous subsidiary chiefs and clan-heads. Included within the king's council was the leading shaman of a particular clan which had a privileged relationship with the chief spirit of the *eqo* cult (the spirits are arranged in a hierarchy). This shaman was in fact the head of the cult for the kingdom as a whole, and incarnated and controlled the leading spirit, known as *Dochay*. Menelik's conquest firmly incorporated Kaffa into the administrative structure of the Ethiopian state. The kingship was abolished and a system of direct rule instituted similar to that in many British colonial territories. Administrative officials, mainly of the ruling Amhara ethnic group, were appointed by the central government and sent to administer Kaffa. Some traditional Kaffa leaders, however, received minor administrative posts.

Despite these radical changes which destroyed the old political superstructure of the Kaffa state, the position of the *Dochay* cult shaman, who was regarded as an essentially religious figure, was left intact. Today under Amhara rule, as in the past, the incumbent of this office consecrates all officially recognized subsidiary clan and lineage shamans. Indeed, as might be expected, the effect of these upheavals, which removed the old temporal authority structure of Kaffa, has been to consolidate and increase the power of this religious office. With the aid of his attendant *Dochay* spirit, it is this paramount shaman who decides between rival claimants for the position of appointed shamanistic leaders of local lineages. And in the context of Amhara domination, this national shaman has become the focus of Kaffa tribal identity. Gifts and tribute are regularly brought to him as the pronouncements of the spirit which he incarnates are anxiously awaited. Virgins are given him as offerings to his spirit. These the god's human vessel deflowers and generously bestows amongst those Kaffa who are too poor to afford wives of their own. Despite these taxing demands on his virility, this tribal shaman is reported to be as corpulent as a bishop. Without question he is the richest individual in Kaffa.

Here, evidently, in an officially Christian environment, we have a central morality possession religion which is led by male shamans who are elected by the spirits and exercise ritual and politico-legal authority at every level of social grouping. Unlike the situation when the Zezuru warmly embraced Christianity and European values, the introduction and partial acceptance of Amhara Christianity has not reduced the status of the traditional Kaffa religion to that of a marginal cult. Rather a subtle, practical symbiosis has occurred which enables the old religious system to continue alongside, and to a certain extent within the new. And with the destruction of the traditional Kaffa political organization by the alien authorities, the old religion and its hierarchically ordered officiants have acquired new political significance. Today, certainly much more than prior to the Amhara conquest, the *eqo* cult serves as a vehicle for Kaffa cultural nationalism, although not, I think, in the same measure nor in the same deliberate and self-conscious manner as amongst the Zezuru in Rhodesia in the 1960s. Nevertheless, it seems highly probable that Amhara colonization and rule play an important part in keeping Kaffa possession on the boil.

VI

These examples will, I hope, show sufficiently how, where it occurs in the context of moralistic ancestor cults and is initially interpreted as an affliction, possession is ultimately construed as ancestral inspiration, and then becomes the basis for the exercise of the shamanistic vocation. Here exactly as in the case of peripheral cults, once possession has been shown to involve the appropriate spirits, and not some other agency, the objective is not to cast out the invader but to reach a viable accommodation with it. The particular diagnosis made here depends less on the symptoms than upon the standing and reputation of the patient. Thus elected, the shaman acts as the appointed mouthpiece of the spirits which sit in judgement upon the conduct of their descendants and dependants.

In this context inspirational possession has an obvious conservative bias, expressing in fact the consensus of public feeling on moral issues. But public opinion can change, and publics differ. Thus, as we have seen, in social units which have grown too large and faction-ridden for comfort, the aspiring leaders of embryonic new groups find in possession an impressive validation for the legitimacy of their aims. And, as with peripheral possession cults, where significant changes occur in the wider geopolitical environment these are mirrored in alterations in the content and meaning of central possession cults as well as in the status of their inspired priests. Whatever its psychological and theological meaning, therefore, this morally inspired enthusiasm is as much a social as an individual phenomenon and is just as easily applied to manipulate others as is peripheral possession.

Of course, in characterizing these as central morality cults, I do not wish to imply that all aspects of public morality are catered for solely by these spirits. In all the examples we have considered in this chapter other sanctions and other agencies of social control also exist. We might expect that the extent to which such spirits exercise a more or less monopolistic control of morality will depend on the presence, or absence, of alternative legal and political mechanisms, and upon the size of the units involved. This is a topic which we shall examine more closely in the next chapter.

Yet, however partial or complete their moral significance, it is nevertheless virtually an article of faith that the spirits concerned here are essentially moralistic, and consequently predictable in their administration of affliction. Unlike peripheral spirits, they do not strike capriciously or haphazardly. Acting either directly as causes of suffering, or indirectly by withdrawing their normal benevolent protection, they ensure that evil deeds do not go unpunished. Their intervention as agents of justice in human affairs is thus pointed, but anticipated, and entirely justified. The moral character which those who believe in them ascribe to these spirits is, consequently, just as consistent with their actual social role as is the case with amoral spirits in peripheral cults. Since I am well aware that these remarks do not apply uniformly to all ancestor spirits, I would emphasize that I am speaking here only of moralistic ancestor cults, and, within this type of religion, only of those which also involve possession.

Chapter Six

POSSESSION AND PUBLIC MORALITY — II OTHER COSMOLOGICAL SYSTEMS

I

Our generalizations of the previous chapter refer only to one type of central possession religion — that addressed to the worship of ancestor spirits. Clearly if our findings are to hold true of morally endowed possession religions generally, irrespective of the nature of the mystical powers concerned, it has to be shown that they apply equally well to other types of shamanistic religion. This chapter will accordingly attempt to extend the range of these conclusions and try to reach a more definitive assessment of the significance of ecstasy by examining its place in central morality cults which are directed to powers other than ancestor spirits.

We shall start with religions where, as in the ancestor cults we have already considered, the spirits which inspire men and also sanctify and protect social morality do so in a straightforward and direct fashion. We shall then discuss other cases where the mystical forces involved are not, at first sight, primarily concerned to uphold morality, or to sanction the relations between man and man, and yet ultimately this result is achieved in a circuitous manner. Such religions where the powers of the cosmos thus obliquely reflect breaches and disharmonies in human relations have important analogies with those cults which we have classified as peripheral. Consequently an examination of their character will bring us back to the problem, which we have already noticed in other contexts, of the relation between these two, seemingly radically opposed, types of religion. This will force us to consider more carefully the significance of these two categories in the analysis of ecstatic religion.

In what follows, I shall deliberately select illustrative material from societies and cultures which are widely separated geographically, which differ substantially in their ways of life and economy, and which exhibit similar contrasts in their political organization and in their religious systems and cosmologies. I shall begin with cases where shamans are by no means the sole holders of political and legal power, and end with examples where they are almost alone in the field. In the process, we shall move from the less familiar territory of African shamanism to the classical shamanistic regions of the Arctic and South America. If, over such a wide area, and in relation to societies which differ in so many other respects, central possession cults can be shown to exhibit fundamentally the same significance, then we can hope to reach conclusions which will be independent of cultural particularities. At the same time, from such comparative evidence, we should be able to uncover some at least of the basic conditions which favour the development and maintenance of an ecstatic emphasis in religion.

With these aims before us, let us begin with another example from Ethiopia. In this case, such is the unusual wealth of historical evidence available that it is possible not only to analyse this religion as it exists today, but also to see how, over several centuries, it has come to assume its present shape. In this instance we are confronted with a main morality religion which, in its earlier phases, did not include ecstasy but now has this character. I am referring to the religion of the Macha Oromo, who live today as cultivators in an area north of the Kaffa and west of Addis Ababa. This people is one of the many sub-divisions of the great Oromo nation which, with a population estimated at some twelve millions, constitutes the largest single ethnic group in Ethiopia. As with the Kaffa and all the other subordinate Ethiopian peoples, the Macha now form part of the Ethiopian empire and are ruled by the Christian Amhara élite.

In contemporary Macha society (Knutsson, 1967, 1975; H.S. Lewis, 1984), men regularly incarnate God (*Waka*) and his various 'refractions', or subsidiary manifestations, which are known as *ayanas*. To the Macha, God is the final guardian of morality and punishes wrongs and misdemeanours, which are considered sins, by withdrawing his protection and thus rendering evil-doers liable to suffer misfortune and sickness. Sacrifices, and prayers for forgiveness and blessing, are regularly made to God and to his subsidiary manifestations through shamans (called *kallus*) who hold priestly offices at all levels of social grouping from that of the extended patrilineal family to the clan. The spirits summoned on these occasions are considered

135

to be refractions of the central deity *Waka*, which is apprehended as a unity at the level of the Macha people as a whole. Shamans who in the recurring rites in honour of their spirits, are often possessed, hold positions which are generally vested in the senior segments of lineages.

These offices are in principle hereditary. Yet an element of achievement is also present, since shamans vie with one another for the leadership of local congregations built round co-resident clusters of kin. And some shamans attain positions of religious leadership which extend far beyond their own immediate circle of patrilineal relatives. In this fashion, competition for power within Macha society is couched in the idiom of possession. If, for example, a family head becomes regularly subject to strikingly histrionic trances, which are interpreted as signs of divine possession, and builds up a reputation for great divinatory powers and success in mediation and dispute settlement, then he is likely to acquire renown at a wider local and lineage level. This gives him a standing which will enable him to bid for recognition as the acknowledged shaman of a much larger group. Typically, those men who are thus striving for wider power and authority experience much more impressive and violent possession trances than those who already hold such positions by right of birth. But success here is often ephemeral. A shaman's position depends upon public recognition, and reputations can be destroyed as easily as they can be built up. Here, as with the Zezuru Shona, but unlike the Korekore and Kaffa, there is no firmly established hierarchy of shamans, and no shamanistic bishopric to adjudicate between the claims of rival competitors.

Each shaman has at least one shrine for the spirit or spirits which he incarnates and it is to these that people of a neighbourhood come in search of help. Inspired by these powers, the shamans hear confessions of guilt at wrongs committed, and receive sacrifices and votive offerings for the spirits. As I have already indicated, alongside the official legal and administrative system of the Ethiopian government they also exercise a certain amount of informal political and legal power. And the judgements which they give in disputes brought to them are backed by the sanction of their spirits. People who defiantly reject a shaman's decision fear his curse.

Side by side with this religion centring on the morally just God, *Waka*, there exist other peripheral cults of spirits (known locally as *muata, atete* (or *Mariam*) which often possess women. But since these involve features with which we are now thoroughly familiar no more need be said about them for the moment. Instead I want to explore the historical events which lie behind the present character of the cult of *Waka*.

Whereas present evidence suggests that the central Kaffa possession religion represents simply an intensification of traditional practices, this is not the case with the Macha. On the contrary, in this case we are fortunate in having secure evidence which shows that, in its present shamanistic form, this main morality cult is a cultural innovation of only a few generations' standing. Before this development, the Macha (who, it will be recalled, form one division of the great Oromo nation) participated in the pan-Oromo cult of *Waka* who was represented on earth, not by an array of inspired shamans, but by a handful of divinely instituted priestly dynasties. Although these lines of priestly mediators were believed to have been endowed by God, and thus to be divinely appointed, the actual incumbents (who were also called *kallus*) did not employ trance and were not considered to be possessed by the power whose authority they exercised.

This 'traditional' pattern of a non-shamanistic priesthood persists today amongst the southern branches of the Oromo nation which remain those most attached to pastoral nomadism and least involved in cultivation. Outside Macha, amongst these more conservative Oromo, this office of tribal priest, which is hereditary, is closely associated with the traditional political structure. This is based primarily upon the generation-set organization which, in the south, is still the main integrating and governmental principle (see Knutsson, 1975). Without going into unnecessary details, this institution provides a mechanism whereby the male population of any autonomous Oromo tribe is divided into sets, each one drawn from men of a different generation, which progress through a number of grades at eight-yearly intervals. Each grade occupied by a set, as its members move through the system, has different roles and obligations assigned to it.

As with age-grade organizations elsewhere, the effect, in this traditionally uncentralized political system, is that every man is given the opportunity of being a warrior and, later, an elder and judge. At any point in time one set, composed of men of the same generation, occupies that grade which supplies the peace-keeping, decision-making and ritual direction for the tribe as a whole. Ideally and in practice, the system is highly democratic and egalitarian. Those who exercise political and legal authority do so only for the eight years that they are in office; power then passes out of their hands into those of the next senior set. And the leaders of each set, who will in their turn briefly rule the tribe as a whole, are elected by all its members. This institution, linked closely to the dynastic *kallu* priesthood which hallows it and endows it with mystical efficacy, is well suited to provide the loose degree of integration and tribal solidarity required by sparsely distributed pastoral nomads.

So much for the traditional Oromo social organization which, as I have said, survives most strongly today amongst those Oromo of southern Ethiopia and northern Kenya who still live as marginal pastoral nomads. Now the Macha, with whom we are concerned here, represent one of the several Oromo groups who moved up into central Ethiopia in the course of the great northern expansion of the Oromo in the sixteenth century. In their new environment they did not succeed in establishing a local *kallu* dynasty of their own. Instead they had to depend upon the great priests of the southern Oromo to whose shrines, before the final imposition of Amhara rule in the late nineteenth century, they used regularly to go on pilgramage.

In their new highland home, however, they gradually adopted cultivation and became subject to pressures of social change sweeping through all northern Oromo society in the late eighteenth and early nineteenth centuries. In the case of the Macha, these led to the breakdown of the traditional and highly democratic political system based on the generation-set organization which was sanctioned and hallowed by the *kallu* priests. Pressure on the land increased, and although lineages were initially land-holding units, the growth of markets and of trade in this period encouraged the rise of a new class of merchant adventurers and military leaders who came to control the land. In some northern areas, the emergence of these 'big men' led to a general development of social stratification with power based primarily on achievement, and ultimately to the formation of monarchies whose rulers tended to adopt Islam as a convenient justification for the new social positions which they had created. But amongst those Macha Oromo discussed here, this process of increasing political centralization had not proceeded to this point before the Amhara conquest supervened and 'froze' the existing situation (cf. H.S Lewis, 1984).

This train of developments, with the rise of 'big men' competing for secular power, was accompanied by parallel changes in religious organization and cosmological beliefs leading ultimately to the

pattern described earlier. As in other conditions of change and dislocation in which possession phenomena flourish, so here, as we have seen,
achieved shamanistic positions, legitimized by possession, replaced the
former attachment of the Macha to the God-given high-priesthoods
of the south. Where formerly inspiration had been fully bounded and
institutionalized in the shape of divinely installed dynasties of priests,
with power incarnate in the office rather than in the person, God was
now in effect breaking out all over. The possession-inspired *kallu*
shaman thus succeeded the *kallu* priest. And, as the generation-set
organization declined in significance, clanship became one of the main
foci of social identity. Thus, at various levels of clan grouping there
developed shamanistic positions paralleling the refraction into
constituent parts of a god who had previously been conceived of as
single and indivisible. Ultimately, therefore, the resulting new *kallu*
institution has come to include ascribed as well as achieved aspects,
thus bringing the wheel of religious change full circle — or nearly so.
Certainly, at least, it is possible to discern the beginnings of what may
eventually become a new *kallu* religious establishment, although trance
and possession still remain at the moment important factors in the
exercise of the religious vocation.

To complete this picture, we must note that, as in Kaffa, a
considerable proportion of the Macha are practising Christians.
Christianity, however, has not displaced their indigenous faith, nor
reduced it to a subsidiary position. On the contrary, both religions
co-exist in a loose syncretic relationship. To many Macha, indeed,
they must appear as parts of a single continuum, rather than as discrete
and contradictory faiths. In this tolerant ecumenical spirit, the Virgin
Mary and a number of leading saints from the Christian tradition,
as well as certain figures from Islam, including even the Prophet
Muhammad, have in fact been assimilated to refractions of *Waka*.
Similarly, the Christian calendar has exerted a considerable influence
upon the rotation of the main public rites addressed to the Macha god.
Hence, if this ecstatic religion voices the local cultural nationalism of
the Macha, it does so to a degree and in a manner which at the same
time admits of a gradual movement towards the assimilative culture
and religion of the dominant Amhara. Though akin to the situation
in Kaffa, these circumstances are rather different from those amongst
the Zezuru.

II

The central possession religion of the Macha cultivators represents, as we have seen, a considerably modified version of their traditional religion. Its shamanistic character is the product of economic and political changes over a period of some three centuries. Despite very considerable differences in cosmology, and although we know little about its earlier history, the classical shamanism of the Tungus reindeer herders of Siberia and the Arctic reveals striking parallels with this Macha cult. In order to clarify the central character of Tungus shamanism and to show how, as in Macha, it is closely associated with the clan system, I now refer to a detailed account of the Evenk Tungus herders by the Soviet ethnographer, Anisimov (Anisimov, 1963, cf. Basilov, 1984; Hamayon, 1984). In this case, the clans involved are smaller, more tightly integrated, and exhibit a higher degree of mutual hostility than in Macha.

In the traditional Evenk setting, sickness and misfortune were believed to be due, either to neglect of the clan spirits, or to the malice of other clans whose protective spirits had been unleashed on their enemies. In the latter event, the shaman treated his afflicted clansmen by exorcizing the demon responsible, and driving it into the lower world. In retaliation for this hostile spirit intrusion, he would then let loose a host of his own clan's guardian spirits, in the form of zoomorphic monsters, sending these out to do battle with the clan which had initiated this spiritual combat. To defend itself against such harassment, each clan shaman was required to fence in the clan lands, protecting them against incursion by a mystical iron curtain consisting of the shaman's spirit watchmen. Alien enemy spirits had first to penetrate this bulwark before they could reach those it sheltered and plague them with illness and death. Aided by his spirit helpers, it was the primary duty of the clan shaman to struggle with trespassing spirits and, having repelled them, to repair the damage done to the clan defences.

This defence work was three-dimensional. In the air, shamanistic bird spirits were ever on the watch; on land, the shaman's animal spirits staunchly stood guard; and in the water, fish spirits were posted as sentries. Each clan was thus thought to possess a sphere of interest which, like that of modern nations, straddled the three worlds: the upper world of the air and heavens, the earth which man inhabited, and the world below into which the rivers flowed. Through the centre of this jealously guarded clan territory flowed the clan's 'watery river road', a spiritual stream whose sources lay in the upper world populated by the supreme nature deities, whose middle course lay in the world of men, and the mouth in the lower world. In this poetic imagery, clan life was viewed as running along this river in a circular process of reincarnation. Neighbouring clans had adjoining rivers of life, and the relations between their mortal representatives were reflected in those on the spiritual plane which the shaman's spirits regulated.

Although each Evenk clan had also a formally installed political leader (called *kulak*), the shaman's position as the interpreter of clan morality and, indeed, as the embodiment of clan well-being, was extremely important. While in principle hereditary, this office could also be obtained, as we have seen, by achievement. The clan spirits were the final arbiters in the selection of the successful candidate who was consecrated in a collective clan ritual which incorporated the themes of rebirth, prosperity in animal husbandry, and success in hunting. Shamans were treated with deference, allocated the most productive areas of clan territory, and helped with their reindeer herding by other clansmen. Paid for their services in gifts, such as a few head of reindeer, they often became as prosperous as they were mystically powerful.

During the period of Russian rule before the revolution, and partly as a result of Christian influence, shamanism declined. But under the new Soviet authorities it acquired a new lease of life. In much the same manner as among the Zezuru of Rhodesia, possession became the vehicle for Tungus cultural nationalism and protest against the policies of their new masters. In this setting, shamans joined forces with the *kulak* clan leaders as agents of local resistance and disaffection.

Amongst the Tungus generally (Shirokogoroff, 1935), the well-being of clansmen depended upon the zealous direction of the cult of their guardian spirits by the clan shaman. If these spirits were neglected, they could themselves wreak havoc; or, as among the Macha Oromo and in other examples we have considered, achieve the same effect by withdrawing their protection, and thus leaving their clan open to attack by hostile enemy powers. These alien spirits were particularly dangerous to women, and women's illnesses were regularly explained in terms of possession by such foreign spirits. Although the literature is not entirely clear on this point, it seems that alongside the central cult of clan guardian spirits, which was directed by men, there also existed a peripheral cult which was mainly concerned with female ailments. It was also, apparently, through alleged association with such amoral evil spirits, that an unpopular shaman might be discredited as a 'witch'. These are features which we have already encountered in a number of our previous examples, and to the significance of which I shall return presently.

Finally, it is of interest to note here that, during the old Russian régime when Christianity exerted a powerful impact, in some areas clan shamanism seems to have degenerated to the status of a marginal cult involving female as well as male shamans. The diffusion of Buddhism, through Manchuria, may earlier have exerted a similar effect.

III

So far, we have concentrated upon cases where male-dominated cults sustain public morality in a direct fashion, the shaman voicing the decisions of moralistic gods which, if they do not simply echo it, are at least highly responsive to the judgement of public opinion. But in our previous examples, the shaman's inspired judgements are only one of several, alternative sources of law, since other authorities and other mechanisms of social control also exist. I want now to examine the role of shamanism in societies which completely lack formal political offices, or courts of law, and where the shaman has virtually no rivals in his inspired ministrations. In such conditions, as we shall see, the shaman's portfolio of functions becomes extremely wide in scope.

I take as my example here the Akawaio Indians of British Guiana, a people living in small autonomous settlements, strung out along the banks of rivers, and practising a mixed economy which includes cultivation, hunting, fishing, and collecting wild fruits. Here, as Audrey Butt breezily says, the shaman 'has many roles, ranging from doctor, military tactician, and priest to lawyer and judge: at one and the same time he is the primitive embodiment of the National Space Agency and the Citizen's Advice Bureau' (Butt, 1967). To appreciate this proliferation of tasks, the background of Akawaio beliefs must be outlined briefly. As with so many other tribal peoples, and to some extent in line with modern psychiatry, the Akawaio believe that animosities between individuals, families, and local communities are a source of sickness, misfortune, and even death. Physical and social disorder and malfunctioning are linked together by the assumption that nature spirits which cause suffering have, as their primary focus of concern, conditions of social disharmony. Hostilities and disputes in personal and social relations are considered to attract the attention of these spirits which then signify their disapproval by afflicting those involved with disease or death.

Such an undesirable state of affairs requires the help of the shaman who, as diagnostician and arbiter of spirit activity, is summoned to investigate the trouble. His task is both medical and politico-legal. He seeks to cure the physical symptoms as well as the more deep-seated social ill which lies behind them. His job is to remove the ostensible cause of suffering and also, with the authority of the spirits, to restore harmonious relations by manipulating the tension-ridden situation which has given rise to the sickness.

Among the Akawaio, nature spirits thus uphold morality by afflicting transgressors with illnesses which may be interpreted either as malign possessions by pathogenic organisms, or as caused by the removal of a vital part of the culprit's body by a spirit. Even theft may be punished in this fashion by the spirits. In fact infringements of ritual prescriptions and taboos are similarly sanctioned, so that the complete gamut of punitive spirit action includes transgressions, omissions, and malpractices in customary behaviour in both the secular and religious spheres. According to Akawaio belief, an illness disappears and the patient recovers when the wrong involved has been righted, when harmony in society and in nature has been restored.

The shaman conducts his inquiry into the causes of affliction through a public séance in the course of which all the relevant evidence is uncovered and analysed. The spirits who speak through the mouth of the possessed shaman act as barristers or prosecuting councillors, extracting information and putting the case against the guilty patient. Their utterances are delivered with a great deal of sagacious wit which is savoured appreciatively by the audience. Those present at the séance act both as witnesses to and judges of the spectacle, the shaman interpreting public opinion with the authority which only the words of the gods can give him. The séance thus both enshrines and expresses the moral conscience of the community and, for the patient, is also the confessional in which the admission of guilt and the agreement to perform such further penances as may be prescribed bring relief and recovery.

When such a séance is held to deal with a sick patient, the shaman's first task is to summon his regular helpers — the spirit of his late teacher, the tobacco spirit, the ladder spirit, tree-bark spirits, mountain bird spirits, and the ghost spirits of dead relatives who are always anxious to lend a hand. Having already taken the powerful tobacco juice which helps him to achieve trance, the shaman begins by conversing with the spirits mentioned as well as with the audience and patient. After a number of other spirits have descended and more tobacco juice has been taken, the shaman goes into full, cataleptic trance. Aided by the ladder spirit, his own spirit has begun to soar aloft on its journey to the sky, to travel among the mountains, in the forests, and under the earth seeking the help of other spirits. Already knowing much of the background to the patient's troubles, with the aid of these spirits the shaman probes further in the séance. Speaking through their human vessel, these spirits interrogate the patient and his relatives as well as other interested parties.

The most searching and pertinent questions are thus publicly put to the patient who is under strong compulsion to reveal all his misdeeds, leaving the shaman's spirits to judge their relevance. If he attempts to cover up his moral failings, he is in danger of being exposed by the audience and is liable to incur a punitive intensification of his illness. As Dr Butt records, 'Intoxicated by tobacco, the rhythm of the swishing leaves (used to induce trance), and his own physical and mental exertions, the shaman must perceive during his state of dissociation a picture of the circumstances which may have created the condition of the patient. A number of possible causes emerge as relevant during his inquiries so that his problem is to recognize the true cause, the generator of sickness. Here the inspiration of the trance must assist his knowledge. Later, if the patient starts to recover it is obvious that the shaman and his spirit aids have indeed diagnosed correctly and found the means of overcoming the enemy: if the patient continues to be ill then another séance must be held and an even deeper investigation into ultimate causation must be conducted.'

Thus in this uncentralized society of small local groups which have no other courts, the séance is a most important mechanism for ventilating and bringing to a conclusion smouldering quarrels and enmities. When the shaman is called in, sources of strife are already present and it only requires the pronouncements of the spirits which speak through him to bring matters to a climax. Here the ready participation of the audience, representing public opinion, is a crucial element. For all those present can listen and participate. Thus, gossip and scandal may be confirmed or denied; actions can be explained and justified; confessions can be forced or retracted. Nor, in this compelling social drama, do the spirits mince their words. They eagerly deliver pious homilies on the importance of correct conduct, denouncing moral failings, condemning transgressions, and generally reducing their victims to acquiescent contrition by a skilful combination of suggestive probes, satire, and sarcasm which might do credit to the techniques of corrective interrogation employed by the Red Guards in the Chinese Peoples' Republic.

In this cross-questioning, in which no holds are barred, a good séance provides an occasion for bringing into the open all the hidden troubles and problems of the local community. Petty disputes and offences are brought to light and pondered, as well as major disruptive issues. Thus the path towards settlement is opened, and a means found to restore harmonious relationships and to reassert general amity. Finally, judgement is delivered by the spirits through the mouth of the shaman, who voices the consensus of the community.

Notwithstanding the heavy emphasis which is placed upon immorality as the cause of sickness, there are, of course necessarily other escape clauses which account for diseases where the patient is generally considered to be guiltless. In much the same fashion as amongst the Tungus, when misfortunes are not satisfactorily explained in terms of moral misdemeanours, their causes are sought outside the community. The Akawaio of each river area believe that some, at least, of their ills are to be traced to the malevolence of other groups. Such external enemies, for relations between different settlements are often hostile, are thought to act as witches sending bad spirits and sickness against their adversaries. In this context, the shaman of each group is seen as the primary agent. As in the Tungus clan, he defends his own people against attack by rival shamans from other regions, and, when they strike, retaliates in kind. Competition is endemic between shamans who symbolize the particularistic loyalties of their communities. A favourite and particularly unpleasant trick employed is for one shaman to cause his opponent's spirit ladder to collapse while its owner is holding a séance. The hapless shaman's spirit is then trapped aloft and deprived of the means of returning to his body. Such soul absence, if prolonged, produces illness and may eventually lead to the death of the unfortunate victim.

IV

In the examples which we have so far considered there is some variation in the extent to which the mystical powers involved are explicitly endowed with moral attributes. But there is little difference in the way in which, in practice, the spirits concerned intervene in human affairs so as to directly sanction public morality. Uniformly, they act in such a way as to maintain and safeguard social harmony. On the one hand, they chastise those who infringe their neighbours' rights; and on the other, they inspire shamans to act as trouble-shooters and law-givers in community relations. Here the moral code over which these spirits so resolutely stand guard concerns the relations between man and man.

We come now to our final type of central possession religion where, although the spirits involved are ostensibly dedicated to other aims, much the same effect is ultimately achieved in a more roundabout way. Here we shall take the Eskimos as our example. Like the Akawaio, the Eskimos live in small, loosely structured communities where, although informal positions of leadership exist, there are no clearly defined political offices. In these circumstances, the shaman once more assumes the centre of the stage as the public diagnostician and curer of afflictions which are attributed to the spirits and which have to be confessed before they can be expiated. Again, all this takes place within a cosmological system where lofty nature spirits play a far more significant role than the ancestors. Whereas, however, among the Akawaio, illness and misfortune are seen as direct consequences of tensions and disharmonies in human society, here they are viewed as the result of contraventions of the code of relations between men and nature. Amongst the Eskimo, it is offences against natural forces, rather than against one's fellow men, which lead to distress and require shamanistic intervention if they are to be alleviated.

The following quotation from an Eskimo recorded by Rasmussen (Rasmussen, 1929, p. 56), could well serve as the motto for their traditional religion and ethos:

We fear the Weather Spirit of earth, that we must fight against to wrest our food from land and sea. We fear Sila (the Weather Spirit). We fear death and hunger in the cold snow huts. We fear Takanakapsaluk, the Great Woman down at the bottom of the sea that rules over all the beasts of the sea. We fear the sickness that we meet with daily around us; not death, but the suffering. We fear the evil spirits of life; those of the air, of the sea, and of the earth that can help wicked shamans to harm their fellow men. We fear the souls of dead human beings and of the animals we have killed.

The final phrase of this baleful catalogue touches on the most crucial theme of all for an understanding of Eskimo conceptions of sin and taboo. For, as Rasmussen's informant continues:

the greatest peril of life lies in the fact that human food consists entirely of souls. All the creatures which we have to kill and eat, all those that we have to strike down and destroy to make clothes for ourselves, have souls, as we have, souls that do not perish with the body and which therefore must be propitiated lest they revenge themselves on us for taking away their bodies.

This is the basic assumption, strongly affecting the way in which the Eskimos seek to control and utilize their environment, upon which their extremely elaborate code of practice regulating the relations between man and nature is built. As long as these rules are meticulously followed, game animals allow themselves to be killed without endangering man. The intricate taboo system which this code embodies turns on the principle that those animals and pursuits with which the Eskimos are concerned in the winter months must not be brought into direct contact or mixed with those of the summer season. Thus the produce of the sea, and of the land, must be kept separate and not brought together unless special precautions are taken. Seals (winter game) and everything pertaining to them must be insulated from all contact or association with caribou (summer game). It is round this seasonal axis of different patterns of hunting and fishing that the whole structure of the taboo system revolves. Infringements which are construed as sins resulting in illness and affliction and endangering the success of the food quest occur whenever any of these rules are broken. Significantly, the most heinous offence that men can commit is the macabre one of engaging in sexual intercourse with animals, especially caribou or seals which they have just killed, or with their dogs. But it is above all women whose lives are especially taboo-ridden, who are the commonest offenders and sources of danger.

These mystical game laws are all the more significant and binding in that their transgression normally affects not merely the individual culprit but also his neighbours and kin in the camp. Sins, indeed, are commonly thought to envelop the guilty person in an evil-smelling miasma which attracts further ills and misfortune and just as surely repels game. Sinfulness has thus an almost tangible quality, and the sinner is a direct danger to his fellows. This baneful state is remedied by the confession of taboo violations and the performance of appropriate redemptive offerings and penances. Concealment of misdeeds only compounds the injury and increases the risk of further suffering. As among the Akawaio and in so many other cases we have examined, such offences are explored and dealt with by means of the séance conducted by the shaman. Without their shamans, who thus treat the sick, secure favourable weather conditions, and forecast weather changes and success in the chase, the Eskimos would, as they themselves admit, be impotent before the multitude of dangers and hostile forces which confront them at every side. Whether misfortune is caused by the Sea Spirit, the weather powers, or the dead, ordinary human beings are powerless. Only shamans can successfully intervene.

Whatever the purpose of the séance, the procedure followed by the shaman conforms to a similar pattern. In trance, and possessed by his helping spirits who speak through his mouth, often while his own soul-spirit is voyaging to the upper world or to the under world, the shaman relentlessly probes into the conduct of the guilty party in his search for breaches of taboo which will account for the calamity which he is called upon to remedy. Following his mystical 'trips', the shaman announces to the receptive audience that he has 'something to say', and receives the eager response: 'Let us hear, let us hear!' All those present are now under strong pressure to confess any taboo violations which they may have committed. Some offences are readily acknowledged; others are only reluctantly divulged as the shaman insistently presses his audience to reveal their misdeeds.

The séance group, and especially women whose taboo infractions have generally more serious consequences, desperately search their consciences and denounce their neighbours in the concerted quest for the uncovering of sins which will account for their present distress. Women named by others are led guiltily forward, shamefaced and weeping, and urged to repentance by the shaman's own cries of self-reproach: 'I seek and I strike where nothing is to be found! I seek and I strike where nothing is to be found! If there is anything, you must say so!' Under this barrage of exhortations, a woman will confess some misdeed. For example, she had a miscarriage but, living in a house containing many other people, concealed the fact because she was afraid of the consequences. Her dissembling, though condemned, is readily understood, for had she revealed her condition custom would have obliged her to have thrown away all the soft skins in her igloo, including the hut's complete internal skin lining. Such is the inconvenience of the ritual purification required that the temptation to conceal a miscarriage is evidently very strong. However, in the séance, forgotten omissions of this sort are forced into the open as the confessional rite proceeds on its cathartic course, cleansing the community of guilt under the enthusiastic direction of the shaman. Once a sufficient number of sins, no matter how apparently esoteric or venial, have been confessed, and the shaman has prescribed the necessary penances, he can assure his audience that the spirits have been appeased and that there will be no lack of game on the morrow.

In the treatment of the sick at public shamanistic séances of this kind it is generally the patient who is thus ceaselessly harangued. The following extracts from a case recorded by Rasmussen (Rasmussen, 1929, pp. 133ff) concerning a sick woman, indicate the general tenor of the proceedings. The shaman begins his diagnosis: 'I ask you my helping spirit whence comes this illness from which this person is suffering? Is it due to something I have eaten in defiance of taboo, lately or long since? Or is it due to my wife? Or is it brought about by the sick woman herself? Is she herself the cause of the disease?' The patient responds: 'The sickness is due to my own fault. I have ill fulfilled my duties. My thoughts have been bad and my actions evil.' Shaman: 'It looks like peat and yet it is not really peat. It is that which is behind the ear, something which looks like the cartilage of the ear. There is something that gleams white. It is the edge of a pipe, or what can it be?'

The audience, impatient to get to the root of the matter, now join in: 'She has smoked a pipe that she ought not to have smoked. But never mind. We will not take any notice of that. Let her be forgiven.' Shaman: 'That is not all. There are other offences which have brought about this disease. Is it due to me, or to the sick person herself?' Patient: 'It is due to myself alone. There was something the matter with my abdomen, with my inside.' Shaman: 'She has split a meat bone which she ought not to have touched.' Audience, magnanimously: 'Let her be released from her offence.' Shaman, who is far from concluding his forensic analysis: 'She is not released from her evil. It is dangerous. It is a matter for anxiety. Helping spirit say what it is that plagues her.' And so the séance continues, often for hours at a stretch, as transgression after transgression is revealed by the afflicted patient. Such treatment is also frequently repeated in further séances held at morning, noon and night, until, after repeated admissions of guilt, the shaman is satisfied that the patient is thoroughly purged and judges that recovery will follow now that so much has been confessed to 'take the sting out of the illness'.

With so elaborate a constellation of minutely detailed proscriptions, which affects all aspects of daily living and which, if neglected, causes the powers of nature to visit man with affliction or withdraw his supply of game, it might be thought that there could scarcely be any Eskimo group at any time without someone amongst its members who would have committed an offence. Yet there are evidently those whose conduct is in all respects impeccable. For in addition to this all-embracing theory of merited misfortune, the Eskimos hedge their bets by recognizing that there also exist mystical forces which can produce undeserved disaster. Death, and other less irreversible calamities, may be due to the malevolence of other living people, particularly to the witchcraft of evil shamans. They may also be caused by capricious malign spirits which act without reference to contraventions of what Rasmussen calls 'the rules of life'. Such terrors are again dealt with by shamans who, at every misfortune, are called upon to intervene to save man from the spiritual tyranny which he has fashioned for himself and superimposed upon the cruel and hazardous physical environment in which he lives.

With the aid of his helping spirits, the shaman entreats, cajoles, threatens, and even does battle, in the most dramatically charged séances, with these constantly menacing powers which he alone has the skill to influence and control. His unique intimacy with these powers is such that on some occasions he sends his own spirit soaring aloft to visit the 'People of Day' for sheer joy. Such séances, which are not necessarily held to remedy any specific affliction, are thrilling dramatic performances when the shaman indulges in those well-known, Houdini-style 'tricks' which have led superficial observers to denounce these skilled Eskimo religious experts as mere charlatans.

These performances are certainly partly aimed at demonstrating the efficacy of a particular shaman's powers and at enhancing his reputation, and are thus examples of what Voltaire, in his ironical way, liked to call 'priest-craft'. Yet they are also poignant religious occasions. They represent joyous rites of communion between the world of mortal men and those who have departed to the happy hunting grounds in the upper world. Here, again, the shaman's vital role as the intermediary between man and the world of spiritual power which surrounds and threatens to engulf him, is dramatically affirmed.

Also, as with the Akawaio, it is evident that through his direction of the séance confessional, the shaman exercises political and legal functions in his manipulation of human crises. Although each individual is held personally accountable for observing the strict code which regulates the relations between nature and man, breaches of these rules endanger other members of the community as well as the miscreant himself. It is in this indirect fashion that the shamanistic religion acquires moral significance in the life of Eskimo communities. The séance fulfils the functions of a public court, investigating the causes of affliction apportioning blame, and purging the affected group through fervid confessions of guilt. It is, after all, the séance audience which denounces those it considers culpable, and judges the extent and severity of their shortcomings. It is moreover in terms of his interpretation of the mood of this public confessional that the shaman decides, through the vehicle of his spirits, that sufficient guilt has been discharged to alleviate the misfortune which he is charged to remedy. He too has the responsibility of determining whether specific afflictions are to be explained in terms of sins committed by a member of the group, or through other malevolent powers which are totally indifferent to the 'rules of life'.

Thus although the older ethnographic sources on which we depend for our understanding of Eskimo society do not clearly show that social disturbances lie at the root of spiritual intervention, as they do amongst the Akawaio, we can at least see that, to a significant extent, the séance here was also a mechanism of social control (cf. Balikci, 1963, pp. 380–96). Its importance in this respect was, moreover, all the greater, because of the paucity among the Eskimos of other institutions with parallel functions — notwithstanding the importance here of the famous song-duels. We should note, however, that in as much as the mystical powers involved are not directly endowed with moral characteristics, and are employed to manipulate human crises, Eskimo shamanism is, from certain points of view, analogous to the peripheral cults we have discussed elsewhere. The difference lies less in the nature of the spirits than in the fact that here a whole society is involved, and not simply one, particularly disadvantaged, subordinate sector.

If then, as it seems we should, we treat this religion as a special form of central morality (cf. Sonne, 1982), we have still to consider the sexual identity of Eskimo shamans. Here we have to acknowledge that the classical accounts for the Eskimos (as well as for the Chukchee and other Siberian peoples) clearly indicate that the shaman's vocation was not restricted solely to the dominant sex. Czaplicka

(Czaplicka, 1914; see also Hamayon, 1984), whose synthesis of this Siberian material represents the classic work on the subject, concludes that, traditionally, female shamans were particularly concerned with evil spirits of foreign origin. If this was in fact the case, it suggests that we again encounter here the same sexual division of labour between main and peripheral cults which we have found elsewhere. Moreover, as Czaplicka emphasizes, most of the primary sources on Siberian shamanism agree that the period at the turn of the century was marked by an upsurge of female shamans. Since this was also a time of great social upheaval, when the impact of external influences and of Christianity was at its height, (Bogoras, 1907, p. 414 records the replacement of 'group' by 'individual' shamanism at this time), we can perhaps infer a tendency for the traditional cult to be relegated to a secondary position where it could be taken up appropriately by women. This at least seems a plausible interpretation, and one that is consistent with the pattern elsewhere.

V

This concludes our detailed examination of possession in central morality religions. Our examples cannot pretend to be exhaustive. But they are, I think, sufficiently representative for us to be able to generalize from them with some confidence.

Let us begin by noting points of difference and of resemblance between these central religions and peripheral cults. First, differences. In peripheral cults, or in separatist religious movements (whose ambiguous character as an intermediary category we have already noted), possession, interpreted as a religious experience, indeed as a benediction, is open to all the participants. In central morality religions, however, inspirational possession has a much more limited currency. It is in fact the hallmark of a religious élite, those chosen by the gods and personally commissioned by them to exercise divine authority among men. Since, moreover, this is the idiom in which men compete for power and authority, there are always more aspirants than positions to fill. In this competitive situation where authentic enthusiasm is a scarce commodity, and where many feel themselves called but few are actually chosen, it is obviously essential to be able to discriminate between genuine and spurious inspiration. It is also necessary to have a foolproof means of discrediting those established shamans who are considered to abuse their power, or who show undue reluctance in making way for younger, up-and-coming aspirants who enjoy a wider measure of public support.

Both these requirements will be satisfied where two alternative and mutually incompatible theories of possession exist. Thus, if the same ostensible symptoms, or behaviour, can be seen, either as an intimation of divine election, or as a dangerous intrusion of demonic power, this will provide an adequate basis for acknowledging the claims of some aspirants while rejecting those of others. Such distinctions will afford a reliable means for controlling access to legitimate shamanistic power.

Now, let us look again at our empirical findings in the light of these considerations. In earlier chapters, we have seen that peripheral possession cults very often exist in societies where inspirational possession plays no part in the central religion. The converse, however, is not necessarily true. Central possession religions may occur alone, or they may be accompanied by peripheral possession cults. Let us deal first with the former possibility, where no subsidiary possession cult is found. As we have seen amongst the Akawaio (and to some extent also, apparently, in the pre-colonial situation of the Eskimo and Tungus), in such circumstances the powers of the cosmos are not neatly arrayed in two opposing ranks, the one beneficent and compassionate, the other malevolent and threatening. On the contrary, all the mystical forces which man acknowledges are felt to be equally ambivalent in character. They can do good, but they can also do great harm. Here the crucial distinction between what constitutes authentic shamanistic ecstasy, and what is merely an undesirable spirit intrusion, ultimately depends upon the ability of the victim to 'master' his affliction in a culturally appropriate fashion. At the same time, those cases of possession which are not seen as signs of genuine illumination are dismissed as illnesses caused by the mystical malevolence of shamans belonging to other groups.

Here those spirits which protect one's own community are the source of sickness elsewhere, and just as they are controlled internally by the shaman, so they are controlled externally in the same way. According to the moral condition of the victim, such externally caused spirit afflictions can be interpreted either as justified punishments for ills committed, or as unmerited misfortunes. Thus, in these relatively monolithic religions, the existing enmities between rival local communities, when projected on to the spiritual plane, provide the means by which true inspiration can be distinguished from those other conditions which are so readily confounded with it.

Now let us examine the second possibility, where, as so often happens, central and peripheral possession cults exist alongside each other. In such dualistic cosmologies possession afflictions are always open to two, similarly conflicting interpretations. Where the subject belongs to the stratum of society from which establishment shamans are drawn, his initial possession experience (the 'primary phase') may be seen, either as a valid indication of divine approval, or as a hostile intrusion by a malevolent peripheral spirit. There is no difference at all in the symptoms, at least initially. What differs is the diagnosis; and this, of course, ultimately reflects public opinion. If the aspiring shaman enjoys a wide measure of local support, the appropriate diagnosis is made, and, barring accidents, his career is assured. If, however, this is not the case, then the authenticity of his experience is denied by attributing it to an evil spirit, and exorcism is prescribed as the appropriate treatment.

Here, obviously, the first interpretation endorses the subject's experience as authentic possession, while the second stigmatizes it as inauthentic. These two diametrically opposed assessments do not pertain to different religious systems (as the folk-view might seem to imply), but, on the contrary, are mutually entailed aspects of a single religious system in which peripheral spirits represent the sinister counterparts of those benign powers which sustain public morality.

Where precisely the same symptoms occur in subjects drawn from lower social strata, then, of course, the second interpretation, involving peripheral spirits, is again selected. But, in this case, the ensuing treatment is not so much designed to expel the possessing agency as to domesticate it, thereby establishing a viable liaison between it and its human host.

These two parallel channels of spirit activity are linked together in an additional and highly revealing manner. When peripheral possession is diagnosed in men of substance this is not the end of the matter. Although this diagnosis effectively disposes of the subject's pretensions to be considered an aspiring shaman, the moral significance of his possession affliction still remains to be determined. If the subject is considered to have sinned, then his complaint can be seen as a judgement, executed by a peripheral spirit, but determined by the gods of the central morality which have withdrawn their protective influence. When, however, the consensus of opinion is that the victim is morally blameless, then his condition can be interpreted as a malicious act of spirit-inspired witchcraft perpetrated by a low class shaman.

These intricate patterns in the anatomy of possession throw into relief the sharp division of labour and of moral responsibility between the two types of ecstatic cult. But the distinction between them is not absolute, as I have repeatedly emphasized, and there is nothing immutable in the characterization of a particular cult as one rather than the other. Some central shamanistic religions are indeed very close to peripheral cults. If, for instance, Eskimo religion seems, in the way it works, to enshrine an implicit morality, it could also be argued that, in effect, peripheral cults do the same. For if the manipulated establishment responds to the spirit-voiced appeals of its subordinates, in the final analysis, it may do so because it recognizes, although this is not made explicit, that these reflect natural justice. There must be some deep-rooted sense of common humanity and moral responsibility in the sentiments which superiors feel towards their subjects. If there were not this underlying sense of *communitas*, as Victor Turner calls it (Turner, 1969), the establishment could treat with impunity these oblique, but often very importunate demands for respect and consideration. Nor, surely, if their consciences were completely clear, would it be necessary for members of the dominant strata to indulge in the whole complicated business of keeping their inferiors at bay by accusing them of witchcraft. Hence, even if peripheral cults involve frankly amoral mystical forces, in practice they cannot be entirely divorced from moral judgement.

Again, as we have repeatedly seen, historically the lines which seperate the two types of cult are not absolute or inviolable. Cults can change their significance and status over time. Just as so many peripheral cults are discarded established religions which have fallen from respectability and grace, so equally those which begin as clandestine curing rites on the fringes of society may evolve into new morality religions. From this perspective, and in a very simplified way, the history of religions can be seen to involve a cyclical pattern of changes in the status and inspirational quality of cults, with movements from and to the centre of public morality according to the circumstances and social settings at different points in time. Sudden outbursts of ecstatic effervescence may thus signal either a decline, or rise, in religious fortunes. Possession may equally well represent the kiss of life or of death in the historical development of religions. And even if they were eventually co-opted by a central male establishment, it seems that peripheral female ecstatics may often have pioneered new religions. Women seem to have played a major if much ignored, role

155

in religious change and innovation.

If, however, religions which are in the process of degenerating into marginal cults tend to attract followers from the lower strata of society by possession, there is an equally well-defined tendency for successful inspirational religions to lose their ecstatic fervour and harden into ecclesiastical establishments which claim a secure monopoly of doctrinal knowledge. As Ronald Knox wryly reminds us: 'Always the first fervours evaporate; prophecy dies out, and the charismatic is merged in the institutional' (Knox, 1950, p. 1). Where this hardening of the spiritual arteries ensues, religious authority is ultimately no longer dependent for its validation upon possessional inspiration, but upon ritual and dogma. Where, before, men were elected by the gods to hold personal charismatic commissions, now these functions are exercised by a self-perpetuating priesthood, recruited by other means, and claiming a divine entitlement to religious authority.

Such a structure implies the notion of a stable capital of religious legitimacy which has been made over by the gods to man to administer. Such legitimacy is a 'limited good', access to which one person gains at another's expense. If inspiration figures at all, it represents little more than a nodding gesture by the gods that they continue to endorse the priestly hierarchy's management of its spiritual endowment. This form of religious organization, officially incarnating the deity, and typically shrouded in a rich panoply of ritual, is clearly more stable, more predictable, and more secure in its religious direction than a shamanistic pattern of inspirational authority. In theory, at least, the latter is always open to dramatic new revelations, to novel messages from the gods, and not merely to re-interpretations of established doctrine. Under these conditions, all that a shaman can bequeath to his heirs is a body of technical expertise which may help a successor to gain privileged intercourse with the gods, but cannot guarantee that this will happen.

It is thus no accident that throughout history, and in many different religions, established churches have sought to control and contain personal inspiration. So if social stability seems to favour an emphasis on ritual rather than on ecstatic expression, this again suggests that enthusiasm thrives on instability.

In the same vein, the circumstances surrounding the rise of new inspirational religions, from messianic eruptions in medieval Europe to Cargo Cults in Oceania, point to the crucial significance of factors of acute social disruption and dislocation. This evidence corroborates our findings on the necessary (if not sufficient) conditions for the rise of those analogous movements which we have called peripheral cults particularly when these are associated with changes which are felt to impose limitations on traditional freedoms and rights, or to benefit one social group or category (e.g. men) at the expense of another (e.g. women). In prompting the ecstatic response, the insecurity bred by disorder may thus, paradoxically, be as potent a factor as the frustration produced by excessive order and control. We are left, then, with the problem of determining to what extent the same or similar pressures are involved in the maintenance of central possession religions. Why do such ecstatic religions not always develop established priesthoods which would render enthusiasm redundant and dangerous? If the extinction of enthusiasm is a built-in political tendency, what other countervailing forces may keep possession on the boil?

Part of the answer again seems to lie in the existence of powerful ecological and social pressures, where social groups are small and fluctuating, and general instability prevails. These are generally the conditions amongst the scattered, hunting and gathering Eskimos, amongst the Tungus and other Arctic and Siberian peoples, and the same holds true of the Veddas and Akawaio. More generally, in Latin America, the prevalence of vigorous shamanic religions (cf. Santos, 1986) among the politically marginalized Indian communities is perhaps not surprising, although we should clearly not discount the ready availability for ritual use of powerful local hallucinogens. In the case of our African examples, the significant pressures seem to arise less from the physical environment than from the external social (and political) circumstances. In both cases, where larger stable groups form, shamanism acquires a more firmly institutionalized character, and there is less emphasis on ecstasy. This is true not only of the Macha in Ethiopia, or of the Korekore Shona (who in contrast to the Zezuru, have a more rigid shamanistic hierarchy), but also of different groups among the Tungus. Shirokogoroff's rich ehtnographic material indicates that while the smaller, more unstable pastoral bands are led by shamans who achieve their positions by ecstatic seizures, the larger Tungus clans have developed stable shamanistic offices where enthusiasm is muted or extinguished.

Hence if religious routinization discourages ecstasy, at the societal level, the ecstatic tendency is likely to be promoted by intrusive external pressures. Where such conditions prevail, each shaman builds up a fund of personal authority which is dissipated with his death, or at least can only be captured anew by a successor, through a new series of ecstatic inspirations. The shaman in main morality religions is thus the religious analogue of the politically influential entrepreneur, or 'big man'; and, as we have seen amongst the Giriama, the Tonga, and to some extent in our Ethiopian examples, as well as among the Eskimos, the two roles may in fact be held by the same person.

This seems to suggest that far from being untypical or even bizarre manifestations of tension and frustration, peripheral cults embody in a specialized way many of the features of central possession religions. Both are forms of religious expression which imply the existence of acute pressures. In periphral cults these pressures arise from the oppression to which subordinate members of the community are subject. The self-assertion which possession represents here is directed against the entrenched establishment, and is ultimately contained in the way we have examined. In central ecstatic religions, the constraints are external to the society as a whole, they are felt by everyone, and possession, which asserts the claims of the possessed to be considered the appointed agents of morally endowed gods, has a significance which is much wider. In peripheral cults, those subordinates who practise as shamans master spirits which, officially at least, have no general moral significance. But in central religions, establishment shamans incarnate and treat as equals the powers which control the cosmos. Here the protest which possession embodies is directed to the gods, as shamanism asserts that ultimately man is master of his fate.

Since we shall pursue these themes further in the following chapter, we can leave them for the present, and turn to summarize our findings on the sexual identity of shamans. Here we may, I think, distinguish three distinct, although not always completely exclusive patterns. First, in central religions, where possession is a precondition for the full exercise of the religious vocation, those selected by the deities are typically men. Secondly, where an established male priesthood, which does not depend upon ecstatic illumination for its authority, controls the central morality cult, women and men of subordinate social categories may be allowed a limited franchise as inspired auxiliaries. Thirdly, these disadvantaged social categories are also those which supply the membership of peripheral possession cults, irrespective of whether ecstasy also occurs in the central religion. Thus in general, it seems that the moral evaluation of possession tends to reflect social and sexual distinctions. Amoral powers select their mounts from women or socially restricted categories of men: those divinities which uphold public morality are less narrowly circumscribed in their choice of human hosts.

But if the spirits of so many different religions appear to show a nice concern for status, we must not forget that in all societies there are psychological 'deviants' — such as effeminate, or homosexual men, for example — whose problems urge them to defy the officially authorized sex-linked roles. Their existence inevitably disturbs this tidy apportionment of spiritual illumination. Thus while drawing the bulk of their members from women and men of the socially appropriate categories, peripheral cults invariably also attract a number of individual men whose participation is less a function of their social placement than of idiosyncratic features in their personality. This raises the complicated problem of the psychological status of possession. So far we have largely evaded this issue: now we must try to confront it squarely.

Chapter Seven

POSSESSION AND PSYCHIATRY

I

If there is one thing which traditionally unites most British social anthropologists it is their fierce antagonism towards psychology and psychiatry and their disregard for the psychological aspects of the social phenomena which they study. In common with their intellectual ancestor Durkheim, they seem to feel a positive obligation to relegate the scope of psychology to individual abnormalities, and thus misrepresent it as a field of study which is generally irrelevant to their preoccupations. In fact, of course, most anthropological theorizing is shot through with ill-considered, and usually unacknowledged psychological assumptions (cf. Lewis, 1977, pp. 1–24; Johoda, 1982). Some leading anthropologists have even developed quite sophisticated defence mechanisms which are designed to protect their Olympian 'naïveté' (as the neglect of psychology is disarmingly called), and to preserve their domain from psychological incursion.

The unprejudiced reader may well ask why considerations which must seem of such fundamental importance in the study of possession have been left to this late stage, before being raised explicitly and examined. I hasten to say, therefore, that although this has been done deliberately, it is not because I wish to follow so many of my colleagues in surreptitiously sweeping psychology under the carpet. It is simply that phenomena we so readily assimilate to the bizarre and abnormal must be approached cautiously if the issues involved in their assessment are not to be prejudged. Nothing after all is easier than leaping to conclusions and projecting our own ethnocentric psychological (or psychoanalytic) assumptions and interpretations on to exotic evidence which may correspond only in superficial detail with apparently similar

160

data from our own culture. It has seemed essential, therefore, to explore the significance of ecstasy and possession in alien cultures in their own setting before attempting to assess how they relate to the often ostensibly similar material described and analysed by psychoanalysts and psychiatrists in our society. With the findings of previous chapters behind us, however, we are now fairly well equipped to venture into this difficult field.

At the end of the last chapter, I referred to the presence in the cults of a certain number of psychologically deviant individuals. This would hardly surprise the majority of those who approach possession and shamanism from a Euro-centric medical stance which, explicitly or implicitly, tends to incorporate a psychoanalytic bias. Indeed one of the best established traditions in the study of shamanism and possession treats these phenomena as abnormalities, and sees them as peculiar cultural elaborations designed by and for the benefit of the mentally deranged. Just as the French psychiatrist, Levy-Valensi, has claimed that in western society the spiritualist séance is often the ante-chamber of the asylum, so shamanism is regularly seen as an institutionalized madhouse for primitives. On this view, possession is not for psychologically normal people, but only for the disturbed: the spirit-possessed shaman is presented as a conflict-torn personality who should be classified either as seriously neurotic or even psychotic.

Assessments of this sort abound in the anthropological as well as psychiatric literature. Many of our authorities on Arctic shamanism, for instance, assert that the shamans they encountered were usually psychologically abnormal. Thus Bogoras reports that the Chukchee shamans with whom he conversed were 'as a whole extremely excitable, almost hysterical, and not a few were half-crazy. Their cunning in the use of deceit in their art closely resembled the cunning of the lunatic' (Bogoras, 1907, p. 415). And in another passage the same authority speaks of these shamans as 'almost on the verge of insanity'. Shirokogoroff who, as a doctor, is a better qualified witness, also judged that some of the Tungus shamans he met were probably insane. More recently, Krader (an ethnographer) has characterized the Buryat shaman as a 'highly nervous person, one subject to nervous disorders' (Krader, 1954, pp. 322–51).

In this style, Ohlmarks has even sought to distinguish between what he calls 'Arctic and Subarctic shamanism' in terms of the degree of psychopathology allegedly exhibited by shamans in the two regions. The same opinions are voiced for other areas by a host of authorities.

At the end of the last century, Wilken proposed that the origins of Indonesian shamanism were to be traced to mental disease. Loeb similarly characterized the shamans of Niue as epileptics, or persons suffering from nervous diseases, and held that they were drawn from families with a history of hereditary nervous instability. More generally, that much respected authority on primitive religion, Paul Radin (Radin, 1937), urged the same equivalence between epileptics and hysterics and medicine-men and shamans. It would be pointless to cite further evidence of this widely held view that, by and large, shamans are mad.

On the basis of this well-established judgement, and of the almost universal fact that induction into the shamanistic career follows a traumatic experience, the psychoanalytically-orientated anthropologist, George Devereux, has powerfully argued that the shaman's 'madness' constitutes a test case in the cross-cultural definition of normality and abnormality. 'How', Devereux, rhetorically asks, 'could anyone's symptoms be more florid than those of the budding Siberian shaman?' Thus he considers that 'there is no reason and no excuse for not considering the shaman as a severe neurotic and even as a psychotic'. Recognizing that shamanism is, to some extent at least, a culturally accepted phenomenon where it occurs, Devereux is thus led to characterize societies where shamanism is prevalent as being in some sense anomic. For, in a 'sick society' he argues, the individual cannot introject the mores of his community effectively, unless he is himself a neurotic. Therefore in the society of the mad, the truly mentally healthy person (in our terms) will be condemned as a lunatic. Hence shamanism is 'culture dystonic', just as the shaman is 'ego-dystonic' (Devereux, 1956, pp. 23–48). In his magnificent study of medieval European millennarian movements, Norman Cohn commits himself to a similar view. He writes:

All phantasies which sustain such movements are those commonly found in individual cases of paranoia. But a paranoic delusion does not cease to be so because it is shared by many individuals, nor yet because those individuals have real and ample grounds for regarding themselves as victims of oppression. (Cohn, 1957, p. 309).

This assessment corresponds closely with Bateson and Mead's well-known characterization of the Balinese as possessing a culture where ordinary psychological adjustment approximates to that degree of maladjustment which, in a western setting, we call schizoid (Bateson and Mead, 1942, p. xvi). In this vein, Silverman (Silverman, 1967, pp. 21–31) has recently produced a vigorously asserted assimilation of the shaman's putative personality to that of the acute schizophrenic. In his judgement, which is based on secondary sources, the shaman's behaviour includes 'gross non-reality ideation, abnormal perceptual experiences, profound emotional upheavals, and bizarre mannerisms' — all features which brand the shaman as a schizophrenic, usually of the 'non-paranoid' type. With Devereux, Silverman acknowledges that the essential difference between the schizoid personality in our society, and that of the shaman in shamanistic societies, is the degree to which in the latter 'abnormal' behavioural characteristics are tolerated, even encouraged, and find an appropriate and approved cultural outlet. As he notes, in western culture the absence of acceptable and realistically valid labels for the feelings which the shaman and schizophrenic are presumed to share leads in the case of the latter to a heightened sense of guilt and to further mental alienation. I shall return to the significance of this point later.

Again, in a series of publications on cases of possession in New Guinea, Langness vehemently claims that these represent 'hysterical psychoses' (Langness, 1965, pp. 258–77). And in an important symposium assessing current research on mental health in Asia and the Pacific, the psychiatrist P.M. Yap delivers the judgement that, in terms of modern psychiatry, 'most instances of possession must be defined as abnormal'. In a review of what he calls the 'culture-bound reactive syndromes', Yap classifies possession as a psychogenic psychosis — by which he means a condition involving a severe degree of abnormal psychic activity which has its origin in an external shock or trauma, rather than in organic pathology (Yap, 1969, pp. 33–53; see also Kiev, 1972; Murphy, 1982; Littlewood and Lipsedge, 1982, 1985).

If, however, there is much in the recent as well as older literature which seems to support these interpretations, there is an equal volume of testimony, and one that is usually better informed and more professionally qualified, which argues the precise opposite. Shirokogoroff, for example, whom I quoted partially earlier, was careful to point out that while he judged some Tungus shamans to be insane, many were in perfect psychological health. Some were egocentric while others were highly socialized; and some exhibited a fervent faith in their calling, whereas others showed merely a conventional acceptance. Similarly and more recently, the Soviet ethnographer

Anisimov reports of Evenk shamans that although some revealed hysterical neurotic characteristics, there were also many who were extremely sober individuals. Likewise, Jane Murphy reports of the Alaskan Eskimo shamans, whose personalities she examined, that psychiatric disorder was definitely not a prerequisite for the assumption of the shaman's role. Well-known shamans were indeed 'unusually mentally healthy' (Murphy, 1964, p. 76). Similarly, *pace* Bateson and Mead, Dr P.M. van Wulfften Palthc, former head of the Dutch psychiatric service in Java, distinguished between schizophrenic and 'normal' hysteric possession, classifying all the Balinese material in the latter category (quoted in Belo, 1960, p. 6). And Nadel, in his classic study of Nuba shamanism to which we shall return again later, categorically insisted that:

> Neither epilepsy, nor insanity, nor yet other mental derangements, are in themselves regarded as symptoms of spirit possession. They are diseases, abnormal disorders, not supernatural qualifications. . . . No shaman is in everyday life an 'abnormal' individual, a neurotic, or a paranoic; if he were he would be classed as a lunatic, not respected as a priest. . . . I recorded no case of a shaman whose professional hysteria deteriorated into serious mental disorders (Nadel, 1946, pp. 25–37).

Similarly in the context of Haitian voodoo, both Herskovits and Métraux — who do not always agree — insist that these phenomena cannot be assimilated to psychopathology. Audrey Butt, likewise, emphatically asserts the psychological normality of Akawaio shamans, stressing that psychopathic symptoms in candidates for the profession, far from being favoured, are considered seriously disadvantageous. Of the Indians she knew who were subject to 'fits' not one was a shaman: and epilepsy was not regarded as having any connection with shamanism (Butt, 1967, p. 40). Careful research by psychiatrists, based on direct study of the personalities of those involved, tends to confirm these findings. Thus in the Bahia cult in Brazil, Stanbrook has shown how while the hysteric who can manage his symptoms in conventional ways may join the *condomblé* rite, the frank psychotic or schizophrenic is screened out during the probationary period. The latter is considered too idiosyncratic and unreliable in his behaviour and symptoms to be successfully absorbed in the cult group (Stanbrook, 1952, pp. 330–35). Again, of the cases which Yap studied in Hong Kong, the majority of those patients presenting what he calls the 'possession syndrome' were hysterics, and a much smaller proportion schizophrenics. This finding is all the more significant in that the sample of patients studied, being those who sought hospital treatment, presumably contained a much higher incidence of serious mental disturbance than that found in the general population who seek relief in traditional possession cults rather than in western psychiatry (Yap, 1960, pp. 114–37).

Finally, we should also note that where spirit possession is a regular explanation of disease, the fact that certain forms of insanity and epilepsy *may* also be regarded as manifestations of possession does not necessarily mean that the people concerned are unable to differentiate between them and other forms of possession. The range of conditions which are interpreted in terms of possession is usually, as we have seen, a very wide one; and within this insanity (or epilepsy) is usually clearly distinguished from other possession states.

II

The disagreement between these two conflicting lines of interpretation is ostensibly resolved, at least in part, by those who consider that the shaman, if he was originally psychologically disturbed, has in assuming his vocation successfully learnt to master his problems. This view was I think first proposed by Ackerknecht and has been authoritatively endorsed by Eliade and other writers on shamanism. As Shirokogoroff puts it: 'The shaman may begin his life career with a psychosis, but he cannot carry on his functions if he cannot master himself.' Even Devereux also grudgingly admits this, though he considers that the shaman, or 'half-healed madman', has only achieved remission of symptoms and is not fully cured. In this more charitable interpretation, the shamanistic healer is thus represented as an 'auto-normal', compensated neurotic, or even psychotic, who has acquired the insight to deal effectively with neurotic or quasi-psychotic symptoms in others. This assessment, which in effect echoes Socrates' judgement that 'Our greatest blessings come to us by way of madness', recalls T.S. Eliot's conception of the 'wounded surgeon'. It also corresponds closely to the emphasis which, as we have so abundantly seen, shamanistic cultures place on traumatic experiences as necessary pre-conditions for the assumption of this vocation.

However, even this modified view of the shaman's mental state does not constitute a fully satisfactory approach to the understanding of possession and shamanism. For whatever the actual mental health of *individual* shamans, this view of the problem is as one-sided as it is ethnocentric, and even smacks somewhat of professional jealousy. It is like discussing, and dismissing Christianity (or any other religion) in terms of psychotic symptoms in priests. Or perhaps more aptly, it is directly comparable to evaluating the whole of psychoanalysis in terms of the psychotic experiences of some analysts. Moreover it is surely bizarre in the extreme to assess mental health in terms of the incidence of syndromes in the *healer* rather than in their *patients.* We do not generally judge the success of advances in medical science in terms of doctors' health!

As Nadel appositely remarks (Nadel, 1946, pp. 25–37), this one-sided approach implies that the significance of shamanism depends upon private experiences which separate the visionary from the rest of his community, whereas in reality this is far from being the case. Thus to reach a more realistic understanding of the true position, we must recall that in the societies with which we are dealing belief in spirits and in possession by them is normal and accepted. The reality of possession by spirits, or for that matter of witchcraft, constitutes an integral part of the total system of religious ideas and assumptions. Where people thus believe generally that affliction can be caused by possession by a malevolent spirit (or by witchcraft), disbelief in the power of spirits (or of witches) would be a striking abnormality, a bizarre and eccentric rejection of normal values. The cultural and mental alienation of such dissenters would in fact be roughly equivalent to that of those who in our western secular society today believe themselves to be possessed or bewitched. Unlike most of their western counterparts in the societies which we have examined, those in whom possession is diagnosed as a presenting symptom are behaving in an accepted and indeed expected fashion. Simply because we do not share their 'fantasies' and find them echoed only in those whom in our own society we label psychotic or mentally deranged gives us no warrant to write off as mad those cultures whose beliefs in spirits and shamanism we have examined in previous chapters.

Consistently with this, as more rigorous recent studies by psychiatrists and psychologists with anthropological training are beginning to show, the majority of those actively involved in peripheral possession cults are only mildly or often temporarily neurotic in any valid sense. And the same applies especially in the case of main morality possession religions where we naturally find a fuller spectrum of the mental health picture of the community. In both types of cult, as we have seen, we do of course meet some genuine schizophrenics and psychotics. But their number is small compared with the mass of ordinary 'normally' neurotic people who find some relief from anxiety and some resolution of everyday conflicts and problems in such religious activity. Here the very marked lack of response to the cathartic therapies employed in possession cults in the case of seriously disturbed individuals, which we shall consider more fully later, is itself a testimony to the robust mental health of the majority of participants. As we have seen repeatedly, the latter have no difficulty at all in communicating their problems. They operate within a culturally standardized medium of communication. Nor, in contrast to the true self-insulated psychotic, do they miss their 'cues'. They respond in the expected way, and others react equally predictably. The manipulated husband's response is just as stereotyped and anticipated as the protesting wife's strategy of possession. Above all, the total symbolism involved is not private or idiosyncratic, but on the contrary public and socially sanctioned.

In peripheral cults, as I have emphasized, the game of possession only works as long as all the players know and observe the rules. Consequently, the person who becomes possessed in response to difficulties is at once provided with a means of coping with his situation which does not alienate him disadvantageously from other members of his community. Far from dismissing the force of the patient's power to influence other members of the community, but bestowing the sea of divine approval possession enhances his influence immeasurably. As Yap points out, this is achieved by 'internalizing a possessing agency with characteristics appropriate to the solution of the conflict'. But to dub this an 'unrealistic' strategy, as he does, seems to me ethnocentric, or biomedically biased. The whole point is that the attributes of the possessing spirit are completely suited to the victim's milieu and position, and in these terms far from 'unrealistic'.

While it cannot be excluded that severely neurotic individuals may, occasionally, achieve prophetic cult status (cf. Littlewood, 1984), more generally it would be wrong to reduce shamanism and spirit possession as total cultural phenomena to expression of the private fantasies of psychotic individuals. And despite the persuasive, and for some no doubt attractive, analogy between the professional trauma which is a prologue to the assumption of the shaman's role and that sometimes followed in induction into the psychiatric, and a *fortiori* psychoanalytic profession, we cannot treat all shamans as simply self-healed neurotics or psychotics. As in psychiatry, this may be the case with some practitioners, but it is not true for all. How then are we to interpret the hysterically coloured afflictions, or seering experiences, which typically herald the onset of the shamanistic vocation?

In all the cases we have considered in previous chapters, these are certainly viewed as dangerous, even terrifying, experiences or as illnesses. Experience of disorder in some form is thus an essential feature in the recruitment of shamans. In peripheral possession cults this initiatory illness looms so large that at first sight it almost completely obscures their positive religious content. In central possession cults, this preparatory experience is most stressed in the case of those aspirants who lack satisfactory ascriptive qualifications for the position of shaman, or with those who, though fully qualified, at first resist the summons of the gods. Here Guy Moréchand's findings on the selection of Hmong shamans in Vietnam and Thailand epitomize the general situation:

> The more he ostensibly refuses this destiny, the more he resists, the more striking will be the signs, the more gripping and dramatic his vocation. . . . Not only have the personal tastes of the individual theoretically no part in this decision to make himself a shaman, but they are also strongly denied. The accent is on the contrary on the (acolyte's) repugnance: the poor persecuted man who could not do otherwise (Moréchand, 1968, p. 208).

In this vein Peter Fry's study of spirit possession among the Zezuru Shona, to which we have already referred, includes a brilliantly detailed account of the onset and development of the professional hysteria which overtook his Shona research assistant and led eventually to his formal installation as an acknowledged shaman. Beginning with peculiar allergies to tobacco smoke and beer, which Fry was able to establish were only operative in relation to other Shona who saw these as manifestations of spirit activity and whom the future medium sought to impress, the new recruit developed a series of arresting dietary abstentions which set him apart from other people. Continually resisting an interpretation of his ailments in terms of possession, the subject maintained his symptoms, consulting a series of different diviners until he had succeeded in gaining a wide measure of attention and expectancy for the ultimate announcement of his calling, which he accepted from a particularly powerful and prestigious shaman.

Thus the shaman's initiatory experience is represented as an involuntary surrender to disorder, as he is thrust protesting into the chaos which the ordered and controlled life of society strives so hard to deny, or at least to keep at bay. No matter how valiantly he struggles, disorder eventually claims him and marks him with the brand of a transcendental encounter. At its worst, in peripheral cults, this is seen as a baneful intrusion of malign power. At its best, in central possession religions it represents a danger-laden exposure to the power of the cosmos. In both cases the initial experience withdraws the victim from the secure world of society and of ordered existence, and exposes him directly to those forces which, though they may be held to uphold the social order, also ultimately threaten it.

But this symbolic wound which asserts the supremacy of the gods as the arbiters of both disorder and of order (since both are in their gift), is a necessary but not a sufficient condition for the assumption of the shamanistic calling. The shaman is not the slave, but the master of anomaly and chaos. The transcendental mystery which lies at the heart of his vocation is the healer's passion; his ultimate triumph over the chaotic experience of raw power which threatened to drag him under. Out of the agony of affliction and the dark night of the soul comes literally the ecstasy of spiritual victory. In rising to the challenge of the powers which rule his life and by valiantly overcoming them in this crucial initiatory rite (cf. La Fontaine, 1985) which reimposes order on chaos and despair, man reasserts his mastery of the universe and affirms his control of destiny and fate.

The shaman is thus the symbol not of subjection and despondency but of independence and hope. Through him the otherwise unfettered power of the world beyond human society is harnessed purposefully and applied to minister to the needs of the community. If by incarnating spirits he embodies the most profound intrusion of the gods into the realm of human society, his mastering of these powers dramatically asserts man's claim to control his spiritual environment and to treat with the gods on terms of equality. In the person of the shaman, man triumphantly proclaims his supremacy over elemental power which he has mastered and transformed into a socially beneficent force. And this hard-won control over the grounds of affliction is re-enacted in every shamanistic séance. This, rather than the repetition of any personal crisis, is the message of the séance. For at the séance the gods enter the shaman at his bidding, and are thus brought into direct confrontation with society and its problems. It is by dragging the gods down to his own level, as much by soaring aloft to meet them, that the shaman enables man to deal with his deities on an equal or almost equal footing.

The essential process in the making of a shaman is thus as follows. Suffering interpreted as possession involves an invasion of the human body which is usurped as a vehicle for the spirit. In trance the host's personality fades away and is replaced by the power of the possessing agent. But while this is a general experience which may befall any socially appropriate member of society, for the shaman it is merely the first indication of his future vocation. By overcoming this spiritual assault a new relationship is forged with the spirit which makes the victim of this experience a shaman with a consequent change in his status. As Eliade rightly insists and as we can now clearly see, this is not to be understood in terms of individual psychopathology, but on the contrary as a culturally defined initiation ritual. In both peripheral and main morality possession cults, the effect is the same. An enhancement of status accrues to the shamanistic candidate who succeeds in mastering the grounds of affliction and thus proves to the world his claim to be considered a healer. The temporary rise in status of the possessed woman or downtrodden man in peripheral possession cults is itself an intimation of the fuller and more permanent rewards which lie in store if the acolyte perseveres to later become a fully-fledged shaman.

Viewed in this light, we can now appreciate how singularly appropriate the idiom of marriage is as a means of expressing the shamanistic relationship. For the transition rite of marriage signifies exactly what has occurred. From being subject, at the whim of the gods, to involuntary, uncontrollable experiences of disorder, the shaman has progressed to a point where he has achieved a stable and dominant relationship with the grounds of affliction. If the shaman is contractually bound as mortal partner to a divinity, that deity is equally tied to its human spouse. Both are inseparably conjoined: each possesses the other.

Elements of other transition rites in the human life cycle are also of course present. Thus the shaman, when possessed and in full trance, has 'died' and is 'born' anew with the personality of the spirit he incarnates. But it seems to me that we can go further in interpreting the significance of the selection of the rite of marriage as the most widely favoured image for the relationship between the shaman and his celestial partner. For while birth and death are both inescapable

POSSESSION AND PSYCHIATRY

events, over which the individual has no control, and to which his lot is simply to submit, marriage at once signals not merely a change of status, but also an alliance, and permits at least some degree of choice. Hence although the official shamanistic ideology emphasizes that it is the gods who make the opening moves, and who relentlessly pursue their victims until the latter submit, there still remains an element of human choice. Not all those upon whom the spirits press their attentions progress to that point of intimacy where they are joined in celestial union. And even when they do, the decision to accept their divine calling is at some level made by the subjects themselves. If, therefore, in this case God proposes, ultimately man disposes. At the same time, as Jean La Fontaine (1985, p. 67) notes, the imagery of conjugal union may also be taken as implying that the possessed shamanic recruit is a product of and a testament to the sexual potency of the gods.

In peripheral cults the catchment area of possession is so circumscribed that those who occupy marginal social positions are strongly at risk. Illness and misfortune are always liable to be interpreted as spirit possession, and this readily leads to induction into the healing cult in this clandestine form of divine election. Of course, the extent to which different individuals of subordinate status are actively involved will depend upon their particular life circumstances, and especially upon the magnitude and severity of the stresses to which they are subject. The happily married wife who is content with her lot is much less likely to resort to possession than her harassed sister whose married life is fraught with difficulty. Successful wives and mothers may occasionally succumb to possession, but they are unlikely to be drawn into permanent involvement in the possession cult groups. The keenest recruits and the most committed enthusiasts are women who, for one reason or another, do not make a success of their marital roles, react against new domestic confinement or who, having fulfilled these roles, seek a new career in which they can give free rein to the desire to manage and dominate others (cf. Constantinides, 1985).

In main morality religions, an initial experience of disorder and its mastering through controlled possession are particularly emphasized in the case of those candidates who lack hereditary qualifications. For such outsiders in the quest for shamanistic office, personal peculiarities and anomalous experiences which society recognizes as expressions of spiritual attention may indeed be exploited with advantage. But they are of no value at all unless they can be conspicuously mastered. The ability to contain and control the grounds of disorder remains the essential requirement; and obviously the greater the apparent trauma which is so mastered, the greater the authority and power of the new shaman.

Some such candidates are undoubtedly people who have found culturally acceptable techniques for controlling private neurotic proclivities. For these, the shamanistic role may well represent a precarious haven within which their eccentricities are tolerated and turned to advantage (cf. Littlewood, 1984). Individuals of this kind, however, seem, on the present evidence to constitute only a small fraction of those who become successful shamans; and the part must not be confused with the whole. Hence, if the idiom which is employed universally to express the role of the shaman is that of the wounded healer, this is above all a stereotype, a professional qualification, which establishes the healer's warrant to minister to his people's needs as one who knows how to control disorder. It does not necessarily tell us anything about his psychiatric condition. What it does purport to guarantee is that such a person has endured the experience of elemental power and emerged, not merely unscathed, but strengthened and empowered to help others who suffer affliction.

III

As has already been suggested, and as Jung himself reminds us in his memoirs, in European culture the profession to which the conception of the wounded surgeon most poignantly and aptly applies is psychoanalysis. With this and other common features in mind, spirit possession and shamanism have also been viewed as a pre-scientific psychotherapy. Thus, remembering that, whatever else they are, spirits are certainly hypotheses used to explain what we would regard as psychological states, such students of hysteria as Ilza Veith have traced the gradual transformation of these mystical theories into those of modern psychiatry (Veith, 1965; Kenny, 981). Here the shaman is seen in a historical perspective as a primitive psychiatrist and his explanations of hysterical and other behaviour are treated as the primitive precursors of the theories of contemporary psychological medicine. The same equivalence has also been proposed on the basis of studies of contemporary shamanism in exotic cultures. Thus in 1946 both Mars (Mars, 1946) and Nadel (Nadel, 1946) independently advanced this view, the first in relation to Haitian voodoo, and the second with respect to possession among the Nuba tribes of the Sudan.

Shamanism, they considered, should be seen as a cathartic mechanism with a crucial role to play in preventive psychiatry. Thus, rejecting the old picture of the crazy shaman, Nadel urged that the institutionalized catharsis of the shamanistic séance might nevertheless have 'the therapeutic effect of stabilizing hysteria and related psychoneuroses, thus reducing a psychopathic incidence which would otherwise be much larger'.

This approach to the problem was in fact also suggested by Shirokogoroff in the context of Tungus shamanism over fifty years ago. As this Russian pioneer in the field of what is now sometimes known as 'trans-cultural psychiatry' notes, shamans in reality treat only the psychological aspects of disease. 'They may strengthen the patient's psychic resolve and determination to recover, and also alleviate distress amongst friends and relatives caused by really serious disease.' They succeed in exercising a positive effect if the community believes that the pathogenic spirits involved are neutralized by being mastered or expelled. And, as he puts it more generally, in terms which those anthropologists (such as Robin Horton) who advocate an intellectualist interpretation of religion would strongly approve:

> Spirits are hypotheses, some of which are admitted by the European complex as well, hypotheses which formulate observations of the psychic life of the people and particularly that of the shaman, and which are quite helpful in the regulation of the psychomental complex to which the Tungus have come after a long period of adaptation. . . . The phenomenon of psychic life is not understood in the same form as modern science would understand it, but it is regulated, and its components are perhaps better analysed (in spirit symbols) than is done by psychologists operating with such conceptions as 'instincts' and 'complexes'. In reality hysteria can be easily regulated (Shirokogoroff, 1935, p. 370).

This assimilation of the shaman's role to that of the psychiatrist has also more recently been enthusiastically endorsed by that modern Heraclitus of ethnology, Lévi-Strauss, whose sedulous search for hidden oppositions and transformations is well known. Claiming that in the séance the shaman always relives his original traumatic experience, in this style Lévi-Strauss concludes that the shamanistic cure is the exact counterpart of the psychoanalytic, but with 'the inversion of all the elements' (Lévi-Strauss, 1968, p. 199). Both aim at inducing an experience and both succeed by re-enacting a myth which the patient has to live or re-live. In psychoanalysis, according to Lévi-Strauss, the patient constructs an individual myth with elements drawn from his past; in the shamanistic séance the patient receives from the outside a social myth which does not correspond to a former personal state. The psychoanalyst listens: the shaman speaks. When a transference is established, the patient puts words into the mouth of the psychoanalyst by attributing to him alleged feelings and intentions. In the shamanistic incantation, on the contrary, the shaman speaks for his patient.

This contrast which sees the psychoanalyst as a passive agent, a mere sounding board for his patient's psyche, and the shaman as an active agent directing his patient's psychic experience, seems to me so contrived and so at variance with the facts that it can have little significance or value. Certainly it does not do justice to that considerable area of psychoanalytic practice where the analyst's role is far from being as passive as Lévi-Strauss supposes. Nor does it take account, as is now well established, of the extent to which the psychoanalyst's mythology both evokes and moulds the putative experiences of his patient. And while it may correspond to the particular South American ethnography from which Lévi-Strauss is generalizing, it is certainly not by any means universally the case that in the shamanistic séance the patient always and inevitably plays merely a passive foil to the active role assumed by the shaman. In both instances patient and healer interact more fully and more subtly in ways which deprive this facile antithesis of explanatory power.

To what extent then can we legitimately assimilate shamanism to psychotherapy or psychoanalysis? The obvious way to begin seeking an answer to this question is to look more closely at the shamanistic séance. As we have seen, the séance is invariably, for part of the time at least, an emotionally highly charged and dramatic performance. In peripheral cults which ostensibly treat illness and where no moral blame attaches to the patient, the séance provides a setting in which free rein is given to the expression of problems and ambitions which refer directly to the participants' normally frustrating social circumstances. The possessing familiar which the patient incarnates, or impersonates, expresses very clearly the frustrated demands of the dependent woman or downtrodden low class man. Women who seek power and aspire to roles otherwise monopolized by men act out thrusting male parts with impunity and with the full approval of the audience. The possessed person who in the séance is the centre of attention says in effect, 'Look at me, I am dancing'. Thus those forced by society into subservience play exactly the opposite role with the active encouragement of the séance audience. Like those of *zar* and *bori*, Haitian voodoo ceremonies are quite clearly theatres, in which problems and conflicts relating to the life situations of the participants are dramatically enacted with great symbolic force.

The atmosphere, though controlled and not as anarchic as it may seem, is essentially permissive and comforting. Everything takes on the tone and character of modern psychodrama or group therapy. Abreaction is the order of the day. Repressed urges and desires, the idiosyncratic as well as the socially conditioned, are given free public rein. No holds are barred. No interests or demands are too unseemly in this setting not to receive sympathetic attention. Each dancer ideally eventually achieves a state of ecstasy, and in stereotyped fashion collapses in a trance from which he emerges purged and refreshed. Where such experiences are genuine psychic adventures (and not, as is often the case for many of the participants on some occasions, merely routine or feigned), clearly a great deal of psychological satisfaction may result. This is the point at which the psychoanalyst's emphasis on 'primary (psychic) gains' becomes significant, although as we have seen the 'secondary gains' in terms of social advantage, and which may be achieved without recourse to genuine trance, are also usually important.

In these terms the regular séances of peripheral possession cults may be seen as danced psychodramas; 'work-outs' in which some measure of psychic compensation for the injuries and vicissitudes of daily life is obtained. Possession in this context is indeed a release, an escape from harsh reality into a world of symbolism which, precisely because it is not inappropriately detached from mundane life, is full of compensatory potentialities and has great emotive appeal (cf. Siikala, 1978; Peters and Price-Williams, 1980). It is not an unrealistic flight from fate, for such psychic benefit as the participants may in different measure gain is supplemented in the more tangible, if from a psychological point of view merely 'secondary', rewards which accrue from this redressive strategy. The shamans who lead the proceedings enter literally into the spirit of the occasion, being themselves possessed by their familiars. They play a dual role. They stimulate and direct the enthusiasm of the participants until the latter achieve a state of full possession (trance, in our terminology), and they elicit the demands which the possessing spirits then make on behalf of their human vehicles. They may also, as in some of the cases we have examined, prescribe a restructuring of the patient's relationships in the best traditions of modern psychotherapy.

In an earlier chapter I referred to possession of this kind as a 'game'. But in so doing I did not wish to imply that it was not a serious game, nor one in which the stakes were invariably of little account. The truth of course is that different participants are psychologically engaged in the possession rituals to different extents. For some individuals it means a great deal, for others very little. Some participants, while enjoying the religious aspects of the cult in a conventional way, have their sights firmly and even consciously and calculatingly set on the ancillary external benefits — the influencing of their superiors and the exaction of propitiatory gifts from them. For others the direct psychic rewards, the 'primary gains' of psychiatry, are of paramount importance. Yet others are so psychologically ill that, try as they will and notwithstanding all the shaman's efforts to induce trance, they do not succeed in achieving this blissful oblivion. As recent studies by psychiatrists show, it is precisely these unfortunate people who cannot fully express their problems in this conventional idiom who are seriously psychologically disturbed. These refractory psychotics and schizophrenics, who do not respond and who cannot satisfactorily enter into the game, are the exceptions proving the rule that spirit possession and shamanism deal essentially not with the hopelessly impaired, but with ordinary 'normally' neurotic people. For the most part, as we have seen, those problems with which peripheral possession is primarily concerned are inherent in the structure of society. It is thus not surprising that a number of psychiatric assessments of the efficacy of these cathartic treatments — such, for example, as that by Kennedy of Sudanese *zar* (Kennedy, 1967, p. 185) — should assert their great therapeutic potential (cf. Leff, 1981). For after all if, as we know from their social context, they involve basically normal people who merely seek more attention and respect, once these are accorded we should expect a good outcome.

Much of what has been said of peripheral possession séances applies equally to those in main morality religions. For here although the patient is in this case regarded as responsible for his plight and is held to be morally culpable, the séance offers abreactive atonement. That insistent refrain of the Eskimo séance — 'Let him be forgiven' — epitomizes the confessional atmosphere of consoling support and understanding in which the afflicted victim is urged to repentance and encouraged to discharge his guilt in the secure knowledge that forgiveness and release are at hand. This, if we like, we can view as a type of 'control' therapy where, contrary to what Lévi-Strauss supposes, the accent is on re-organizing and re-orientating the patient in terms of an ethos which is as compassionate as it is comprehensive but does not absolve him of responsibility for his condition. The stress on confession thus appears as a direct consequence of the importance of moral obligation in central possession cults, where illness is a sin — not merely an unkind stroke of fortune. Here the possession illness does not constitute a legitimate escape or evasion of duty or of authority. On the contrary, it amounts to an admission of guilt, a recognition that authority and obligation have been wantonly ignored. Nevertheless as soon as treatment commences, and once guilt has been admitted, it proceeds as a cathartic abreaction. In opposition to this, the shaman's controlled possession, which is not an illness, represents an assertion of authority, a demonstration of his moral fitness to act both as a leader of men and as a spokesman of the gods.

The foregoing suggests that a persuasive argument does in fact exist for equating shamanism with psychotherapy (or psychoanalysis). But there are other factors which must also be taken into account. Although with this assimilation in mind, a number of writers have claimed (Loudon, 1959; Yap, 1960 and 1969) that in the illnesses in which possession is diagnosed and for which the shamanistic cure is prescribed only psychogenic complaints are involved, this is far from being the general case. While shamanistic therapy may in reality only accomplish what it claims in the case of psychiatric disorders, the range of illnesses which are attributed to possession is far wider than this. In many, if not most of the exotic cultures with which we are concerned, medical specialization has obviously hardly proceeded to the point it has reached in our culture. Consequently, unlike the western psychiatrist, the shaman's practice frequently includes patients with real organic lesions, as well as those who are not so much physically ill as the victims of misfortune. The shaman is moreover asked to placate and control elemental nature, and to divine and prophesy in a manner and to a degree which would daunt even the most optimistically omniscient psychiatrist. Hence as Shirokogoroff correctly saw, but as so many other students of shamanism have failed to appreciate, the parallel applies only in respect of such aspects of the shaman's practice as concern the treatment of tensions, fears and conflicts which are, in reality, readily susceptible to psychotherapeutic control. In a word, the shaman is not less than a psychiatrist, he is more.

In this argument in which I have followed others over the same ground to reach generally different conclusions, I have assumed, as they have, that psychiatry is a latent function of shamanism. It is one of the things it does, although it is not fully aware of doing it. From a different point of view, I gladly concede that spirit possession and shamanism (as is also the case with witchcraft beliefs) may be said to represent over-determined theories of psychiatric causation. They seem to assume that psychogenic and other mental disturbances have their roots in inter-personal and social conflict — as much of functional psychiatry does today to a significant extent (see e.g. Leff, 1981; Murphy, 1982). But they also hold that the causes of purely organic disorders, as well as of misfortunes generally, can again be traced to the same nexus — and to that extent they constitute an over-determined psychiatry. Again, however, this brings us back to the same conclusion: shamanism is more than psychiatry.

Thus the more meaningful equivalence is that psychiatry, and especially psychoanalysis, as Jung would perhaps have admitted much more freely than most Freudians would care to, represent limited and imperfect forms of shamanism. The theme is developed in a very interesting way to highlight the cultural relativity of western psychiatry by Littlewood and Lipsedge (1986), mainstream British psychiatrists who include anthropology in their expertise. Their basic aims are the same: to maintain harmony between man and man, and between man and nature. Hence we can, if we wish, group shamanism and psychoanalysis (if not the whole of psychiatry) together under the genus religion. But, if we choose to look at psychoanalysis and shamanism in this light, we must remember that the abreaction of the confessional is also employed by other faiths and ideologies.

IV

We are now left with the most formidable problem of all: why possession? In previous chapters we have come some way towards answering this question in sociological terms. We have now to see what depth psychology has to say on the matter and whether its interpretations agree or clash with ours. The clue here lies in the 'professional' hysteroid character of possession, and the key to the psychiatric interpretation of hysteria is of course Freud and Breuer's classic study (Freud, 1912). As is well known, these founders of modern psychiatry explained hysteria as the result of a conflict between the ego and some forbidden desire which is therefore suppressed. Since the repression is only partial, the desired aim is expressed indirectly and covertly, through 'conversion reactions' — the oblique strategy which we have seen in operation in so many cultures. This view has been skilfully deployed by Yap in his study of what he calls the 'possession syndrome' in Hong Kong. Possession, Yap argues, is a condition where problem-solving processes result in an unusual dramatization of a certain part of the 'me' aspect of the self, that part being constituted by forced and urgent identification with another personality credited with transcendental power. The nature of the possessing personality, or agency, can be understood psychologically — and we have reviewed abundant examples of this — in the light of the subject's own personality needs, his life situation, and cultural background which determine the normality or otherwise of the condition.

From this eminently reasonable standpoint, Yap sees the dramatic elements of possession as an adaptive, problem-solving behaviour ranging from the acting out of a wish-fulfilment through an experimental probing type of conduct, with various degrees of abreactive satisfaction, to the direct manipulation of other persons involved in the subject's problems. Again in accordance with much of our findings, Yap also recognizes that possession may appear in the symptoms at a superficial level, with the achievement of secondary gains without any true psychopathological significance.

For possession to occur, Yap holds, the following conditions are necessary. The subject must be dependent and conforming in character, probably occupying a position in society that does not allow for reasonable self-assertion. He must be confronted with a problem which he sees no hope of solving. Similarly from a more thorough-going psychoanalytic position, Charles Rycroft has argued that what he calls the hysterical defence is a type of submission in which normal self-assertive tendencies are suppressed and satisfaction is obtained and others influenced by ingratiation and manipulation. The basis for this response, he suggests, lies in a deep conviction of defeat and insignificance acquired in early childhood (Rycroft, 1968).

Both these interpretations fit closely the facts we have examined in earlier chapters in relation to peripheral possession. They are indeed only slightly different, and less positive ways of expressing the notion that peripheral possession represents an oblique aggressive strategy.

They can also be seen to correspond fairly closely to the fact that in main morality religions the intensity of the future shaman's professional hysteria is in direct proportion to his lack of the requisite hereditary qualifications and his ostensible resistance to accepting his vocation. More generally, the sociological distinction which we have been forced to draw between peripheral possession and witchcraft is echoed in the contrast which psychiatrists draw between their underlying ideologies — the introjective character of possession, and the projective nature of witchcraft scapegoating. These two ideologies may, however, as we have seen, be combined together as different facets of the same role. For the paradox of the shaman's position is that he is credited with being capable of causing what he has learnt through suffering to cure.

This ambivalence in the shaman's role Devereux purports to explain from a psychoanalytic stance in terms of an inferred degradation in the personality of the 'half-healed' shaman. Initiation into the ranks of the possession group and the assumption of a leading position in it have only provided remission of symptoms and the primary defence of such fundamentally distorted personalities soon breaks down. Thus healing shamans degenerate into aggressive witches. This seems an unconvincing explanation of what as we have seen earlier is a general sociological process. For whatever the true personality and inner feelings of the shaman it is society which regards him ambivalently as at once a healer and, potentially at least, a witch. The peripheral possession shaman who is branded as a witch is the leader of a protest cult, and the accusation of witchcraft is designed to contain this oblique aggression which has become too openly overbearing and threatening to be safely tolerated. In psychological terms, consequently, the explanation is not that of Devereux, but rather that the resentment and aggression which peripheral possession invariably arouses among the manipulated establishment fastens on those thrusting shamans who, in daring to control spirits, make a bid for the tenure of roles and status from which they are normally excluded because of the low social categories to which they belong. In terms of Mary Douglas' convenient explanatory slogan (Douglas 1966), they represent 'matter out of place', and have therefore to be put back in it by the accusation of witchcraft. All this, of course, is not to say that there are not cases where through psychiatric problems relapses occur, occasioning eccentric behaviour which may fit into cultural stereotypes of witchcraft.

These distinctions and transformations between peripheral possession and witchcraft are perhaps relevant in a different way to our own
psychological theories, which, of course, as I have been repeatedly
emphasizing, are themselves merely hypotheses rather than final truths.
Although frankly hysterical reactions are generally considered to be
out of fashion at the moment in western society, it does seem that many
temporary or mildly neurotic responses to conflict and tension in our
society lead to attention-seeking behaviour (even if this simply means
going to visit one's family doctor). This may achieve the effect of a
satisfactory rallying round of friends and relations and even perhaps,
as some psychiatrists advocate, lead to an actual modification or
restructuring of relations towards the subject. Laing and others,
however, have suggested that sometimes in the case of those patients
who are rendered more seriously ill and are committed to a mental
hospital, they are to some extent being offered up as scapegoats in
a stressful situation (Laing and Esterson, 1964). As Lipsedge and
Littlewood (1982) have convincingly shown, this regularly applies
particularly to the high levels of what is diagnosed as florid
'schizophrenia' or 'acute psychosis' in patients from the immigrant
black community in the British Isles. Where this is so, the patient's
condition is no longer analogous to that of the peripherally possessed
subordinate, but rather to that of the aggressive 'witch' who protests
too openly and too much.

I make these tentative suggestions to stress again how it is frequently
both more appropriate and more illuminating to assimilate psychiatry
to shamanism and witchcraft — although the latter deal primarily with
culturally normative forms of 'paranoia' — than to read the equation
in the opposite direction. It is reassuring that such authoritative
psychiatrists as Littlewood and Lipsedge (1987) should consider it
worthwhile to pursue this theme.

V

Psychiatric or psychoanalytic theories of hysteria which attempt to
explain possession negatively as aggression on the part of the socially
repressed, or of the ascriptively unqualified shamanistic recruit who
protests his unfitness and reluctance to assume his high calling, only
solve part of our problem. They leave out of account those possession
religions which enshrine morality and where to a large extent the office
of shaman is filled ascriptively by candidates who, far from being

drawn only from the margins of society, are of perfectly respectable background. In terms of what was said earlier of the significance of the shaman's professional trauma, to account for possession in both these very different social contexts we have to realize, I think, that possession most generally expresses aggressive self-assertion. That in both these contexts possession should assume the psychological colouring which western science identifies as hysteria is no longer surprising. For, as Weber clearly saw, it is not only in exotic marginal cults, or indeed in 'primitive' society generally, that leadership is tinged with hysteria. Many of those who today study politics under the banner of 'games theory', or of 'transactional analysis', assume that political man is little more than a manipulative, power-hungry 'hysteric' — a view which differs very little from that held by Hobbes or, more recently, Adler. Only our received view of hysteria inhibits our perception of the many forms which hysterical manipulation may assume.

If we are right, thus, in seeing possession as primarily a response to oppressive conditions, then as our evidence suggests, we may expect to find central shamanic cults in societies whose members are, in their total eco-political setting, under acute pressure. Such pressure may result from external encapsulating forces when a whole society is marginal or marginalized, and becomes itself peripheral in relation to a wider, over-arching political system. (The terms 'central' and 'marginal' are, as we need to remember, themselves relative.) The stimulus here, as in most peripheral cults, is an excess of oppressive structure. Paradoxically, as others have argued (e.g. Douglas, 1970), lack of structure and socio-political indeterminacy may very well have much the same effect: after all, over- and understimulation are equally effective triggers for states of altered consciousness (cf. Lewis, 1977). Thus it is not surprising that radical social change should so often have featured prominently in the settings in which we have found possession and shamanism flourishing.

Here, I believe we should return to Nadel's view of shamanism as an attempt to enrich the spiritual armoury of a community beset by chronic environmental uncertainty, or rapid and inexplicable social change. As he correctly saw, generally instability provides the fertile soil in which shamanism flourishes. This, however, is not necessarily to thrust shamanism into the gaping maws of that low grade explanatory catch-all 'anomie', for none of the societies which we have considered can plausibly be characterized as truly normless. Such a state would in fact be the antithesis of central shamanism with its strong moral emphasis. The problem is therefore to identify the minimum degree of insecurity (or excessive security) and pressure which is required to elicit the possession reaction.

I do not pretend to have achieved this. But it does seem that the pressure of adverse circumstance must be considerably higher than that which is adequately met by other theologies and cosmologies where possession is not enlisted as a basic feature in religious expression. Belief in spirits is much more widespread than belief in possession: and certainly religions which employ ecstasy seem much more sensitive to the impact of changing circumstances than those which do not. In line with this contrast, possession, as we have seen, represents an assertion, in the most direct, dramatic, and conclusive form that the spirits are mastered by man. What is proclaimed is not merely that God is *with* us, but that He is *in* us. Shamanism is thus the religion *par excellence* of the spirit made flesh, and this reassuring doctrine is demonstrably substantiated in each incarnatory séance, which as Zempleni (1977), de Heusch (1985), and others have observed, is, of course, also a sacrifice of the human self to the spiritual other. (Skultans, 1987, describes an intriguing Indian case where such sacrificial possession is offered on behalf of a relative of the possessed person rather than for the benefit of the possessed person herself.) Yet it is difficult to avoid the suspicion that for all its confident optimism, shamanism protests a little too much. For it, as I am arguing, possession is essentially a philosophy of power, it also seems tinged with a kind of Nietzschian desperation. If this is a valid inference, it seems again to confirm the high threshold of adversity to which shamanism appears to respond.

In the sense of mediating recurrent and novel stress (whether of endogenous or exogenous origin) in the consoling idiom of possession, shamanism may well contribute to mental health by stabilizing the incidence of nervous disorders, since it affords a means of ostensibly controlling the powers which are believed to activate these destructive forces. By identifying ecstatically with disturbing new experiences, or with recurrent hazards which are impossible to withstand otherwise, those who hold this spiritualistic philosophy yield pliantly to the savage onslaughts of innovation and change and to the recurrent buffets of fate. In thus bowing to the inevitable, and accepting it, as it were, with open arms, they soften its impact, making it seem that they passionately desire what they cannot avoid. And, if for those who do not believe in spirits, all this can be no more than a kind of heroic shadow-boxing, it nevertheless has significant psychological effects which permit the endurance of pressures that could not otherwise be tolerated. Ultimately, therefore, we have to acknowledge that to a certain extent in common with the unconscious and so many of our other psychological concepts, spirits are at least hypotheses which, for those who believe in them, afford a philosophy of final causes and a theory of social tensions and power relationships. Our concentration in this book on the politics of possession does not, of course, mean that we wish to devalue or deny the important intellectual, aesthetic, dramatic, and moral aspects which we have also touched on.

To conclude, let me refer again to our own religion. Traditional Christianity portrays God as all-powerful and omnipotent, making man seem puny and weak. This has led the Christian faith (and I exclude Christian enthusiasm here) to be peculiarly vulnerable to advances in science and technology. For, as man has acquired increasing mastery over his environment, so those things which were thought to be controlled only by God have passed out of His keeping. God's stature has thus inevitably diminished. Shamanistic religions do not make this mistake. They assume from the start that, at least on certain occasions, man can rise to the level of the gods. And since man is thus, from the beginning, held to participate in the authority of the gods, there is scarcely any more impressive power that he can acquire. What the shamanistic séance thus protests is the dual omnipotence of God and man. It celebrates a confident and egalitarian view of man's relations with the divine, and perpetuates that original accord between God and man which those who have lost the ecstatic mystery can only nostalgically recall in myths of creation, or desperately seek in doctrines of personal salvation.

BIBLIOGRAPHY

Ackerknecht, E., 'Psychopathology, primitive medicine, and primitive cultures', *Bulletin of the History of Medicine*, 14, 1943.
—— *Medicine and Ethnology*, Baltimore, John Hopkins Press, 1971.
Ahlberg, N., 'Some psycho-physiological aspects of ecstasy in recent research', in N.G Holm (ed.), *Religious Ecstasy*, Stockholm, Almquist and Wiksell, 1982, pp. 63–73.
Alpers, E.A., 'Ordinary household chores: ritual and power in a nineteenth-century Swahili women's spirit possession cult', *International Journal of African Historical Studies*, 17, 4, 1984, pp. 677–702.
al-Shahi, A., 'Spirit possession and healing: the *zar* among the Shaygiyya of the Northern Sudan', *Bulletin, British Society for Middle Eastern Studies*, vol. 11, No. 1, 1984, pp. 28–44.
Anisimov, A.F., 'The shaman's tent of the Evenks and the origin of the shamanistic rite', in H.N. Michael (ed.), *Studies in Siberian Shamanism*, Toronto University Press, 1963.
Balikci, Asen, 'Shamanistic behaviour among the Netsilik Eskimos', *South Western Journal of Anthropology*, 19, 1963.
Banyai, E.I., 'On the technique of hypnosis and ecstasy: an exceptional psychophysiological approach', in M. Hoppal (ed.), *Shamanism in Eurasia*, Göttingen, Edition Herodot, 1984.
Bargen, D.G., 'Jugao: a case of spirit possession in *The Tale of Genji*', *Mosaic*, xix, 3, 1986, pp. 15–24.
Barnett, MG., *Indian Shakers: a messianic Cult of the Pacific North-West*, Carbondale, 1957.
Basilov, V.N., 'The Study of Shamanism in Soviet Ethnography' in M. Hoppal (ed.), *Shamanism in Eurasia*, Göttingen, Edition Herodot, 1984, pp. 46–66.
—— 'The *Chiltan* spirits', in M. Hoppal (ed.), *Shamanism in Eurasia*, Göttingen, Edition Herodot, 1984, pp. 253–67.
Bastide, R., *African Civilisations in the New World*, London, 1971.
Bateson, G. and Mead, M., *Balinese Character*, New York, 1942.
Belo, J., *Trance in Bali*, New York, 1960.
Berger, I., 'Rebels or status-seekers? Women as spirit mediums in East Africa',

in N.J. Hafkin and E.G. Bay, *Women in Africa*, Stanford University Press, 1976, pp. 157–82.

Berger, I., *Religion and Resistance: East African Kingdoms in the Pre-Colonial Period*, Tervuren, Musée Royale de l'Afrique Centrale, 1981.

Berreman, G., *Hindus of the Himalayas: Ethnography and Change*, Berkeley, 1972.

Besmer, F.E., *Horses, Musicians and Gods: the Hausa Cult of Possession-trance*, Massachussets, Bergin and Garvey, 1983.

Bjerke, S., *Religion and misfortune: The Bacwezi complex and the other spirit cults of the Zinza of northwestern Tanzania*, Oslo, Universitetsforlaget, 1981.

Blacker, C., *The Catalpa Bow: A Study of Shamanistic Practices in Japan*, London, 1975.

Bogoras, W., *The Jesup North Pacific Expedition, Vol. 11, The Chukchee*, Leiden, 1907.

Bourguignon, E., 'World distribution and patterns of possession states', in R. Prince (ed.), *Trance and Possession States*, Montreal, 1967.

—— *Possession*, San Francisco, Chandler, 1976.

Brown, G. and Harris, T., *Social Origins of Depression: A Study of Psychiatric Disorder in Women*, London, 1978.

Burkert, W., *Greek Religion*, Oxford, Blackwell, 1985.

Butt, A., Wavell, S., and Epton, Nina, *Trances*, London, 1967.

Caplan, A.P., *Choice and Constraint in a Swahili Community*, London, 1975.

Carstairs, G.M. and Kapur, R.L., *The Great Universe of Kota: Stress, Change and Mental Disorder in an Indian Village*, London, 1976.

Clark, W., 'Temporary madness as theatre in the eastern central highlands of New Guinea', *Oceania*, 43, 1973, pp. 198–214.

Cohn, N., *The Pursuit of the Millennium*, London, 1957.

Colson, E., 'Spirit possession among the Tonga of Zambia', in J. Beattie and J. Middleton (eds), *Spirit Mediumship and Society in Africa*, London, 1969.

Constantinides, P., 'Ill at ease and sick at heart: symbolic behaviour in a Sudanese healing cult', in Lewis, I.M. (ed.), *Symbols and Sentiments*, London, 1977, pp. 61–84.

—— 'Women heal women: spirit possession and sexual segregation in a Muslim society', *Social Science Medicine*, Vol. 21, No. 6, 1985, pp. 685–92.

Courlander, H. and Bastien, R., *Religion and Politics in Haiti*, Washington, 1966.

Crapanzano, V. and Garrison, V., *Case Studies in Spirit Possession*, New York, Wiley, 1977.

Crapanzano, V., *The Hamadsha: A Study in Moroccan Ethnopsychiatry*, Berkeley, University of California Press, 1973.

Culley, R.C. and Overholt, T.W., 'Anthropological perspectives on Old Testament prophecy', *Semia* 21, 1982.

Czaplicka, M.A., *Aboriginal Siberia*, Oxford, 1914.

Davis, W., *Dojo: Magic and Exorcism in Modern Japan*, Stanford, Stanford University Press, 1980.

Delaby, L., *Chamanes Toungouses*, Nanterre, Centre d'Etudes Mongoles, 1976.

Dermenghem, E., *Le Culte des saints dans l'Islam maghrebin*, Paris, Gallimard, 1954.

Derrett, J.D.M., 'Spirit-possession and the Gerasene Demoniac', *Man*, 14, 2, 1979, pp. 286–93.

Devereux, G., 'Normal and abnormal: the key problem of psychiatric anthropology' in J.B. Casagrande and T. Gladwin (eds), *Some Uses of*

Anthropology: Theoretical and Applied, Washington, 1956.

Dodds, E.R., *The Greeks and the Irrational*, Berkeley, University of California Press, 1951.

Douglas, M., *Purity and Danger*, London, Routledge, 1966.

—— *Natural Symbols: Explorations in Cosmology*, London, Barrie and Rockcliff, 1970.

Dube, K.C., 'A Study of prevalence of mental illness in U.P. India', *Acta Psychiat. Scand.*, 46, 1970, pp. 327–59.

Echard, N., 'La pratique religieuse des femmes dans une société d'hommes: les Hausa du Niger', *Revue francaise de sociologie*, xix, 1978, pp. 551–62.

Edsman, C.M. (ed.), *Studies in Shamanism*, Stockholm, 1967.

Eliade, Mircea, *Le Chamanisme et les techniques archaiques de l'extase*, Paris, Payot, 1951.

Elwin, V., *The Religion of an Indian Tribe*, London, 1955.

Fairchild, W.P., 'Shamanism in Japan', *Folklore Studies* (Tokyo), 21, 1962.

Fakhouri, H., 'The *zar* cult in an Egyptian village', *Anthropological Quarterly*, 41, 1968, pp. 49–56.

Farah, Nuruddin, *From a Crooked Rib*, London, Heinemann, 1970.

Ferchiou, S., 'Survivances mystiques et cultes de possession dans le maraboutisme tunisien', *L'Homme*, 12, 3, 1972, pp. 47–69.

Fields, K., *Revival and Rebellion in Colonial Central Africa*, Harvard, Harvard University Press, 1985.

Firth, R., 'Problem and assumption in an anthropological study of religion', *Journal of the Royal Anthropological Institute*, 39, 1959.

—— *Tikopia Ritual and Belief*, London, 1967.

—— 'Ritual and drama in Malay spirit mediumship', *Comparative Studies in Society and History*, ix, 2, 1967, pp. 190–207.

Freeman, D., *Shaman and Incubus*, Australian National University (mimeo.), 1965.

Freud, S., *Selected Papers on Hysteria and other Psychoneuroses* (trans. A.A. Brill), New York, 1912.

Fry, P., *Spirits of Protest: Spirit Mediums and the Articulation of Consensus amongst the Zezuru of Southern Rhodesia*, Cambridge, Cambridge University Press, 1976.

Furst, P.T. (ed.), *Flesh of the Gods: the Ritual use of Hallucinogens*, New York, 1972.

Gallini, C., *I Rituali dell'Argia*, Padua, CEDAM, 1967.

Garbett, K.G., 'Spirit mediums as mediators in Valley Korekore society', in J. Beattie and J. Middleton (eds) *Spirit Mediumship and Society in Africa*, London, 1969.

Giannattasio, F., 'Somalia: La terapia coreutico-musicale del Mingis', *Culture Musicali*, anno *11*, 1983, pp. 93–119.

Giles, L. 'Possession cults on the Swahili coast: a re-examination of theories of marginality', *Africa*, 57, 2, 1987, pp.2 34–58.

Gomm, R., 'Bargaining from weakness: spirit possession on the South Kenya Coast', *Man* (NS), 10 December, 1975, pp. 530–43.

Goodman, F.D., Henney J.H., and Pressel, E., *Trance, Healing and Hallucination*, New York, Wiley, 1974.

Gough, K., 'Cults of the dead among the Nayars', *Journal of American Folklore*, 71, 1958.

Graham, H., 'The social image of pregnancy: pregnancy as spirit possession', *The Sociological Review*, May, 1976, pp. 291–308.

Grof, S., 'The implications of psychedelic research for anthropology: observations from LSD psychotherapy', in Lewis, I.M. (ed.), *Symbols and Sentiments*, London, 1977, pp. 141–74.

Gussow, Z., 'Pibloktoq (hysteria) among the Polar Eskimo', in *Psychoanalysis and the Social Sciences*, 1, New York, 1960.

Hamayon, R., 'Is there a typically female exercise of shamanism in patrilinear societies such as the Buryat?', in M. Hoppal (ed.), *Shamanism in Eurasia*, Göttingen, Edition Herodot, 1984, pp. 307–18.

Harner, M.J. (ed.), *Hallucinogens and Shamanism*, New York, 1973.

Harper, E.B., 'Spirit possession and Social Structure', in B. Ratman (ed.), *Anthropology on the March*, Madras, 1963.

Harris, G., 'Possession "hysteria" in a Kenyan tribe', *American Anthropologist*, 59, 1957.

Harvey, Y. Kim, *Six Korean Women: The Socialization of Shamans*, American Ethnological Society Monograph 65, Minnesota, West Publishing Co., 1979.

Helman, C., *Culture, Health and Illness*, Bristol, Wright, 1984.

Heusch, L. de, 'Cultes de possession et religions initiatiques de salut en Afrique', *Annales du Centre d'Etudes des Religions*, Brussels, 1962.

—— *Le Rwanda et la civilisation interlacustre*, 1966.

—— *Pourquoi l'epouser?*, Paris, Gallimard, 1971.

—— *Sacrifice in Africa*, Manchester, Manchester University Press, 1985.

Hexham, I. and Poewe, K., *Understanding Cults and New Religions*, Michigan, Eerdmans, 1986.

Hippler, A.E., 'Possession and trance cults: a cross-cultural perspective', *Transcultural Psychiatric Research*, 10, 1973, p. 21.

Hitchcock, J.T. and Jones, R.L. (eds), *Spirit Possession in the Nepal Himalayas*, Warminster, 1976.

Holden, P. (ed.), *Women's Religious Experience*, London, Croom Helm, 1983.

Holm, N.G. (ed.), *Religious Ecstasy*, Uppsala, Almquist and Wiksell, 1982.

Hoppal, M., *Shamanism in Eurasia*, Göttingen, Edition Herodot, 1984.

Hori, Ichiro, *Folk Religion in Japan: Continuity and Change*, Chicago, University of Chicago Press, 1968.

Humphrey, C., *Karl Marx Collective*, Cambridge, Cambridge University Press, 1983.

Jahoda, G., *Psychology and Anthropology*, New York, Academic Press, 1982.

Jahoda, G. and Lewis, I.M. (eds), *Acquiring Culture: Cross-cultural Studies in Child-Development*, London, Croom Helm, 1987.

Jeanmaire, H., *Le Culte de Dionysus*, Paris, 1951.

Jones, E., *On the Nightmare*, London, 1949.

Kapferer, B., *A Celebration of Demons*, Bloomington, Indiana University Press, 1983.

Katz, R., *Boiling Energy: Community Healing among the Kalahari Kung*, Cambridge, Mass, Harvard University, 1982.

Kehoe, A.B. and Giletti, D.H., 'Women's preponderance in possession Cults: the calcium-deficiency hypothesis extended', *American Anthropologist*, 1981, 83, pp. 549–61.

Kendall, L., *Shamans, Housewives and other Restless Spirits*, Honolulu, University of Hawaii Press, 1985.

Kennedy, J.G., 'Nubian Zar ceremonies as psychotherapy', *Human Organization*, 1967.

Kenny, M.G., 'Multiple personality and spirit possession', *Psychiatry*, 44, 4, 1981, pp. 337–58.

Kessler, C.S., 'Conflict and sovereignty, in Kelantanese Malay spirit séances', in Crapanzano, V. and Garrison, V. (eds), *Case Studies in Spirit Possession*, New York, 1977, pp. 295–332.

Kiev, A., *Transcultural Psychiatry*, New York: The Free Press, 1972.

Kleinman, A., *Patients and Healers in the Context of Culture*, Berkeley, University of California Press, 1980.

Knox, R.A., *Enthusiasm, A Chapter in the History of Religion*, Oxford, 1950.

Knutsson, K.E., *Authority and Change: A Study of the Kallu Institution among the Macha Galla of Ethiopia*, Goteborg, 1967.

—— 'Possession and extra-institutional behaviour: an essay in anthropological micro-analysis', *Ethnos*, 1975, 40, pp. 244–72.

Koritschoner, H., 'Ngoma ya Sheitani: an East African native treatment for physical disorder', *Journal of the Royal Anthropological Institute*, 66, 1936.

Koss, J.D., 'Spirits as socializing agents: a case study of a Puerto Rican girl reared in a matricentric family', in Crapanzano, V. and Garrison V. (eds), *Case Studies in Spirit Possession*, New York, 1977, pp. 365–82.

—— 'Social process, healing, and self-defeat among Puerto Rican spiritists', *American Ethnologist*, 4, 3, 1977, pp. 453–69.

Krader, L., 'Buryat religion and society', *Southwestern Journal of Anthropology*, 10, 1954.

Kramer, F.W., *Der rote Fes: Uber Bessessenheit und Kunst in Afrika*, Frankfurt, Athenaum, 1987.

Kuba, M., 'A psychopathological and socio-cultural psychiatric study of the possession syndrome', *Psychiatrica et Neurologica Japonica*, 75, 1973, p. 169.

La Barre, W., *The Ghost Dance*, New York, Doubleday, 1970.

La Fontaine, J.S., *Initiation: Ritual Drama and Secret Knowlege Across the World*, Harmondsworth, Penguin Books, 1985.

Laing R.D. and Esterson, T. *Sanity, Madness and the Family*, London, 1964.

Lambek, M., *Human Spirits: A Cultural Account of Trance in Mayotte*, Cambridge University Press, 1981.

Lan, D., *Guns and Rain: Guerillas and Spirit Mediums in Zimbabwe*, London, James Curry, 1985.

Langley, M., 'Spirit-possession, exorcism and social context: an anthropological perspective with theological implications', *Churchman*, 84, 3, 1980, pp. 226–45.

Langness, L., 'Hysterical psychosis in the New Guinea highlands: a Bena-Bena example', *Psychiatry*, 28, 1965.

Lanternari, V., *The Religions of the Oppressed*, New York, Mentor Books, 1965.

Larose, S., 'The meaning of Africa in Haitian Vodu', in Lewis, I.M. (ed.), *Symbols and Sentiments*, London, 1977, 85-115.

Last, M., 'Some economic aspects of conversion in Hausaland (Nigeria)', in N. Levtzion, *Conversion to Islam*, New York, Holmes and Meier, 1979, pp. 236-46.

Leacock, S. and R., *Spirits of the Deep: A Study of an Afro-Brazilian Cult*, New York, 1972.

Leff, J., *Psychiatry Around the Globe: A Transcultural View*, New York, Marcel Dekker, 1981.

Leiris, M., *La Possession et ses Aspects Theatraux Chez les Ethiopiens de Gondar*, Paris, 1958.

Lévi-Strauss, C., *Structural Anthropology*, London, 1968.

Lewis, H.S., 'Spirit possession in Ethiopia: an essay in Interpretation', in S. Rubenson (ed.), *Proceedings International Congress of Ethiopian Studies*, Uppsala, 1984.

Lewis, I.M., 'Spirit-possession and deprivation cults'. *Man*, 1, 1966, pp. 307-29.

—— 'Spirit-possession in northern Somaliland', in J. Beattie and J. Middleton (eds), *Spirit Mediumship and Society in Africa*, London, Routledge, 1969.

—— (ed.), *Symbols and Sentiments: Cross-cultural Studies in Symbolism*, London, Academic Press, 1977.

—— 'Spirit-possession and biological reductionism: a rejoinder to Kehoe and Giletti', *American Anthropologist*, 85, 1983, 2, pp. 412-17.

—— *Religion in Context: Cults and Charisma*, Cambridge, Cambridge University Press, 1986.

Lindblom, G., *The Akamba in British East Africa*, Uppsala, 1920.

Littlewood, R., 'The imitation of madness: the influence of psychopathology upon culture', *Social Science and Medicine*, Vol. 19, 7, 1984, pp. 705-15.

Littlewood, R. and Lipsedge, M., *Aliens and Alienists*, Harmondsworth, Penguin Books, 1982.

—— 'Culture-bound syndromes', in K. Granville-Grossman (ed.), *Recent Advances in Clinical Psychiatry* , Edinburgh, Churchill Livingstone, 1985, pp. 105-42.

—— 'The Butterfly and the Serpent: culture, psychopathology and biomedicine', *Culture, Medicine and Psychiatry*, 11, 1986, pp. 43-89.

Loeb, E.M., 'The Shaman of Niue', *American Anthropologist*, 26, 1924, pp. 393-402.

Loudon, J.B., 'Psychogenic disorder and social conflict among the Zulu', in M.K. Opler (ed.), *Culture and Mental Health*, New York, 1959.

Mair, L., *Witchcraft*, London, 1969.

Maquet, J., *The Premise of Inequality in Rwanda: A Study of Political Relations in a Central Africa Kingdom*, Oxford University Press, 1961.

Marazzi, U., *Testi dell Sciamanesimo, Siberiano e Centroasiatico*, Turin, Unione Topografico-editrice Tourinese, 1984.

Mars, L., *La Crise de possession dans le voudon: essai de psychiatrie comparée*, Port-au-Prince, 1946.

Marshall, L., 'The medicine dance of the 'Kung Bushmen', *Africa*, 39, 1969.

Martino, E. de, *La Terre du remords*, Paris, 1966.

Marwick, M., 'The social context of Cewa witch beliefs', *Africa*, 22, 1952.

Mary, A., 'L'alternative de la vision et de la possession dans les sociétés religieuses et therapeutiques du Gabon', *Cahiers d'Etudes Africaines*, 91, xxiii-3, 1983, pp. 281-310.

Masters, R.E.L. and Houston, J., *The Varieties of Psychedelic Experience*, London, 1967.

Messing, S., 'Group therapy and social status in the *zar* cult of Ethiopia', *American Anthropologist*, 60, 1958.

Métraux, A., *Voodoo in Haiti (English translation)*, London, 1959.

Mischel, W. and F., 'Psychological aspects of spirit possession in Trinidad', *American Anthropologist*, 60, 1958.

Mitchell, J., 'Women: the longest revolution', *New Left Review*, November-December 1966.

Monfouga-Nicolas, J., *Ambivalence et culte de Possession*, Paris, Editions Anthropos, 1972.

Morichand, G., 'Le Chamanisme des Hmongs', *Bulletin de l'Ecole Francaise de l'Extreme-orient*, 1968, p. liv.

Morris, B., 'Hill gods and ecstatic cults: notes on the religion of a hunting and gathering people', *Man in India*, 1981, 61, pp. 203-36.

Morsy, S.A., 'Sex differences and folk illness in an Egyptian village', in L. Beck and N. Keddie (eds) *Women in the Muslim World*, Harvard, Harvard University Press, 1977, pp. 599-616.

—— 'Sex roles, power, and illness in an Egyptian village', *American Ethnologist*, Vol. 5, No. 1, 1978, pp. 135-50.

Morton, A., 'Dawit: Competition and Integration in an Ethiopian Wugabi Cult Group', in V. Crapanzano and V. Garrison (eds), *Case Studies in Spirit Possession*, New York, John Wiley, 1977.

Murphy, H.B.M., *Comparative Psychiatry: The Internatinal and Intercultural Distribution of Mental Illness*, Berlin, Springer, 1982.

Murphy, J., 'Psychiatric aspects of shamanism on St Lawrence Island, Alaska', in A. Kiev (ed.), *Magic, Faith and Healing*, 1964.

Nadel, S., 'A study of Shamanism in the Nuba Hills', *Journal of the Royal Anthropological Institute*, 76, 1946.

Ngubane, H., *Body and Mind in Zulu Medicine*, London, Academic Press, 1977.

Nicolas, G. *Dynamique Sociale et Appréhension du Monde au Sein d'un Société Hausa*, Paris, Institut d'Ethnologie, 1975.

Nicolas, J., *Les Juments des Dieux: Rites de possession et condition feminine en pays Hausa*, Niger, Etudes Nigeriennes, No. 21, 1967.

Obeyesekere, G., 'The Idiom of Demonic Possession: a case study', *Social Science and Medicine*, July 1970, pp. 97-112.

—— *Medusa's Hair: An Essay on Personal Symbols and Religious Experience*, Chicago, University of Chicago Press, 1981.

O'Brien, Elmer, *Varieties of Mystic Experience*, Mentor-Omega Paperbacks, London, 1965.

O'Connell, M.C., 'Spirit-possession and role stress among the Xesibe of Eastern Transkei', *Ethnology*, 1982, xxi, pp. 21-37.

Oesterreich, T.K., *Possession, Demoniacal and Other, among Primitive Races, in*

Antiquity, the Middle Ages and Modern Times, London, 1930 (authorized translation of the 1921 original in German).

Ohlmarks, A., *Studien zum Problem des Schamanismus*, Lund, 1939.

Onweujeogwu, M., 'The cult of the Bori spirits among the Hausa', in M. Douglas and P. Kaberry (eds), *Man in Africa*, London, 1969.

Opler, M.E., 'Spirit-possession in a rural area of northern India', in W.A. Lessa and E.Z. Vogt (eds), *Reader in Comparative Religion*, New York, 1958.

Orent, Amnon, *Lineage Structure and the Supernatural: the Kaffa of Southwest Ethiopia*, unpublished PhD thesis, Boston University, 1969.

Paques, V., *L'Arbre cosmique dans la pensée populaire et dans la vie quotidienne du nord-ouest africain*, Paris, 1964.

Parkin, D., 'The politics of ritual syncretism; Islam among the non-Muslim Giriama of Kenya', *Africa*, 40, 1970.

Parkin, D.J., *Palms, Wine and Witnesses*, London, Intertext Books, 1972.

Peters, L.G. and Price-Williams, Douglass, 'Towards an experiential analysis of shamanism', *American Ethnologist*, 1980, 7, 397–418.

Pressel, E., 'Negative spirit possession in experienced Brazilian Umibanda spirit mediums', in V. Crapanzano and V. Garrison (eds), *Case Studies in Spirit Possession*, New York, Wiley, 1977, pp. 333–64.

Prince, R.H., 'The problem of spirit possession as a treatment for psychiatric disorders', *Ethos*, 2, 1974, pp. 315–33.

—— (ed.) *Shamans and Endorphins* (special issue of Ethos), *Ethos*, 10, 1982.

Radin, P., *Primitive Religion: Its Nature and Origin*, New York, 1937.

Raqiya, H.D. Abdalla, *Sisters in Affliction. Circumcision and Infibulation of Women in Africa*, London, Zed Press, 1982.

Rasmussen, K., *The Intellectual Culture of the Iglulik Eskimos*, Copenhagen, 1929.

Reichel-Dolmatoff, G., *Amazonian Cosmos*, Chicago, University of Chicago Press, 1971.

Reminick, R.A., 'The evil eye belief among the Amhara of Ethiopia', *Ethnology*, 13, 1974, pp. 279–91.

Rouch, J., *La Religion et le Magie Songhay*, Paris, 1960.

Rouget, R., *La Musique et la transe. Esquisse d'une théorie générale des relations de la musique et de la possession*, Paris, Gallimard, 1980.

Rycroft, C., *Anxiety and Neurosis*, London, 1968.

Santos Granero, F., 'Power, ideology and the ritual of production in Lowland South America', *Man*, 1986, 21, pp. 657–79.

Sardan, J.P. Olivier de, *Les sociétés Songhay-Zarma*, Paris, Karthala, 1984.

Sargant, W., *The Mind Possessed*, London, 1973.

Sartre, J.P., In F. Fanon, *The Wretched of the Earth*, London, 1967.

Saunders, L.W., 'Variance in Zar experience in an Egyptian village', in V. Crapanzano and V. Garrison (eds), *Case Studies in Spirit Possession*, New York, John Wiley, 1977.

Scharer, H., *Ngaju Religion* (Translated by R. Needham), The Hague, 1963.

Schoffeleers, M., *Pentecostalism and Neo-traditionalism*, Amsterdam, Free University Press, 1985.

Scholem, G., *Major Trends in Jewish Mysticism*, New York, 1941.

Schultes, R.E. and Hofmann, A., *Plants of the Gods: Origins of Hallucinogenic*

Use, London, Hutchinson, 1980.

Seligman, C.G. and B.Z., *The Veddas*, Cambridge University Press, 1911.

Shack, W., *The Gurage*, London, Oxford University Press, 1966.

Shirokogoroff, S.M., *Psychomental Complex of the Tungus*, London, 1935.

Siikala, A.L., *The Rite Technique of the Siberian Shaman*, Helsinki, FF Communications, Vol. 93, No. 220, 1978.

Silverman, J., 'Shamans and acute schizophrenia', *American Anthropologist*, 69, 1967.

Skultans, V., *Intimacy and Ritual: A Study of Spiritualism, Mediums and Groups*, London, Routledge, 1974.

—— 'Trance and the management of mental illness among Maharashtrian Families', *Anthropology Today*, Vol. 3, No. 1, 1987.

Sonne, B., 'The professional ecstatic in his social and ritual position', in N.G. Holm (ed.), *Religious Ecstasy*, Uppsala, Almquist and Wiksell, 1982, pp. 128–50.

Spencer, P., *The Samburu, A Study of Gerontocracy in a Nomadic Tribe*, London, Routledge & Kegan Paul, 1965.

Spiro, M.E., *Burmese Supernaturalism*, New Jersey, 1967.

Stanbrook, E., 'Some characteristics of the psychopathology of schizophrenic behaviour in Bahian society', *American Journal of Psychiatry*, 109, 1952.

Stayt, H., *The Bavenda*, London, 1937.

Stewart, K., 'Spirit-possession in native America', *Southwestern Journal of Anthropology*, 2, 1946.

Stirrat, R.L., 'Demonic possession in Roman Catholic Sri Lanka', *Journal of Anthropological Research*, 33, 2, 1977, pp. 133–57.

Strathern, M., Women-in-between: female roles in a male world: Mount Hagen, New Guinea, London, Seminar Press 1972.

Strobel, M., *Muslim Women in Mombasa, 1890–1975*, New Haven, Yale University Press, 1979.

Sundkler, B., *Bantu Prophets in South Africa*, London, 1961.

Swantz, M.L., *Ritual and Symbol in Transitional Zaramo Society*, Uppsala, 1970.

Taylor, D.M., *The Black Caribs of British Honduras*, New York, 1951.

Taylor, R., *The Death and Resurrection Show*, London, Anthony Blond, 1985.

Teja, J.S., Khanna, B.S. and Subrahmanyam, T.B., 'Possession states in Indian patients', *Indian Journal of Psychiatry*, 21, 1970, p. 71.

Todd, D., 'Problems of comparative ecstasy', *Northeast African Studies*, 1, 3, 1979–80, pp. 49–57.

Tremearne, A.J.N., *The Ban of the Bori*, London, 1914.

Tubiana, J., 'Quete de Sawbadayt', in J. Tubiana (ed.), *Guirlande pour Abba Jerome*, Paris, Le Mois en Afrique, 1983.

Turner, V.W., *The Ritual Process: Structure and Anti-Structure*, London, 1969.

Veith, I., *Hysteria, the History of a Disease*, Chicago, 1965.

Voigt, V., 'Shaman — person or word?', in M. Hoppal (ed.), *Shamanism in Eurasia*, Göttingen, Edition Herodot, 1984, pp. 13–21.

Wadley, Susan S., 'The spirit "rides" or the spirit comes: possession in a north Indian village', in A. Bharati (ed.), *The Realm of the Extra-human: Agents and Audiences*, The Hague, Mouton, 1976, pp. 233–52.

Walker, S.S., *Ceremonial Spirit Possession in Africa and Afro-America*, Leiden: E.J. Brill, 1972.

Wavell, S., Butt, A. and Epton, Nina, *Trances*, London, 1967.

Whisson, M.G., 'Some aspects of functional disorders among the Kenya Luo', in A. Kiev (ed.), *Magic, Faith and Healing*, London, 1964.

Whyte, S.R., 'Men, women and misfortune in Bunyole', *Man*, 16, 3, 1981, pp. 350–66.

Wijesinghe, C.P., Dissanayake, S.A.W. and Mendis, N., 'Possession trance in a semi-urban community in Sri Lanka', *Australian and New Zealand Journal of Psychiatry*, 10, 1976, pp. 135–9.

Wilken, G.A., *Het Shamanisme bij de Volken van den Indischen Archipel*, 1887.

Wilson, P.J., 'Status ambiguity and spirit possession', *Man*, 2, 1967.

Wilson, R., *Prophecy and Society in Ancient Israel*, Philadelphia, Fortress Press, 1980.

Woldetsadik, T., 'The cult of Damwamwit and the Mwayat organization', Social Research fieldworkers' meeting, Addis Ababa, 1967 (ms).

Worsely, P., *The Trumpet Shall Sound*, London, 1957.

Wyllie, R.W., 'Introspective witchcraft among the Effutu of southern Ghana', *Man*, 8, 1, 1973, pp. 74–9.

Yap, P.M., 'The culture-bound reactive syndromes', in W. Caudill and Tsung-yi Lin (eds), *Mental Health Research in Asia and the Pacific*, Honolulu, 1969.

—— 'The possession syndrome — a comparison of Hong Kong and French findings', *Journal of Mental Science*, 106, 1960.

Young, A., 'Why Amhara get Kureynya: sickness and possession in an Ethiopian *zar* cult', *American Ethnologist*, 2, (3), 1975, pp. 567–84.

Young, J., *The Drugtakers*, London, Paladin, 1972.

Zaehner, R.C., *Mysticism, Sacred and Profane*, Oxford, 1957.

Zempleni, A., 'From symptom to sacrifice: the story of Khady Fall', in V. Crapanzano and V. Garrison (eds), *Case Studies in Spirit Possession*, 1977, pp. 87–140.

INDEX